Animals Count

Whether their populations are perceived as too large, just right, too small or non-existent, animal numbers matter to the humans with whom they share environments. Animals in the right numbers are accepted and even welcomed, but when they are seen to deviate from the human-declared set point, they become either enemies upon whom to declare war or victims to be protected.

In this edited volume, leading and emerging scholars investigate for the first time the ways in which the size of an animal population impacts how they are viewed by humans and, conversely, how human perceptions of populations impact animals.

This collection explores the fortunes of amphibians, mammals, insects and fish whose numbers have created concern in settler Australia and examines shifts in these populations between excess, abundance, equilibrium, scarcity and extinction. The book points to the importance of caution in future campaigns to manipulate animal populations and demonstrates how approaches from the humanities can be deployed to bring fresh perspectives to understandings of how to live alongside other animals.

Nancy Cushing is associate professor in History at the University of Newcastle, Australia. An environmental historian most interested in relations between humans and other animals, she is co-author, with Kevin Markwell, of *Snake-bitten, Eric Worrell and the Australian Reptile Park* (2010), co-editor of *Radical Newcastle* (2015) and is writing a history of meat eating in colonial Australia.

Jodi Frawley is an honorary research fellow in the Department of History at the University of Western Australia, Australia. She is interested in understanding the cultural implications of environmental change in all its guises, from globally mobile biological matter to the ways that race relations impact the environment. Her current project is a history of fishing in the Great Sandy Strait, Queensland.

Routledge Environmental Humanities
Series editors: Iain McCalman and Libby Robin

Editorial Board
Christina Alt, St Andrews University, UK
Alison Bashford, University of Cambridge, UK
Peter Coates, University of Bristol, UK
Thom van Dooren, University of New South Wales, Australia
Georgina Endfield, University of Nottingham, UK
Jodi Frawley, University of Sydney, Australia
Andrea Gaynor, The University of Western Australia, Australia
Tom Lynch, University of Nebraska, Lincoln, USA
Jennifer Newell, American Museum of Natural History, New York, USA
Simon Pooley, Imperial College London, UK
Sandra Swart, Stellenbosch University, South Africa
Ann Waltner, University of Minnesota, USA
Paul Warde, University of East Anglia, UK
Jessica Weir, University of Western Sydney, Australia
International Advisory Board
William Beinart, University of Oxford, UK
Sarah Buie, Clark University, USA
Jane Carruthers, University of South Africa, Pretoria, South Africa
Dipesh Chakrabarty, University of Chicago, USA
Paul Holm, Trinity College, Dublin, Republic of Ireland
Shen Hou, Renmin University of China, Beijing, China
Rob Nixon, Princeton University, Princeton, NJ, USA
Pauline Phemister, Institute of Advanced Studies in the Humanities,
    University of Edinburgh, UK
Deborah Bird Rose, University of New South Wales, Sydney, Australia
Sverker Sorlin, KTH Environmental Humanities Laboratory,
    Royal Institute of Technology, Stockholm, Sweden
Helmuth Trischler, Deutsches Museum, Munich and Co-Director,
    Rachel Carson Centre, Ludwig-Maximilians-Universität, Germany
Mary Evelyn Tucker, Yale University, USA
Kirsten Wehner, National Museum of Australia, Canberra, Australia

The *Routledge Environmental Humanities* series is an original and inspiring venture recognising that today's world agricultural and water crises, ocean pollution and resource depletion, global warming from greenhouse gases, urban sprawl, overpopulation, food insecurity and environmental justice are all *crises of culture*.

The reality of understanding and finding adaptive solutions to our present and future environmental challenges has shifted the epicentre of environmental studies away from an exclusively scientific and technological framework to one that depends on the human-focused disciplines and ideas of the humanities and allied social sciences.

We thus welcome book proposals from all humanities and social sciences disciplines for an inclusive and interdisciplinary series. We favour manuscripts aimed at an international readership and written in a lively and accessible style. The readership comprises scholars and students from the humanities and social sciences and thoughtful readers concerned about the human dimensions of environmental change.

Animals Count
How Population Size Matters in
Animal-Human Relations

Edited by Nancy Cushing and
Jodi Frawley

First published 2018
by Routledge
2 Park Square, Milton Park, Abingdon, Oxon OX14 4RN

and by Routledge
711 Third Avenue, New York, NY 10017

Routledge is an imprint of the Taylor & Francis Group, an informa business

© 2018 selection and editorial matter, Nancy Cushing and Jodi Frawley; individual chapters, the contributors

The right of Nancy Cushing and Jodi Frawley to be identified as the authors of the editorial material, and of the authors for their individual chapters, has been asserted in accordance with sections 77 and 78 of the Copyright, Designs and Patents Act 1988.

All rights reserved. No part of this book may be reprinted or reproduced or utilised in any form or by any electronic, mechanical, or other means, now known or hereafter invented, including photocopying and recording, or in any information storage or retrieval system, without permission in writing from the publishers.

Trademark notice: Product or corporate names may be trademarks or registered trademarks, and are used only for identification and explanation without intent to infringe.

British Library Cataloguing-in-Publication Data
A catalogue record for this book is available from the British Library

Library of Congress Cataloging-in-Publication Data
Names: Cushing, Nancy, editor. | Frawley, Jodi, editor.
Title: Animals count : how population size matters in animal-human relations / edited by Nancy Cushing and Jodi Frawley.
Description: Abingdon, Oxon ; New York, NY : Routledge, 2018. | Series: Routledge environmental humanities | Includes bibliographical references and index.
Identifiers: LCCN 2018007508 (print) | LCCN 2018022479 (ebook) | ISBN 9781351210645 (eBook) | ISBN 9780815381365 (hbk) | ISBN 9781351210645 (ebk)
Subjects: LCSH: Animal populations—Australia. | Human-animal relationships—Australia. | Wildlife conservation—Social aspects—Australia.
Classification: LCC QL752 (ebook) | LCC QL752 .A66 2018 (print) | DDC 591.7/880994—dc23
LC record available at https://lccn.loc.gov/2018007508

ISBN: 978-0-8153-8136-5 (hbk)
ISBN: 978-1-351-21064-5 (ebk)

Typeset in Goudy
by Apex CoVantage, LLC

Every effort has been made to contact copyright-holders. Please advise the publisher of any errors or omissions, and these will be corrected in subsequent editions.

Contents

List of figures	vii
Notes on contributors	viii
Acknowledgements	xi

1 Why count animals?   1
NANCY CUSHING AND JODI FRAWLEY

PART I
Excess   13
The man from Menindie – D. H. Souter

2 Cane toads as sport: conservation practice and animal ethics at odds   15
LIBBY ROBIN

3 Taking locust country   26
ANDREA GAYNOR

4 On the ant frontier: ontological conflict with *Iridomyrmex humilis* in post-war Sydney   41
ADAM GALL

5 A swarm of sheep: colonising the Esperance bioregion   56
NICOLE CHALMER

PART II
Abundance   71
Life hath its charms

6 Optimism unlimited: prospects for the pearl-shell, bêche-de-mer and trochus industries on Australia's Great Barrier Reef, 1860–1940   73
ROHAN LLOYD

vi *Contents*

7 Swamplands: human-animal relationships in place   85
EMILY O'GORMAN

8 'Pain for Animals, Profit for People': the campaign against
live sheep exports, 1974–1986   99
GONZALO VILLANUEVA

PART III
Equilibrium   111

The Ento(M)-usician – Emma Carmody

9 "Cunning, intractable, destructive animals": pigs as co-colonisers
in the Hunter Valley of New South Wales, 1840–1860   113
NANCY CUSHING

10 Wine worlds are animal worlds too: native Australian animal vine
feeders and interspecies relations in the ecologies that host vineyards   126
JULIE MCINTYRE

11 Defending nature: animals and militarised landscapes in Australia   139
BEN WILKIE

PART IV
Scarcity   153

Homecoming (Alpine Strata) – Emma Carmody

12 A slow catastrophe? Fishing for sport and commerce in
colonial Victoria   155
DAVID HARRIS

13 The palatability of pests: redfin in the Murray-Darling Basin   168
JODI FRAWLEY

PART V
Extinction   181

'Tis the last fly of summer

14 After none: memorialising animal species extinction through
monuments   183
DOLLY JØRGENSEN

Index   201

Figures

1.1	This image tracks wool imports into Britain and indirectly counts Australian sheep	5
2.1	The cane toad	16
3.1	The war on locusts in south-eastern Australia, as depicted in *Argus*, 25 November 1953	27
5.1	Sheep flock moving inland from Israelite Bay, east of Esperance, circa 1890	63
6.1	Opening pearl shells on Thursday Island, 10 February 1907, postcard	80
7.1	Detail of a map from 1857 showing Toowoomba swamps	87
10.1	This design for a table mat, and one for a larger and more complex tea cloth, captured the popular association of silvereyes with vineyards in the 1930s	132
11.1	The Puckapunyal military training area, circa 1940, showing the initial degradation of the environment	143
12.1	Packing fish for Melbourne, circa 1886. Photographer, N. J. Caire	159
12.2	Ballarat Fish Hatchery, circa 1890	159
14.1	'Endling' at the National Museum of Australia, Canberra, February 2016	184
14.2	Memorial to the passenger pigeon in Wyalusing State Park, Wyalusing, Wisconsin, March 2017	187
14.3	Passenger pigeon memorial in the Cincinnati Zoo, Cincinnati, Ohio, June 2017	189
14.4	Passenger pigeon bronze from the Lost Birds project in place at the Audubon Center, Columbus, Ohio, June 2017	190
14.5	Monument to Extinction. Above: full work; below: two panels close-up, artist Bob Lockhart, Louisville Zoo, Louisville, Kentucky, June 2017	192
14.6	Carver at work on a sculpture of a cycad for the Mass Extinction Memorial Observatory (MEMO) project, Dorset Centre for Creative Arts, Dorchester, May 2017	194
14.7	The Life Cairn on the top of Mount Caburn near Lewes, England, was in a rather dilapidated state, so founder Andreas Kornevall is setting a stake to reclaim the location, May 2017	195

Notes on contributors

Emma Carmody is a lawyer at Australia's oldest public interest environmental law centre, the Environmental Defenders Office New South Wales, as well as a legal adviser to the secretariat of the Ramsar Convention on Wetlands in Switzerland. Emma holds a PhD in creative writing, awarded by the University of Adelaide, Australia. She publishes in both English and French.

Nicole Chalmer has undergraduate qualifications and experience in zoology and agriculture and is completing an environmental history PhD at the University of Western Australia, Australia. Her thesis, "Consuming Eden: Food, Culture and Nature in the Esperance Mallee-Recherche Bioregion (late Pleistocene to present)", examines past interactions between ecosystems and social ecological systems as people have produced food in this region.

Nancy Cushing is associate professor in history at the University of Newcastle, Australia. An environmental historian most interested in relations between humans and other animals, she is co-author, with Kevin Markwell, of *Snakebitten, Eric Worrell and the Australian Reptile Park* (2010), co-editor of *Radical Newcastle* (2015) and is writing a history of meat eating in colonial Australia.

Jodi Frawley is an honorary research fellow in the Department of History at the University of Western Australia, Australia. She is interested in understanding the cultural implications of environmental change in all its guises, from globally mobile biological matter to the ways that the politics of race impact the environment. Her current project is a history of fishing in the Great Sandy Strait, Queensland.

Adam Gall is an interdisciplinary researcher based in Sydney. He teaches Australian environmental history at NYU, Sydney, and academic writing and research at the University of Sydney, Australia. His current research deals with the relationship between mediated attachment and ethico-political commitment in settler-colonial city and suburban environments.

Andrea Gaynor is associate professor and head of history at the University of Western Australia, Australia. Primarily an environmental historian, her recent publications include an essay on human relationships with 'nature' in Australian home gardens and *Never Again: Reflections on Environmental Responsibility After Roe 8* (2017), co-edited with Peter Newman and Philip Jennings.

David Harris is an environmental historian who works at La Trobe University, Australia. He is interested in social constructions of nature, Australian colonial fisheries, acclimatisation and the spaces where politics and technology intersect with the environment.

Dolly Jørgensen is professor of history at the University of Stavanger in Norway. Her research interests lie at the intersections of the environment, technology and human cultures, and she currently works on issues related to ecological restoration, reintroduction, rewilding and de-extinction. She is the co-editor of *Northscapes: History, Technology, and the Making of Northern Environments* (2013), *New Natures: Joining Environmental History with Science and Technology Studies* (2013) and *Visions of North in Premodern Europe* (2018) as well as the immediate past president of the European Society for Environmental History (2013–2017).

Rohan Lloyd is an environmental historian based in Townsville. His PhD was a history of settler Australian perceptions of the Great Barrier Reef from Captain Cook to the establishment of the Great Barrier Reef Marine Park in 1975. His research mostly addresses North Queensland environmental history and histories of environmentalism. He has also worked as a public historian for the Townsville City Libraries, Australia, high school teacher and lecturer and tutor at James Cook University, Australia.

Julie McIntyre is a research fellow in history at the University of Newcastle, Australia. Her publications to date focus on the growing, making, selling and drinking of grape wine as a window to human desire and identities. Her new projects are settlers in the empire of science, global Newcastle and Australia's Atlantic.

Emily O'Gorman is an environmental historian with interdisciplinary research interests within the environmental humanities. Her research focuses on how people have lived with rivers, wetlands and climates. Currently a senior lecturer at Macquarie University, Australia, she holds a PhD from the School of History at the Australia National University and undertook a postdoctoral candidacy at the Australian Centre for Cultural Environmental Research at the University of Wollongong, Australia.

Libby Robin is a historian of science and environmental ideas. She is professor at the Fenner School of Environment and Society at the Australian National University and holds affiliations with the National Museum of Australia and the Royal Institute of Technology, Stockholm. She has published widely in the history of science, international and comparative environmental history and the ecological humanities, winning national and international prizes

x *Notes on contributors*

in history, zoology and literature. She was elected fellow of the Australian Academy of Humanities in 2013. Her most recent book is *The Environment: A History* (with Paul Warde and Sverker Sörlin, 2018).

Gonzalo Villanueva is a Gilbert Postdoctoral Career Development Fellow at the University of Melbourne, Australia. He is the author of the 2018 book *A Transnational History of the Australian Animal Movement, 1917–2015.*

Ben Wilkie is a social and environmental historian and an honorary fellow at the School of Humanities and Social Sciences at Deakin University, Australia. Having published on the Grampians National Park and the Scots in Australia, he is currently working on the intersections between environmental and military history.

Acknowledgements

Even more than usual, this is a book made possible by the efforts of many people. It began with the inaugural Green Stream at the Australian Historical Association in Ballarat, Victoria, in July 2016, convened by Jodi Frawley, Chris McConville and Nancy Cushing. The theme of the conference was "Boom and Bust", and environmental historians responded enthusiastically, engaging with and contesting this concept as it applied to their areas of interest. Encouraged by discussion with Libby Robin over hot coffees in that wintry city, this collection became one of the first projects of a reinvented Australian and New Zealand Environmental History Network, which interested readers are warmly invited to join. We would like to thank Libby Robin and Tom Griffiths for generously allowing us to extend the good work they had been doing through the network for many years as well as our colleagues on the interim executive committee, several of whom have chapters in this volume, for their support and encouragement.

On behalf of our contributors, we would like to thank the team at Routledge for clear and cheerful advice and the many librarians and archivists who make our research so much easier. Thank you to our respective families, workmates and post-graduate students for forbearance as work on this collection took us away from other tasks.

1 Why count animals?

Nancy Cushing and Jodi Frawley

One crow sorrow, two crows joy
Three crows a letter, four crows a boy
Five crows silver, six crows gold
Seven crows a secret that should never be told[1]

John Berger, in his influential 1977 essay "Why look at animals?", argued that until the nineteenth century, other animals were with humans at the centre of their worlds, not only economically and productively but also imaginatively, spiritually and emotionally.[2] He posited that as modernisation occurred in the West, real animals were increasingly marginalised from these roles, leaving Western peoples still talking about other animals, thinking with animal metaphors and nostalgically looking at representations of animals – in Disney films, nature documentaries, zoos and children's toys. The impulse to count animals is closely linked with this habitual looking, a means of systematising it, and like looking, it is associated with our continuing practices of seeking meaning from them. The traditional English rhyme which opened this chapter invokes the oracular properties of animals, offering a set of rules by which to understand the message conveyed by the crows, who predict the future on a personal scale.

Expanding the scope of such predictions to the level of communities or whole regions, the size of animal populations is also understood as foreshadowing prosperity or bad fortune. Whether animal populations are perceived as too large, just right or too small, their numbers matter to the humans with whom they share environments. Animals at the human-declared set point are accepted and even welcomed, but as they deviate from it, they become enemies upon whom to declare war or victims to protect. We count animals as we look at animals, in part to reassure ourselves of their continued presence in our lives. Counting animals shapes the ways we interact, manage, protect, love and vilify these environmental companions.

Animal numbers have been of particular interest in Australia, a continent colonised by Europeans just as the process of marginalising animals discussed by Berger was beginning.[3] Australia is unique in having a highly distinctive fauna, with 87% of its mammal species, 45% of birds, 93% of reptiles and 94% of frogs

2 Nancy Cushing and Jodi Frawley

being endemic, but also as an entire continent governed since 1901 by a single political entity, the Commonwealth of Australia.[4] As a nation, Australia is still emergent, not having yet entirely escaped the influence of the colonising nation, Great Britain. Australians struggle with their contemporary racial and cultural diversity and to achieve reconciliation with their First Nations, the Aboriginal and Torres Strait Islander peoples. From the perspective of its non-human animal population, despite its large landmass, Australia shares characteristics with other smaller islands which can make them both refuges from predators and disease but also places of particular vulnerability when ecologies are disrupted. Being an island nation has encouraged a high level of awareness of the distinction between native and introduced species and a tendency to identify the nation with native animals. These features have made animal studies an area of great interest amongst Australian environmental humanities scholars and Australian-based studies useful points of comparison and contrast for animal studies researchers internationally.[5]

In this collection, we explore how the size of an animal population impacts the ways in which they have been viewed in settler colonial Australia, and, conversely, how perceptions of the correctness of animal populations have effects on animals. Playing on the double meaning of our title, we also seek to demonstrate that just as animals are not passively looked at but actively return that gaze, they are not only objects to be counted but also subjects who count. Although Berger argued that animals in the postmodern world were incapable of looking back at humans, others have rejected this premise, including Derrida, who reflected on the meaning of the shame he felt when looked upon, naked, by his cat.[6] The unflinching appraisal by the cat reminds us that animals have their own historical roles and take actions that have consequences. In both regards, drawing attention to how animals count is timely in the Anthropocene, as awareness grows of precipitous falls in the numbers of many free-living species, unprecedented rises in populations of intensively farmed animals and shifts in the populations of those being pushed into new areas by habitat loss and climate change. Animals will continue to count and be counted as we struggle to learn how to share dwindling living space and resources.

Animal typologies: invasive and native, free-living and domestic

The animal subjects of this book existed in varying relationships with the settler colonial society established in Australia from 1788. These were new and separate from the relations between non-human species and Australia's First Nations peoples, the Aboriginal and Torres Strait Islander groups who had inhabited the continent together for some 60 000 years. Indigenous Australians understood animals not as resources but as partners in their social and spiritual lives. They kept their country healthy through ritual techniques which encouraged biodiversity and accepted population fluctuations as part of annual and climatic cycles. When faced with novel introduced species post contact, the First Nations peoples accommodated themselves to the new situation rather than resisting it, harvesting different animals to meet their needs and incorporating new species into their dreamings.[7]

Australia's settler-colonists have been more interventionist and less successful at coexisting with other animals. The issue of invasive species dominates public and scholarly debate about animals in Australia where native species are understood as vulnerable and in need of protection and introduced species as excessively robust.[8] Troubling this distinction, our studies show how some native animals, like locusts, thrived in the changed conditions of colonisation while exotics, including sheep, had to be carefully nurtured.[9] Regardless of their place of origin, Australian animals defy simple categorisations, becoming pests to some human groups and resources for others.

Most of our studies are of free-living animals, including the cane toads and redfin perch that arrived as a result of colonists deliberately introducing them for economic and cultural reasons. These two animals, and many others like them, are now labelled pests.[10] Libby Robin's shows how, in the cane toad's case, the category of pest has created local approaches to the animals that deny care and encourage cruelty.[11] Cane Toad Musters that promote the removal of the threat by killing them "one toad at a time" are juxtaposed with the approach of scientist Rick Shine, whose extensive fieldwork with his team of researchers has been enabling them to recommend a more nuanced approach to managing the toad's presence in particular ecosystems. The story of the redfin, on the other hand, shows a different set of local and scientific approaches to a pest species. Jodi Frawley grapples with the varying ways that fishing communities in the Murray-Darling Basin and scientific advocates for native fish saw redfin. The meaning and importance of the category "pest", with its superficial connotation of overpopulation, is challenged by the complexity of local stories set in specific histories and environments.

Carefully imported species that have thrived in Australian conditions are not the only invasive species whose numbers cause concern.[12] Others have arrived uninvited, accidentally loaded on ships and planes with more favoured cargo. Like the Argentine ants whose Sydney history is detailed by Adam Gall, having evaded Australia's notoriously strict border controls, many reproduced sufficiently to climb to numbers which exceeded the tolerance for them. Gall shows how the lives of these invasive ants intersected with changing ideas about domestic spaces in the mid-twentieth century. In suburban Sydney, the shifting understandings of the effect of poisons modified the view of the ant numbers, as the original motive of protecting the environment from the ants was replaced by a concern to protect the wider ecology from the poison being used against them. Advocates for eradication make skilful use of numbers in a wide range of debates about invasive animals.

Some native species have made themselves similarly unwelcome within the settler society, especially those whose numbers bloomed in the changed conditions of a new Australia. Locusts, always present in Australia, thrived in the settler colonial agroecologies established in Victoria and Western Australia.

4 *Nancy Cushing and Jodi Frawley*

Andrea Gaynor explores this phenomenon, pointing out that Aboriginal peoples' oral traditions include stories of locust plagues associated with the boom-and-bust conditions that became more widespread with colonisation. Gaynor shows how the increased numbers of locusts were met with shifting military approaches that mirrored Australia's changing war strategies through the twentieth century. Mosquitos, another insect native to Australia, were seen as excessive when settlements developed near wetlands and waterways that carried large populations of these animals. Emily O'Gorman investigates the swamplands that underpin the urban development of Toowoomba in Queensland. The mosquito, as a disease vector, became entangled in the medical and health trajectories of this city's growth. Although myriad urban practices had made the swamps "unhealthy" in the nineteenth century, it was the environmental controls targeting excessive volumes of mosquitoes that forever changed the wetlands.

Other native animals, including silvereyes and thylacines, were equally subject to measures designed to reduce their numbers in the nineteenth century. The thylacine did not withstand this onslaught, but the silvereye, as shown by Julie McIntyre, lived on to share the special cultural status accorded to natives from the mid-twentieth century which nominally earns them greater tolerance and even protection.[13] Silvereyes are one of several opportunistic native feeders on the introduced grapes which, along with a small range of animals introduced with vine stock, McIntyre argues are absent from the rhetoric of the wine industry which prefers to hide its toll on fauna. Although the silvereye is a good example of a resilient and adaptive native species, many others are now threatened or endangered because of relentless competition for space and resources. Australia's Environment Protection and Biodiversity Conservation Act list of endangered species stands at 503, including 54 mammals, birds, fish and amphibians that have become extinct since colonisation.[14]

The politicisation of animal numbers is most evident in debates over how to address what are seen as damagingly excessive populations of introduced species that have become naturalised. Formerly domesticated animals, including pigs, camels, donkeys, horses and goats, grew as a concern warranting counting in the twentieth century. In some instances, these animals greatly expanded their numbers largely unobserved, resulting in a negative impact on the environment and Indigenous people. As Nancy Cushing shows, this was an unintended consequence in the case of pigs, as the pigs were offered and accepted a high level of autonomy within the animal husbandry practices of the nineteenth century.

How to count animals

The counting of this range of native and introduced animals has a long history in settler Australia. The most heavily counted have been those raised in commercial operations primarily for food and wool. Settlers counted the ancestors of these animals onto and off of the ships that brought them to Australia and carefully tracked their rising numbers as a measure of the success of the colonies.[15]

As the nursery rhyme "The Man from Menindie" recalls, sheep were repetitively counted in and out of stockyards, night-time hurdles (enclosures) and saleyards. Such counting was in some cases undertaken by Aboriginal people working in the pastoral industry, who applied traditional methods of counting – such as counting by fives and then grouping the fives into tens – enabling them to "give the exact number of cattle in a group up to four or five hundred almost without a moment's hesitation".[16] Historians using colonial records found sheep numbers to be a useful means of representing progress and employed them to demonstrate the rate of expansion into Aboriginal land, growth in employment and rising prosperity (see Figure 1.1). Although steep reductions in sheep numbers, as during the 1890s depression, served as shorthand for the still-fragile hold on the continent,[17] Richard Waterhouse notes the impact of the apparent abundance of sheep, arguing that practices like washing wool before shearing by holding sheep under water in creeks persisted into the 1870s because, although some individuals drowned, sheep as a group were plentiful.[18] Individual animals count for

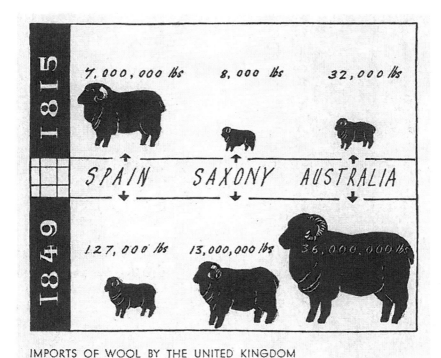

Figure 1.1 This image tracks wool imports into Britain and indirectly counts Australian sheep.

Source: Hugh Anderson (text) and R. G. Edwards (illustrations), *Sheep and Wool*, from Australian Industries Series (Melbourne: Lothian, 1970), 14.

6 Nancy Cushing and Jodi Frawley

little within populations perceived to be abundant or excessive. Nicole Chalmer investigates the impact of the introduction of sheep in the south-west of Western Australia and finds that in the Esperance bioregion, sheep numbers were managed by being incorporated into pre-existing socio- and agrecologies as Aboriginal people's knowledge and pathways were melded with animal husbandry and mobile shepherding based on European practices. Only when these methods were set aside did their numbers overwhelm the region's resources

Manual counting became less important as farmed animals were increasingly permanently numbered. An ear tag or tattoo now marks them with a number by which owners can track their lives from birth to slaughter. Their days are numbered as well – from day-old chick to broiler at 60 days, repeated 116-day pregnancies for sows, lives capped at 6 months for spring lamb and 18 months for beef. Some, as explored by Gonzalo Villanueva, continue to be counted onto ships as part of Australia's live animal export trade, the largest in the world. Villaneuva shows how the availability of large numbers of sheep allowed the development of a long-distance live export trade, starting with ships which carried 6000 animals each in the 1960s and growing to 92 000 in a single shipment in 1980. It was opposed by both the trade union movement, seeking to protect meat workers' employment, and the animal rights movement which objected to the breach to duty of care for the sentient animals that suffered in this trade.

The next most carefully counted animals were those thought to be interfering with the production of livestock or crops. In the nineteenth century, these were principally native species, including grubs, caterpillars, parrots, wallabies and dingoes.[19] Estimates of their numbers were rough and often alarmist but were made concrete for some species in the number of bounties paid for their scalps and ears.[20] Many of these species were resilient in the face of mass killing, but at least one, the Tasmanian tiger (thylacine), was pushed towards extinction by it.[21] Dolly Jørgensen explores memorialisation of extinct animals, including the thylacine, in Australia, North America and Europe and why it is essential that we remember what has been lost.

There were, of course, biases in estimates of animal numbers made by people with vested interests. Drawing upon memory and chance encounters, they formed impressionistic conclusions about whether numbers were too high, too low or sufficient to allow them to continue harvesting. Both numbers of pest species and of prized animals were likely to be exaggerated. As Rohan Lloyd demonstrates, overly optimistic perceptions of animal numbers were often sustained in cases where overharvesting had led to precipitous and unsustainable declines in populations. Claims related to the abundance of pearl-shell and bêche-de-mer supported the exploitation of these fisheries from the late nineteenth through to the mid-twentieth century.

An increasing sophistication of methods by which free-living animals are counted flowed from the rise of biological sciences in the early twentieth century.[22] Accurate population counts give a sense of the scale of a community and a starting point from which to determine whether it is increasing, stable or declining and why. They can lead to the discovery of unacknowledged animal populations, such as those on land set aside for military use, as shown by Ben Wilkie. Making a case study of the large army base at Puckapunyal in Victoria, Wilkie shows that the Australian defence establishment has taken its conservation role seriously and effectively manages the wide range of both flora and fauna on its bases, despite the overall damage to animal populations caused by war.

Scientific counting techniques vary to suit the size of the animal and the scale of the census. Small populations of large animals are counted comprehensively, with individuals uniquely identified to avoid double counting. Larger populations are systematically sampled and overall populations extrapolated from them. Studying red kangaroos on the plains north of the MacDonnell Ranges in the Northern Territory in the early 1960s, ecologist A. E. Newsome pioneered the aerial survey, sectioning off his 7000-square kilometre research area into blocks which varied according to vegetation type, flying over it at an altitude of 90 metres in parallel lines and writing down the tally of kangaroos seen every ten seconds, at the sounding of a buzzer.[23] Satellite imagery and digital camera traps are newer methods being applied to identify the presence and density of less visible animal populations. When the scientists cannot count animals directly, evidence of their presence, including footprints, burrows and DNA in hair and scat, are used to gain a sense of how many animals are living in an area.

Using animal numbers

Such systematic counts of animal populations have removed some of the bias from assessments of population size, but the numbers they produce are ripe for politicisation. As Theodore M. Porter observed, drawing attention to the subjective role of what is so often cloaked in claims of objectivity, "Numbers . . . create new things and transform the meanings of old ones".[24] Scientific assessments of population size hold an authority that lay people and politicians seize upon to support claims for action, whether to protect, harvest or deliberately reduce animal populations. David Harris shows how different groups preying on one type of animal can provide evidence of the politics embedded in places like the Gippsland Lakes. Commercial and recreational fishing communities were variously vilified and revered in Victoria as they fought over the number of fish each could take. The politics around this issue masked warnings of aquatic environmental change and the advice from locals that might have protected the populations of table fish that went to market.

Official counts of "feral" animals have furthered the demonisation of many, including cane toads, mynahs and cats. As on other continents, this includes the use of race and racial epithets.[25] The mynah, a small opportunistic urban-dwelling bird, is often called an Indian mynah, at once conjuring its native land and the Australian cultural politics of race. Many would be accepting of the killing of these birds by other animals (including humans), but a 2017 study which found that feral and pet cats kill one million native birds a day in Australia was greeted with outrage.[26] The researchers concluded that the impacts on bird population viability and conservation were difficult to interpret, with the kill rate amounting

8 *Nancy Cushing and Jodi Frawley*

to 4% of the 11 billion-strong bird population annually. Nonetheless, the one million figure was seized upon by the popular media and the public and used to advocate the killing of cats. This parallels Robin's study of the cane toad which shows that the death of the amphibian has always been argued to be justified to preserve the lives of native animals and their habitats.

Just as potent as systematically calculated estimates of animal populations are the conclusions drawn from animal counts based on personal observation. Many Australians monitor the numbers of animals in their immediate environments, assessing current sightings against those remembered from the past and taking a particular interest when changes in numbers seem to intersect with contemporary issues around extinction, environmental degradation and the management of feral animals. In December 2016, the absence of the Christmas beetle, a group of scarabs (*Anoplognathus*) with metallic-coloured shells that were familiar visitors during past holiday seasons, concerned many Sydney residents. Turning to the expertise of museum-based entomologists, the scarcity of the beetles was explained as linked with the disappearance of their favoured open woodland territory to suburban development combined with prolonged drought.[27] Others note the addition of whale watching to the annual calendar in eastern Australia, recalling that in their youth, there was no such whale activity or tourism to go with it. More frequent sightings are taken to signal improvements in human relations with animals, with the cessation of regional commercial whaling in 1962 having allowed numbers to begin to recover. This interest has led to citizen science projects, such as one conducted by the New South Wales Office of Environment and Heritage in which volunteers count humpback whales from Cape Solander in the Kamay Botany Bay National Park, near a former whaling station.[28] At the same time, scientists are returning to the nineteenth-century whaling ships' log books to track their catches, and through them, the historic decline in whale populations.[29]

In other cases, perceived rises in animal numbers can be related instead to additional stress having been placed on habitat, forcing animals into territory now shared with humans. Wildlife sightings in urban areas, from regular incursions by brush turkeys in Sydney's northern suburbs to a swamp wallaby trapped after having crossed the Sydney Harbour Bridge early one January morning in 2018, are seen popularly as reflecting the robust presence of native animals when instead they can signal the lack of alternative habitats and declining populations. Informal knowledge based on oral accounts and personal memory has always been an essential aspect of managing relations with animals, but traditional knowledge is poised to draw new attention in the Anthropocene as dramatic shifts create disconnections with what we know from the past.[30]

Animals count

This volume is divided into five sections that capture the principal ways in which animal numbers are perceived from the standpoint of the settler society. It begins with Excess, the state in which animal populations are much greater than what is seen as desirable by those making judgments about them. In these numbers, they may serve as competitors to more desired animals, interfere with such economic enterprises as the growing of crops, act as disease vectors or merely be perceived as a nuisance. Excessive animals created a particular kind of relationship of anxiety in settler-colonial Australia, addressed by putting in place measures to reduce their mobility through fencing, denying access to food, slowing rates of reproduction or directly killing them. As the chapters in this section show, settler Australians have invested large amounts of time, ingenuity and resources in reducing the numbers of animals seen to be in excess, often achieving only temporary results and causing significant collateral damage.

The next section is Abundance, again suggesting large numbers of animals but framed more positively as a resource to be harvested. Efforts to achieve abundance by introducing new animals into environments are often very successful in the short term, especially in areas free of diseases and predators for that species, but require careful management to avoid subsequent sharp declines. Abundance is a way of seeing an environment itself as a resource, and it has in many instances caused a myopic view of the real effects of economic enterprise. Abundance, like excess, means that little value is placed on the welfare of the individual, leading to inhumane practices and overharvesting and making abundance a rarely sustainable position.

Equilibrium captures the state in which animal numbers sit in a range acceptable to human observers. Animals in balance can be disruptive but are still viewed with some affection, indulgence or sense of their usefulness. When animals numbers are too high or too low, they demand action, but animals that are in balance do not warrant the same sort of attention. Equilibrium is a number to aspire to, a balance that Australians actively seek in relation to some animal populations. Within this range, animals are often beneath notice, enabling some to live their lives with minimal intervention.

Scarcity occurs when the balance in animal numbers begins to tip and awareness of the limits of animals' resilience grows. These animals can induce anxious worrying about the state of their populations and the overall health of environments with which they are associated. Attempts to protect and preserve these animals emerge in a range of ways, including recognition of depopulation, exposure of excessive exploitation and acknowledgement of the ways some practices might support one human group's livelihood but infringe on the ability for others to continue to make a living in particular ways. At its most powerful, scarcity is articulated in animals as endangered species, thereby triggering legislative and policy interventions into stabilising populations.

Finally, Extinction describes a state in which no animals remain to be counted. Australia's claim to have the largest number of species which have been made extinct since colonisation makes it of interest as the world hurtles towards the sixth extinction event. Extinction is already here, and animal studies scholars are at the forefront of addressing what this means for humanity. As twenty-first century life brings the consequences of historical actions, globalisation, reduced habitat and encroaching urbanisation, how we count in the time of extinctions

10 *Nancy Cushing and Jodi Frawley*

will matter. From the depths of the oceans to the tops of the mountains, humans still have much to learn from animals on how to inhabit this world. As part of this effort to retain and learn from past understanding and misunderstandings, this collection brings together creative and scholarly works in which animals were counted and in which animals count. They show how important the size of animal populations, as understood by humans, has been and how decision making has been directed by these often-mistaken assumptions.

Notes

1 There are many versions of this rhyme. Some omit the reference to crows, and likely the original referent bird was a magpie, as discussed by John Brand and Henry Ellis in *Observations on Popular Antiquities* (London: FC and J Rivington and others, 1813), which included the rhyme as: One for sorrow, two for mirth, three for a wedding, four for a birth.
2 John Berger, 'Why Look at Animals', *About Looking* (New York: Pantheon Books, 1980), 1–2.
3 See Libby Robin, *How a Continent Created a Nation* (Sydney: University of New South Wales Press, 2007); Geoffrey Bolton, *Spoils and Spoilers: A History of Australians Shaping Their Environment* (Sydney: Allen and Unwin, 1992).
4 A. D. Chapman, *Numbers of Living Species in Australia and the World*, 2nd edition (Toowoomba: Australian Biodiversity Information Services, 2009), www.environment. gov.au/science/abrs/publications/other/numbers-living-species/executive-summary (accessed 24 January 2018).
5 See, for example: Deborah Bird Rose, *Nourishing Terrains: Australian Aboriginal Views of Landscape and Wilderness* (Canberra: Australian Heritage Commission, 1996); Deborah Bird Rose et al., 'Thinking through the Environment, Unsettling the Humanities', *Environmental Humanities*, 1 (2012): 1–5; Thom van Dooren, 'Invasive Species in Penguin Worlds: An Ethical Taxonomy of Killing for Conservation', *Conservation and Society*, 9.4 (2011): 286–98.
6 Jacques Derrida, *The Animal That Therefore I Am* (New York: Fordham University Press, 2008), 4.
7 Adrian Franklin, *Animal Nation: The True Story of Animals and Australia* (Sydney: UNSW Press, 2006), 168–69; 172–73.
8 Banu Subramaniam, 'The Aliens Have Landed! Reflections on the Rhetoric of Biological Invasions', *Meridians*, 2.1 (2001): 26–40; Karen Middleton, 'Renarrating a Biological Invasion: Historical Memory, Local Communities and Ecologists', *Environment and History*, 18 (2012): 61–95; Chris T. Smout, 'The Alien Species in 20th-Century Britain: Constructing a New Vermin', *Landscape Research*, 28.1 (2003): 11–20; Rachel Sanderson, 'Re-writing the History of Australian Tropical Rainforests: "Alien Invasives" or "Ancient Indigenes"?', *Environment and History*, 14 (2008): 165–85.
9 Fiona Probyn-Rapsey, 'Five Propositions on Ferals', *Feral Feminisims* (2016), www. feralfeminisms.com/five-propositions-on-ferals/ (accessed 28 January 2018).
10 Jeffrey A. McNeely (ed.), *The Great Reshuffling: Human Dimension of Invasive Alien Species* (Gland, Switzerland: International Union for Conservation of Nature and Natural Resources, 2001), 43–54.
11 Libby Robin, 'Culling and Care: Ferals, Invasives and Conservation Icons in Australia', *Australian Zoologist* 39.1 (2017): 103–13.
12 Paul Robbins, 'Culture and Politics of Invasive Species', *The Geographical Review*, 94.2 (2004): iii–iv; Harold A. Mooney, 'Invasive Alien Species: The Nature of the Problem', in Harold A Mooney et al. (eds.), *Invasive Alien Species: A New Synthesis*

(Washington, DC: Island Press, 2005), 1–15; Lesley Head and Pat Muir, 'Nativeness, Invasiveness, and Nation in Australian Plants', *The Geographical Review*, 94.2 (2004): 199–218; Sarah Johnson (ed.), *Bioinvaders: Themes in Environmental History* (Cambridge: The White Horse Press, 2010); Tim Low, *Feral Future: The Untold Story of Australia's Exotic Invaders* (Ringwood: Penguin Books, 2001).

13 Franklin, *Animal Nation*, 113.

14 Australia Department of the Environment and Energy, EPBC Act List of Threatened Fauna, www.environment.gov.au/cgi-bin/sprat/public/publicthreatenedlist.pl#other_animals_endangered (accessed 29 January 2018).

15 Nancy Cushing, 'Animal Mobilities and the Founding of New South Wales', in Christof Mauch, Ruth Morgan and Emily O'Gorman (eds.), *Visions of Australia, Environments in History* (Munich: Rachel Carson Centre, 2017).

16 Mary Gilmore, *Old Days Old Ways: A Book of Recollections* (1934) quoted by Ray Norris in 'Why Old Theories of Indigenous Counting Just Won't Go Away', *The Conversation*, 5 September 2016, https://theconversation.com/why-old-theories-on-indigenous-counting-just-wont-go-away-64173 (accessed 27 March 2018).

17 See, for example, Richard Waterhouse, *The Vision Splendid: A Social and Cultural History of Rural Australia* (Perth: Curtin University Books, 2005), 75–86.

18 Waterhouse, *The Vision Splendid*, 79.

19 Warwick Frost, 'European Farming, Australian Pests: Agricultural Settlement and Environmental Disruption in Australia, 1800–1920', *Environment and History*, 4 (1998): 129–43.

20 For example, Stubbs calculated that bounties were collected on 18 464 kangaroos, 10 615 wallabies and 91 031 pademelons between 1881 and 1894 by Pastures and Stock Protection Boards at Grafton, Casino and Lismore (Brett J. Stubbs, 'From "Useless Brutes" to National Treasures: A Century of Evolving Attitudes towards Native Fauna in New South Wales, 1860s to 1960s', *Environment and History*, 7.1 (2001): 31.

21 Thylacines were blamed for killing sheep and eating animals trapped for their fur. Paddle provides a tally of 2209 thylacines for which bounties were paid between 1888 and 1909, while emphasising the role of epidemic disease, habitat destruction and environmental degradation in their extinction (Robert Paddle, 'The Thylacine's Last Straw: Epidemic Disease in a Recent Mammalian Extinction', *Australian Zoologist*, 36.1 (2012): 78.

22 This paragraph and the following one draw on the overview of current animal counting techniques and findings in Cheryl Lyn Dybas, 'Counting Whales in the Seas, Trees in the Forests, and Mountain Lions on the Ridges', *BioScience*, 66.12 (2016): 1013–22. This topic is treated in more detail in a wide range of textbooks, including John R. Skalski, Kristin E. Ryding and Joshua Millspaugh, *Wildlife Demography: Analysis of Sex, Age, and Count Data* (London: Elsevier Science, 2005).

23 Thomas Newsome and Alan Newsome, *The Red Kangaroo in Central Australia: An Early Account by A. E. Newsome* (Canberra: CSIRO, 2016), Chapter 3, 'Distribution and Abundance'.

24 Theodore Porter, *Trust in Numbers: The Pursuit of Objectivity in Science and Public Life* (Princeton: Princeton University Press, 1995), 28.

25 Gary Alan Fine and Lazaros Christoforides, 'Dirty Birds, Filthy Immigrants and the English Sparrow War: Metaphorical Linkage in Constructing Social Problems', *Symbolic Interaction*, 14.4 (1991): 375–93; Fiona Probyn-Rapsey, 'Dingoes and Dog-whistling: A Cultural Politics of Race and Species in Australia', *Animal Studies Journal*, 4.2 (2015): 55–77.

26 J. C. Z. Woinarskia, B. P. Murphy, S. M. Legge, S. T. Garnett, M. J. Lawes, S. Comer, C. R. Dickman, T. S. Doherty, G. Edwards, A. Nankivell, D. Paton, R. Palmer and L. A. Woolley, 'How Many Birds Are Killed by Cats in Australia?', *Biological Conservation*, 214 (2017): 76–87.

12   *Nancy Cushing and Jodi Frawley*

27   Chris Reid, 'Where Have All the Christmas Beetles Gone?', https://australianmuseum. net.au/christmas-beetles (accessed 19 January 2018); Jennifer Ennion, ''Tis the Season for Christmas Beetles', *Australian Geographic*, 21 November 2016, www. australiangeographic.com.au/topics/wildlife/2016/11/australias-christmas-beetles (accessed 21 January 2018).

28   The Cape Solander Whale Migration Study began in 1997. It recorded 3032 humpback whales swimming north between 24 May and 31 July 2016. 'Highest Ever Number of Humpbacks Recorded at Cape Solander', NSW Office of Environment and Heritage, 8 August 2016, http://www.environment.nsw.gov.au/news/highest-ever-number-of-humpbacks-recorded-at-cape-solander (accessed 22 January 2018).

29   Emma L. Carrole, Jennifer A. Jackson, David Paton and Tim D. Smith, 'Two Intense Decades of 19th Century Whaling Precipitated Rapid Decline of Right Whales around New Zealand and East Australia', *PLoS ONE*, 9.4 (2014): 1–13, doi:10.1371/journal. pone.0093789.

30   Canadian environmental historian put out a half-joking call for interviews with "veterans of the Holocene" with memories of life before the start 1945 date of the Anthropocene in "The Alanthropocene", part of the blog series 'Canada's Anthropocene', 15 January 2018, http://niche-canada.org/2018/01/15/the-alanthropocene/#_edn6 (accessed 21 January 2018).

Part I

Excess

The man from Menindie

The man from Menindie was counting sheep;
He counted so many he went to sleep.
He counted by threes and he counted by twos,
The rams and the lambs and the wethers and ewes;
He counted a thousand, a hundred and ten –
And when he woke up he'd to count them again.

> – D. H. Souter, published in
> *Australian Nursery Rimes, Selected from
> the Bulletin for the Children's Hospital,*
> Sydney, 1917

2 Cane toads as sport
Conservation practice and animal ethics at odds

Libby Robin

Introduction

The ugly and unloved cane toad creates tensions for people concerned about environmental management. Toads have a bad reputation in the Anglophone world, where there are adverse literary allusions from Shakespeare to Kenneth Grahame.[1] In *Wind in the Willows*, a children's bedtime story, Mr Toad is arrogant and selfish. 'Toadying' is not endearing behaviour.

Politics, both local and national, has been touched by the cane toad invasion across northern Australia. Here is an introduced animal with a rapidly expanding range that has invaded a huge swathe of country (about a third of Australia – or the area of Spain, France, Germany, Italy, Norway and Sweden combined). It is an animal that is easy to hate. Even in places where political views are polarised and communities share little common ground, eradicating cane toads is perceived as a good thing. The 'toad menace' has motivated volunteer efforts and citizen science from diverse communities, including remote Aboriginal communities, urban Darwin and smaller and larger settlements in between. Local newspapers have monitored the arrival of the toads as they have spread across northern Australia, from mid-Queensland in the 1930s to Broome on the Western Australian coast in 2010. They are also travelling south, with sightings at Hawks Nest, just north of Newcastle, in 2017.[2] This chapter considers the recent history of the toads and the practices for managing the environment they inspire. The cane toad irruption, especially the recent rapid geographical spread across northern Australia, has created a 'crisis' as well as discussions about emergency management.

What is a cane toad?

The large terrestrial toad *Rhinella marinus* (formerly *Bufo marinus*) is widely distributed internationally. It is a native of South and Central America. Its vernacular names include 'giant neotropical toad' or, confusingly, 'marine toad'. Despite its scientific name, it is a land dweller. It varies in size enormously, but all have poison glands on the backs of their necks (see Figure 2.1). Even the tadpoles are poisonous to most mammals, but it is the bigger toads that, if eaten, can kill a

Figure 2.1 The cane toad.
Source: CSIRO Science Image, Photographer: David McClenaghan.

pet dog or a goanna and can make an adult human very sick indeed. The biggest toads are the size of large rabbits, with huge poison sacs. They are ugly and scary – as federal parliamentarian Julie Bishop discovered when she met the well-named "Rabbit" at a political function in Darwin in 2010.[3] Bishop was quick to pass the monster on to the local Northern Territory candidate who was used to coping with constituents with strange pets.

The animal is called a 'cane toad' only in Australia. It was introduced to protect sugar cane from damaging beetles in Queensland in 1935. Calling the new biological control agents cane toads (rather than giant neotropical toads) probably made them more acceptable in the anxious white Australia of the 1930s, where 'giant tropical' things were generally feared.[4]

Evidence for the effectiveness of the toads in controlling beetles was slight. In the sugar plantations of Puerto Rico, some said that toads ate the cane beetles, although the evidence was very limited.[5] Nonetheless, entomologist Reg Mungomery introduced 101 young cane toads from Honolulu to Meringa in North Queensland, without the normal protocols for introducing animals from elsewhere. The introduction had full public support: the *Cactoblastis* moth had just successfully provided a biological control over the Prickly Pear (*Opuntia* spp.) invasion. One 'lucky break' inspired the move for the next, as historian Jodi Frawley argues: 'Storytelling that centralised luck enabled continuity of land practices that repeated the disasters associated with nineteenth-century introduction of exotic biota'.[6] Such luck gave optimism even in the face of failure. Luck also forced science to go beyond its evidence.[7] Biological controls had become a proud part of 'national progress' as Australia's identity was closely tied to its primary industries, agriculture and pastoralism. Cane toads spread throughout northern Australia from 1935, but their spread accelerated in the late 1980s. Indeed, the toad invasion outstripped the scientific models for it in the twenty-first century.[8] By 2008, the spread of toads across the Northern Territory was exponential, not linear.[9] No one anticipated that toads could get to the shore of the Indian Ocean so quickly, but they arrived in 2010, decades ahead of the modelled predictions.

As Trigger and colleagues have argued, what belongs and what does not is complex and cultural.[10] While biological scientists argue for the eradication of invasive species because they threaten biological diversity, citizen scientists and policymakers use the term 'biodiversity' more loosely – some even use it interchangeably with 'nature'. They seek to eradicate species that 'don't belong', targeting 'non-natives' because they have evolutionary origins elsewhere. Which animals and plants are 'native' is sometimes constructed scientifically, sometimes culturally and sometimes science is an argument that serves cultural purposes. A preference for 'native' species may not have any basis in local ecology. For example, 'native gardens' were widely promoted in Australia from the 1940s to the 1970s[11] – but they grew very different plants from what we now call 'indigenous gardens', which include only ecologically local species. Indeed, the list of garden escapees that are classified as weeds include many that are native to Australia but that invade beyond their original ecosystem. Even our 'national floral emblem', Golden Wattle (*Acacia pycnantha*), is regarded as invasive in parts of Australia. We are now encouraged to celebrate Wattle Day not by planting the national emblem but rather by planting a local wattle suitable to our region.[12]

The very different ecologies of different parts of Australia make national policy-making from the south-east corner (where the nation's capital, Canberra is located) unpopular in the north and the west of the continent. Nonetheless, concepts like National Reserves – a collective term that includes national parks, state forests and private nature reserves – can bring new voices to environmental policymaking. Indigenous Protected Areas (IPAs), owned and managed by Traditional Owners, account for a very significant part of the area of National Reserves.[13] Although ecologists might consider the functioning of the ecosystem with humans included only as a disruptive force, Aboriginal managers are concerned first about the functioning of 'country', including its people. Indigenous perspectives on conservation are mainstream in northern Australia. Toad management affects the health of the country and the people, and Aboriginal people are very engaged with these concerns.

The unnatural toad and sport in the national interest

In 1988, the cane toads attracted international fame through the documentary film *Cane Toads: An Unnatural History*, directed by Mark Lewis.[14] The 'unnatural' of the film became part of conservation discussions. The film put toad irruption into popular consciousness, and the 'unnatural' stuck. When 'invasive species eradication' deals with 'unnatural' phenomena, it can lose sight that they are animals.

18   *Libby Robin*

In the Kimberley, conservation science met the 'violent brand-new sport' of toadbusting, in the words of wry singer-songwriter Dana Lyons. Lyons plays light-heartedly with serious issues, exposing how nature is constructed culturally in his song the 'Cane Toad Muster'.[15] The Kimberley Toad Busters (as they call themselves), with patriotic pride, defend their country against the invasive cane toad that has 'decimated' the Northern Territory and Western Australia.[16] Cane toads, Lyons suggests, are something to 'hate together' (whatever your political views).[17] The volunteer effort that goes into toadbusting is closely tied to Friday-night beers and building a consensus about what it means to 'be Australian'. The killing sport of the 'Cane Toad Muster' is a source of national pride, like the cattle industry from which it takes its name. It aims to eradicate the menace, to kill every last toad. This is the Australian way to do conservation.

If killing cane toads is constructed as a national duty, it becomes heroic to eradicate the ugly animal, to cleanse the landscape of an undesirable element, to somehow make the whole ecosystem 'more Australian'. The 'twisted sports idea' of hitting them with golf clubs or driving over them with SUVs depends on toads being unnatural. If the muster is a game, the toads are akin to Pokémon avatars, things to collect as a game. If the rules are like a computer game in a virtual world, the toads themselves are mere gizmos, nameless gadgets, not animals deserving of ethical consideration. How they die is not important – be it in a freezer bag or under the wheels of a heavy vehicle. Toads can be busted *any which way*. The important thing is the *muster*, the gathering of people doing their national duty.

Yet if we could disentangle patriotism and ideas of national progress from conservation practices, we might recall that cane toads are, after all, *animals*. Even if they breed rapidly and change ecosystems in undesirable ways, they are sentient beings.

Killing toads in this way can create a virtual reality of its own. Although it is good to get children away from their computer games and into the great outdoors, it is odd to kill animals in a way that is just another game of little real or ethical consequence. This is hardly the sort of participation that will build great citizens. Nor is it likely to eradicate the fecund toad.

Darwin is surely the only town in the world where a Lord Mayor was elected on a political platform that included leadership in toadbusting and promoting toad-whacking safaris as a tourist gimmick.[18] Toad politics had a time and place. In 2008, the month before the relevant mayoral elections, an international team of scientists documented the fact that toads were spreading faster than even the models had predicted.[19] This exceptional behaviour called for an exceptional political leader with a concern for conservation.

Belonging and not belonging

Metaphors are important to sustainability efforts, as Canadian geographer Brendan Larson argues.[20] What is crucial in the cane toad story is what 'belongs' and what doesn't. Animals 'belong' (or not) in Australia as *native* or *alien*, categories often based on specimens kept in museums half a world away. Cane toads change ecosystems suddenly. This is an 'unnatural' and seemingly alien animal. But the question of what belongs and what doesn't in a settler society is not simply based on Linnaean classifications.

The cane toad was deliberately introduced to Queensland in 1935 to attack a native Australian Greyback Beetle *Dermolepida albohirtum*, a recognised sugar cane pest. As a 'biological control agent', the cane toad belonged to the category of an 'industry animal' (like sheep or cattle), an instrument for furthering the economy, invisible as biota.[21] The French cane beetle *Lepidiota frenchi* was also perceived as a problem in the sugar industry, but there was no differentiation between the Australian and the non-Australian beetle: they were both just pests. The option for biological control was better than using poison: beetles could not be poisoned without also killing beneficial (native and non-native) insects at the same time, so the cane toad was welcomed initially. The cane toad offers an extreme example of invasiveness, but its story is typical of deliberate introductions. It was one of many introductions designed to meet specific needs of the settler economy either by supplying deficit items (most famously, rabbits and foxes for hunting or birds for their songs) or for pest control. As Eric Rolls put it in the title of his 1969 history of acclimatisation, *They All Ran Wild*.[22] Introductions were for biological control in the service of the settler economy, and when they went wrong, they went 'wild'. The *good* here was the economy; the *bad* was when nature flourished excessively. Nature, of course, behaves the way it does irrespective of human economic aspirations. Cosmopolitan biota will always do well in an ancient, isolated continent where there are no natural predators or competition.

Cane toads are 'ecosystem wreckers'. They invade at a landscape scale – indeed, nearly a *continental* one. Yet 'busting' eradicates individuals, *one toad at a time*. 'A toad a minute', as Ian Vigger, one Adelaide River buster put it, 'is just doing my bit'.[23] The population explosion is not something citizen science can tackle alone.

Prey as threat

Some people think toads are stalking the north, eating wildlife. In fact, toads are only dangerous when *eaten*. The poison glands on the toad kill the predator. Thus, the most dangerous toad is the *first one* to arrive on the frontier, the one that native animals think is food and have never before experienced as poisonous. This is the danger that toads pose for biodiversity. Yet it is not only wildlife that eat toads. Pet dogs regularly die from eating toads, and sometimes cats as well, yet the toad eradication rhetoric focuses on 'protecting native wildlife'. In most other contexts, cats and dogs themselves are constructed as enemies of native animals,[24] but this conservation effort is attractive to pet owners, as eliminating toads as an accidental food source benefits pets and wildlife alike.

Rick Shine, winner of the prestigious Prime Minister's Prize for Science in 2016, knows a lot about defending the rights of unfashionable animals.[25] He is Australia's leading snake expert and long-time student of the animals of the Top

20   *Libby Robin*

End. His study site at Fogg Dam, Humpty Doo, is an hour's drive south-east of Darwin. It is a 'paradise for snakes' and a place where he has worked for more than three decades.[26] The cane toad arrived at Humpty Doo in December 2004: the local paper records this.[27] Fogg Dam *was* the cane toad frontier in 2005, when Shine took up his Federation Fellowship (a major research prize), moving there to set up a major ecological experiment with his group of scientists affectionately known as Team Bufo.[28] The team moved straight into the former rice research station. Their work included toads but also their interactions with snakes, goannas, marsupials and the whole ecosystem. Being physically on an invasion frontier provided an opportunity for Shine to look at how toad invasions worked and how to model them. The work was important because it also compared toads with other invasive species and built ways to manage invasive species in wet tropical ecosystems. Shine began with the *history* of toad invasions and documented how they changed over time:

> In the early years (up to the 1960s or so), the toad invasion front advanced fairly slowly – about 10 km each year. But then it began to speed up, and has kept accelerating. The front now moves at about 40 to 60 km per year. Our radio-tracking shows that this is because individual toads at the front travel longer distances (sometimes more than a kilometre) each night – and do so every night. This is an incredible rate for an amphibian: cane toads at the Aussie invasion front travel much, much faster and further than any other frogs or toads that have been studied elsewhere in the world.[29]

This most important conclusion from this history is not so much about the environmental damage to the ecosystems but about the fact that such an invasion drives rapid evolution not only of cane toads but also of native animals responding to them:

> We know that toads kill lots of native predators that try to eat the toxic invaders, but cannot tolerate the toads' poisons. Animals that try to eat big toads, like quolls and goannas, are in the biggest trouble (because big toads have a <u>lot</u> more poison than small toads). However, not every predator is equally vulnerable. Some are reluctant to try to eat toads; others are a bit more tolerant than usual of the toads' poison, and so forth. In evolutionary biology jargon, this means that cane toads in Australia are a "selective pressure" [on evolution].[30]

Shine's management strategy was to focus on the vulnerable predators: he trained them to avoid the toads. He realised the big animals were the only ones that could eat a big cane toad, but that if there were small toads arriving before the big ones, the big animals could be given an aversive dose of poison that would make them sick but not kill them. They would learn that these toads are not food. The toad frontier normally advanced led by big fat strong toads, with smaller ones in their wake. He reversed this, successfully introducing small toads ahead of the big ones, which reduced the poisoning deaths of goannas and snakes and quolls. By modifying the behaviour of the predators, he saved enough of the native animals for their populations now to be recovering.

Shine is always gentle when he speaks of the animals. His low-key style is very different from the machismo around toadbusting. He supports the work of the toadbusters with science but does not endorse the tone. His website includes a fact sheet debunking myths about toads.[31] His most powerful insight is that if a female toad can lay 30,000 eggs in a single night, killing 'one toad at a time', even one a minute, as Ian Vigger offered, is not going to make a difference, unless the toad happens to be pregnant. Pregnant toads are seldom on the frontier – they follow the leaders. Shine's conservation strategies have concentrated on retraining native animals in anticipation of the frontier. Scientists also fence waterholes to limit opportunities for huge breeding events – without water there can be no breeding event.[32]

Shine works closely with citizen science, extending its capacity. He has addressed the wasting of bodies in 'culling' operations that has been widely criticised by ethicists and animal rights campaigners.[33] Toadbusters can help behavioural retraining of native animals by *collecting* the animals they kill. Shine recommends toads be killed 'humanely' in freezers so that they can then be minced into sausages for his taste aversion conservation program. Involving people who want to help and caring about what happens to the bodies, rather than leaving them flattened on the road, is better for the toads, for the native animals, for science and for the killers of toads.[34] It extends the role of conservation practice to include the community, but it does not let it become just a killing game.

Nature in crisis

In 1985, ecologist Michael Soulé described conservation biology as a science of 'crisis', likening it to emergency medicine, where not everything can be done at once, and quick decisions must support the most critical cases.[35] The term 'biodiversity' itself was introduced into international conservation biology in 1986 as a device to help policymakers count species loss, to make extinctions visible in the policy environment and to help with prioritising the spending of the limited conservation funding.[36] International Union for Conservation of Nature (IUCN) 'red lists' were part of a wider 'trust in numbers'[37] that was part of evidence-based policy development. But counting species is very different from assessing how any one invasive species affects a whole ecosystem and its evolutionary future, as Tim Low has argued cogently.[38] What does crisis and uncertainty do for science? Increasingly, it makes for conversations with philosophical, ethnological and anthropological scholars – like Deborah Rose, who writes of how she learns about being in nature from Aboriginal teachers; like Donna Haraway, who argues for a 'more than human' conservation that works at the level of the multi-species organism; and like semiologists Jacob von Uexküll and Kalevi Kull, who argue that relations with nature should not exclude the consciousness of non-human others. Already in Australia, ecologist Adrian Manning draws on von Uexküll's

22   *Libby Robin*

philosophy in developing practical conservation plans for Mulligans Flat, country on the urban/rural edge of Canberra.[39]

New conservations question the scale of operation. Should one save species? Landscapes? Organisms? Ecosystems with porous edges? It is often the non-scientific extended peer community that frames the funding and the scale of operation, not just conservation science or ecological principles. Judges of what constitutes 'good conservation practice' include community action groups, citizen scientists, environmental policy wonks and officers working for government or corporate instrumentalities. For example, as Wilkie explores in Chapter 11 of this volume, the army manages significant areas of Crown land in Australia for conservation purposes. Working with the 'politically possible' and trying to align as much as possible with the scientifically desirable has always been the tightrope walk of public science and policy.

Science, with its probabilistic and pragmatic approaches to the world – including modelling and scenario making – has become increasingly important in understanding 'hyperobjects' like climate change and extinction, which are the flashpoints of sciences of crisis like conservation biology. Humanist and philosopher Timothy Morton defines a *hyperobject* as something that is too big and abstract to be seen by any human eye or comprehended by human rules. Hyperobjects can be inferred mathematically and logically, but they are neither life nor 'other than life'. They are seldom concrete. Yet as things that one can compute and think, but neither see nor touch, they can still be scary and emotive.[40] In a world of hyperobjects, reason itself is no longer a merely humanist endeavour 'but rather something larger and more intractable than we had supposed', Morton argues.[41] Like the natural scientists, humanists argue that we need new transdisciplinary conversations that forge unusual and innovative alliances and that broaden the expertise to include the humanities. Partnerships need to include artisanal scholarship, too. The practical skills of conservation, right down to making toad sausages, are increasingly important in a mix where not everything can be funded.[42]

Concepts like *nature* and *environment* take on new meanings and demand different understandings if the distinction between humans and other-than-humans is porous and the environment is *within* and not just 'around' us. Ecological science alone is not enough. There have never been enough ecologists to do all the work or even to supervise it. Volunteer workforces and philanthropic benefactors are essential to conservation, and engaging their support involves explaining the science but also listening to their passion, concern and care. Funding bodies and governments far from the conservation situation may set an agenda without understanding the motivations of either science or the volunteers. Learning about how an organism lives in its environment can inspire warm responses that are helpful to ethical conservation practice.[43]

Conclusions

The precautionary principle demands 'first do no harm'.[44] This includes not riding roughshod over the concerns of people who live locally on the scales where the consequences of programmatic plans will be felt.[45] Assuming any invasive biota needs *eradicating* is an extreme position. There is also a place for Donna Haraway's humanistic approach of reframing the question and 'staying with the trouble', by which she means acknowledging the problem, but continuing to work with it, rather than finding 'solutions' that bring their own problems.[46] Accelerating climate change demands constant rethinking and new thinking about relations *between* biota. Important among these are relations between people and other animals. Variability is becoming more pronounced as climate change advances. Uncertainty is increasing. What is 'normal' or 'natural' is changing fast. Climate modelling also suggests increasing monsoons and cyclones in northern Australia, spreading the wet further inland. Cane toads, which travel with the wet, will be probably winners in such changing circumstances. More diverse approaches are already needed and, encouragingly, are happening on the ground. Nature's future, the health of the country and climate justice can all benefit from imaginative practices that extend ethical care to animals, even toads.

Notes

1 Shakespeare, *As You Like It* features toads 'ugly and venomous' as signs of adversity. Kenneth Grahame, *Wind in the Willows* (London: Methuen, 1946).

2 Each 'first' sighting is reported as headline news in local papers – for example, Chalpat Solti, 'Cane Toad Found in Broome', *WAtoday.com.au*, 19 July 2010; 'A Cane Toad Has Been Spotted in Hawks Nest', *Great Lakes Advocate*, 15 June 2017.

3 Eleni Roussos, 'He's Blowing Up: Huge Toad Shocks Julie Bishop', 9 August 2010, www.abc.net.au/news/2010-08-09/hes-blowing-up-huge-toad-shocks-julie-bishop/937756 (accessed 13 February 2018).

4 David Walker, *Anxious Nation: Australia and the Rise of Asia 1850–1939* (Brisbane: University of Queensland Press, 1999); Warwick Anderson, *The Cultivation of Whiteness: Science, Health and Racial Destiny in Australia* (Melbourne: Melbourne University Press, 2005); Libby Robin, *How a Continent Created a Nation* (Sydney: University of New South Wales Press, 2007).

5 In fact, it has now been established that toads eat everything in sight – not just beetles but wood and car tyres and other things not usually regarded as food at all.

6 Jodi Frawley, 'A Lucky Break: Contingency in the Storied Worlds of the Prickly Pear', *Continuum: Journal of Media and Cultural Studies*, 28.6 (2014): 760–73, quote 770.

7 It was also important to international scientific networks. As Frawley observed, Australia was not the end of the line for introductions; it was a step on the way to global science. After the success with Prickly Pear in this era, Australia went on to supply *Cactoblastis* to South Africa, Ceylon (Sri Lanka), New Caledonia and the Dutch East Indies (Indonesia).

   The introduction of *myxomatosis* to fight rabbits was forced upon CSIRO by the pressures of the influential Jean Macnamara and international pressure. Macnamara whipped up desperate local farmers (and they spread the virus before the CSIRO was ready to release it). But because it was a success, the scientists were quick to claim it, as the future of CSIRO depended on stories like this one. See Brian Coman, *Tooth & Nail: The Story of the Rabbit in Australia* (Melbourne: Text, 2010).

8 Mark Urban et al., 'A Toad More Traveled', *American Naturalist*, 171.3 (2008): E134–48.

9 Urban et al., 'A Toad More Traveled', E145, put it this way: 'Cane toads reached the western Northern Territory in 2006, a full 21 years before' [Freeland and Martin had predicted their arrival in 1985]. Freeland and Martin's earlier modelling had been based on constant (linear) expansion rates.

24 *Libby Robin*

10 David Trigger, Jane Mulcock, Andrea Gaynor and Yann Toussaint, 'Ecological Restoration, Cultural Preferences and the Negotiation of "nativeness" in Australia', *Geoforum*, 39 (2008): 1273–83.

11 Libby Robin, Joslyn Moore, Sharon Willoughby and Sara Maroske, 'Aliens From the Garden', *Proceedings of the State of Australian Cities Conference*, Melbourne, 30 November–2 December 2011, http://apc.org.au/node/59951; Libby Robin, *Building a Forest Conscience: An Historical Portrait of the Natural Resources Conservation League of Victoria, 1944–1990* (Springvale: Natural Resources Conservation League, 1991).

12 Libby Robin, 'Wattle', in Melissa Harper and Richard White (eds.), *Symbols of Australia: Uncovering the Stories behind the Myths* (Sydney: UNSW Press/NMA Press, 2009), 114–19; Jane Carruthers et al., 'A Native at Home and Abroad: The History, Politics, Ethics and Aesthetics of *Acacia*', *Diversity and Distributions*, 17.5 (2011): 810–21, doi:10.1111/j.1472–4642.2011.00779.x; Dave Kendal et al., 'Led up the Garden Path? Weeds, Conservation Rhetoric and Environmental Management', *Australasian Journal of Environmental Management*, 24.3 (2017): 228–41, doi:10.1080/14486563.2017.130 0954.

13 IPAs represent over half of the land in reserves in the Northern Territory.

14 Mark Lewis, *Cane Toads: An Unnatural History* (Film Australia/Ronin Films, 1988). Documentary, 47 minutes.

15 Song-writer Dana Lyons, performed by Dana Lyons with Jack Tinapple on drums (Technical Production Charles Darwin University, Darwin), www.youtube.com/watch?v=6n0PUbV0Q_U (accessed 10 December 2017).

16 See www.canetoads.com.au/. The Kimberley Toad Busters manage this site.

17 See 'Cane Toad Muster' (2013): www.youtube.com/watch?v=6n0PUbV0Q_U.

18 See Alyssa Betts, 'Toad Killing Safaris Could Boost Tourism', *NT News*, 4 June 2010, www.couriermail.com.au/news/toad-killing-safaris-could-boost-tourism/news-story/2039b1643ddf49c2bae497c4d23447dd (accessed 10 December 2017).

19 Urban et al., 'A Toad More Traveled'.

20 Brendon Larson, *Metaphors of Sustainability* (New Haven: Yale University Press, 2011).

21 Lesley Head makes a similar argument for why wheat does not appear on 'vegetation maps'. It is a product, not a plant. Lesley Head, Jennifer Atchison and Alison Gates, *Ingrained: A Human Biogeography of Wheat* (Abingdon: Ashgate, 2016).

22 Eric Rolls, *They All Ran Wild* (Sydney: Angus and Robertson, 1969).

23 Richard Nelson, n.d. 'Cane Toad', *Encounters* radio program. http://podbay.fm/show/304284997/e/1265839467?autostart=1 (accessed 24 March 2018).

24 See, for example, Australian Government, 'Tackling Feral Cats', Fact Sheet, 2015, www.environment.gov.au/system/files/resources/8bde0309-4f18-4bab-bda8-fc3d78bb5c75/files/factsheet-tackling-feral-cats.pdf (accessed 10 December 2017).

25 Marcus Strom, 'Professor Rick Shine Wins Prime Minister's Prize for Science for Work on Cane Toads', *Sydney Morning Herald*, 19 October 2016, www.smh.com.au/technology/sci-tech/professor-rick-shine-wins-prime-ministers-prize-for-science-for-work-on-cane-toads-20161017-gs4jqq.html.

26 Margaret Throsby interview with Professor Richard Shine, ABC podcast, recorded 31 October 2016, www.abc.net.au/radionational/programs/archived/throsby/professor-rick-shine/7976190; Terry Lane interview with Rick Shine, 'Toads on the Evolutionary Road', recorded 2005, *Inside Story* podcast, http://insidestory.org.au/toads-on-the-evolutionary-road/.

27 'They're Here!', *The Litchfield Times*, 20.48 (14 December 2004): 1.

28 The genus for cane toads then was *Bufo*. Now it is *Rhinella*.

29 'Cane Toads in Oz,' www.canetoadsinoz.com/invasion.html (accessed 10 December 2017). This website gathers together a range of scientific and popular sources, including ABC interviews with Shine as well as maps and graphs of invasion patterns. It is set out for popular audiences, including schoolchildren.

30 See www.canetoadsinoz.com/invasion.html. For an example of the science, see Ben L. Phillips and Richard Shine, 'An Invasive Species Induces Rapid Adaptive Change in a Native Predator: Cane Toads and Black Snakes in Australia', *Proceedings of the Royal Society B (Biological Sciences)*, 273.1593 (2006): 1545–50, doi:10.1098/rspb.2006.3479.

31 See www.canetoadsinoz.com/debunkingcanetoadimpactmyths.html.

32 Darren Southwell's team is fencing waterholes south of Broome to try to prevent toads crossing the desert, www.abc.net.au/news/2016-09-04/cane-toad-barrier-gives-hope-in-battle-to-stop-pests-spread/7795342 (accessed 10 December 2017).

33 On the ethics of killing, see Thom van Dooren, 'Invasive Species in Penguin Worlds', *Conservation and Society*, 9.4 (2011): 286–98; Jonathan L. Clark. 'Uncharismatic Invaders', *Environmental Humanities*, 6 (2015): 29–52.

34 Erin Parke, 'Cane Toad Sausages on the Menu', 14 November 2016, www.abc.net.au/news/2016-11-14/cane-toad-sausages-to-help-protect-native-species-in-wa-north/8024904.

35 Michael E. Soulé, 'What Is Conservation Biology?' *Bioscience* 35.11 (1985): 727–34; Libby Robin, Sverker Sörlin and Paul Warde (eds.), *The Future of Nature: Documents of Global Change* (New Haven: Yale University Press, 2013): 363–6.

36 Libby Robin, 'The Rise of the Idea of Biodiversity: Crises, Responses and Expertise', *Quaderni* (Journal of l'Institut des Sciences Humaines et Sociales du CNRS); Special Issue: *Les promesses de la biodiversité*, 76.1 (2011): 25–38.

37 Theodore Porter, *Trust in Numbers: The Pursuit of Objectivity in Science and Public Life* (Princeton: Princeton University Press, 1995); Ursula K. Heise, *Imagining Extinction: The Cultural Meanings of Endangered Species* (Chicago: University of Chicago Press, 2016).

38 Tim Low, *Feral Future: The Untold Story of Australia's Exotic Invaders* (Melbourne: Penguin 1999).

39 Deborah Rose, *Reports from a Wild Country* (Sydney: University of New South Wales Press, 2005); Donna Haraway, *Staying with the Trouble: Making Kin in the Chthulucene* (Durham, NC: Duke University Press, 2016); Andreas Roepstorff, Nils Bubandt and Kalevi Kull (eds.), *Imagining Nature: Practices of Cosmology and Identity* (Aarhus: Aarhus University Press, 2003); Adrian Manning et al., 'Continua and *Umwelt*', *Oikos*, 104.3 (2004): 621–7. On the rise of environmental humanities and multispecies thinking, see Libby Robin, 'Environmental Humanities and Climate Change: Understanding Humans Geologically and Other Life Forms Ethically', *WIREs Climate Change*, 26 October 2017, e499, doi:10.1002/wcc.499.

40 Timothy Morton, 'This is Not My Beautiful Biosphere', in Tom Bristow and Tom Ford (eds.), *A Cultural History of Climate Change* (Abingdon: Routledge, 2016): 229–38.

41 Morton, 'This is Not My Beautiful Biosphere', 229.

42 Robin, 'Environmental Humanities and Climate Change', 9.

43 John Turner, professor of botany and plant physiology at the University of Melbourne (1938–1973), argued that you could not but be a 'conservationist' if you understood biology (Turner interview with author 1991). This view was widespread among conservation activists in the twentieth century.

44 Libby Robin, 'A History of Global Ideas about Environmental Justice', Anna Lukasiewicz et al. (eds.), *Natural Resources and Environmental Justice* (Melbourne: CSIRO Publishing, 2017), 13–25.

45 Libby Robin, 'Culling and Care: Ferals, Invasives and Conservation Icons in Australia', *Australian Zoologist* (2017), Online advance https://doi.org/10.7882/AZ.2016.024.

46 Haraway, *Staying with the Trouble*.

3 Taking locust country

Andrea Gaynor

It is 1953 and eastern Australia is in the grip of a major outbreak of the Australian plague locust, *Chortoicetes terminifera*. Arriving in a dense, whirring fog, they devour pastures and lawns, even entering homes and chewing on clothing and furnishings. As the locusts swarm southward, the Victorian government responds with a military campaign mobilising Royal Australian Air Force (RAAF) and civilian personnel and aircraft to spray the organochlorine pesticide Gammexane. The Melbourne-based *Argus* newspaper reports the hopper 'invasion' with a map depicting the swarms moving relentlessly through Dubbo, Parkes and Forbes towards the Murrumbidgee River. There they would be met by the RAAF planes and poison baits protecting the fruit and sheep beyond; more poison awaited the invaders at the Murray River (see Figure 3.1).[1]

There are manifold historical connections between war and nature, from Emperor Probus's deployment of Roman soldiers to drain marshlands and the US Army Corps of Engineers' ongoing efforts to tame the Mississippi to the use of natural features in military strategy and the ecological consequences of warfare.[2] Environmental historian Edmund Russell, who has examined relationships between war and nature through insect pests and pesticides, proposes that 'war and control of nature coevolved', and each influenced the other in the areas of ideas, materials and organisations.[3] This is borne out in the case of agricultural development in Australia, where many settlers found the vegetation and climate harsh and alienating. Metaphors of war were commonplace in their descriptions of the struggle to create farms and produce crops. There were also material connections – for example, in the use of ex-military tanks to clear southern Australia's mallee woodlands for farming in the 1950s.[4] The response to locusts, however, stands out due to the strength and ubiquity of its material and metaphorical militarisation: it was a literal war waged against nature using the same strategies, techniques and even personnel and vehicles deployed in war on humans.

Responses to swarming locusts have been deeply entangled with warfare and statecraft in other national and imperial contexts. Claude Peloquin, for example, has shown how the French resistance in the Second World War used locust control to bolster its claims for geopolitical legitimacy by presenting the French colonial empire as a constructive and benevolent techno-scientific federation that united its members against both non-human (locust) and human (Axis)

Figure 3.1 The war on locusts in south-eastern Australia, as depicted in *Argus*, 25 November 1953.

Source: 'Layout of the Big Battle', *Argus*, November 25, 1953. National Library of Australia, http://nla.gov.au/nla.news-article23302361.

enemies.[5] John Thistle has demonstrated how locust irruptions acted as a field for consolidation of social power using military means and metaphors in the interior of British Columbia, while Ted Deveson's extensive environmental and scientific historical research notes the widespread use of war metaphors in describing the effects of, and responses to, locusts in southern Australia.[6]

28 *Andrea Gaynor*

In this chapter, I propose that the Australian war on locusts presents an extreme case of the general pattern of agricultural and pastoral colonisation of Australia, which involved occupation of country and pacification of the indigenous plants, animals and people through military, scientific and other means. From the beginning of colonisation, military metaphors and strategies have been deployed to achieve control of unruly and insurrectionary spaces and especially indigenous threats from the interior. This settler-colonial mindset combined with long-standing associations between locusts and warfare to make the Australian war on locusts a potent symbol of settler ambitions. This chapter follows the ways in which conceptual and material connections between war on people and war on locusts changed with Australia's various military engagements, from the colonial invasion and occupation of Indigenous territory to the early twenty-first-century war on terror. As James Scott points out, 'the nature of military threat requires clearly defined and easily monitored and patrolled state spaces'.[7] As the potential extent of locust outbreak areas in the interior was increasingly recognised in the mid-twentieth century, so was the state's inability to monitor, let alone control, such vast areas. But from the 1970s, after three decades of almost uninterrupted engagement in warfare overseas, Australia was finally achieving the centralised control and increasingly the technological means to make the unruly inland a state space. As the ongoing locust threat, and the cane toads discussed in Chapter 2 suggest, however, this project is far from complete.

Long locust histories

Chortoicetes terminifera ('the locust') and the taxonomically related small plague grasshopper, *Austroicetes cruciata*, are both native to Australia, with a range extending across the continent. They are herbivorous and live on inland grassy open woodland and tussock grassland, with a preference for establishing egg beds on compact soil and bare ground. The locust can complete two or three generations over the warmer months of the year, with autumn-laid eggs remaining dormant throughout winter.[8] It is exquisitely adapted to take advantage of the scanty and sporadic rainfall of the Australian interior. When conditions are warm and moist, females mature rapidly and eggs develop and hatch without delay. Where there is a low population density, the insects are solitary, but dense populations sustained by sufficient green feed can become gregarious, maintaining mutual attraction and moving in a coordinated way. Once mature, locusts can undertake migratory night flights of up to 700 kilometres at altitudes of up to 3000 metres. If they land in an area where conditions are favourable, further breeding can occur; where hatching and survival rates are high, large swarms will form, with high destructive potential in pastoral and agricultural landscapes.[9] As the locust relies on rainfall to produce sufficient moisture and vegetation to sustain large migratory swarms, these 'plagues' often occur in La Niña years. Although we tend to think of locusts as armoured, winged and hungry automatons, they have individual food preferences and show a capacity for rapid learning in laboratory conditions. In the field, as Ted Deveson puts it, they 'know when they are being pursued'.[10]

The locust forms part of Australian Aboriginal traditions in the arid interior – for example, as a totem of the Ngalea people of what is now north-western South Australia; they were also an occasional food source.[11] However, Aboriginal people were perplexed by the first 'locust' irruptions recorded by colonists in Australia, occurring around Adelaide in the 1840s.[12] These animals were almost certainly *A. cruciata*. The colonists hypothesised that Aboriginal burning regimes had previously kept them in check, and as these ceased, the insects were able to proliferate.[13] It was only from the 1870s that the locust became the more widespread and economically significant species. The burgeoning quadruped populations that spread across southern Australia from the early nineteenth century compacted the soil and reduced the extent of dense grass cover, producing the hardened and bare soils favoured for locust egg beds. Clearing of woodland and forest for agricultural development created more of the locust's favoured grassland habitat, amplifying the trend. The resulting large outbreaks were, to a considerable extent, of the colonists' own making.[14]

'Locust plagues' would have been familiar to the colonists through the Judeo-Christian tradition, in which the swarming behaviour of the desert locust (*Schistocerca gregaria*) of Africa and the Middle East was seen as warlike. In biblical scriptures, locusts appeared as one of the armies of God. The Book of Joel (one of the minor Old Testament prophets), for example, evocatively describes a locust outbreak:

> Their appearance is like the appearance of horses,
> and like war horses they run.
> . . .
> like a powerful army
> drawn up for battle.
> Before them peoples are in anguish;
> all faces grow pale.
> Like warriors they charge;
> like soldiers they scale the wall.
> They march each on his way;
> they do not swerve from their paths.[15]

In the face of this invasion, when the people of Zion assemble the congregation and pray to God, He has pity on them and relents, saying:

> I will restore to you the years
> that the swarming locust has eaten,
> the hopper, the destroyer, and the cutter,
> my great army, which I sent among you.[16]

For the prophet, locusts are the Lord's army, and in their sheer numbers and destructiveness a potent symbol of His might. This conception of locusts was probably due in no small part to the locusts' mobile hyperabundance and physical features. The mass movement of a perceived excess of anonymous bodies with

30   *Andrea Gaynor*

tough exoskeletons saw them readily placed in a military frame, particularly in an era in which Roman infantry wore segmented or scale metal armour and formed well-organised wide fronts in battle.

Bringing war to Australian locusts

In Australia, settlers tended not to regard grasshoppers and locusts as a symbol of God's power, perhaps because of the predominance of Protestantism and its emphasis on the New Testament; presumably also as the settlers upon whom these 'plagues' were visited believed themselves to be virtuous cultivators rather than sinners courting divine punishment. Although locusts were regarded largely in secular terms, the military frame established within the Bible remained. The language of war was evident in the first recorded grasshopper outbreak around Adelaide in 1844 and in subsequent locust irruptions in the 1870s, 1888, 1891 and 1908.[17] Some landholders responded actively with fire and the plough, ripping up egg beds. Some despaired, regarding locusts as a foe they could do no more about than frost or hail. By the twentieth century, state agricultural departments were encouraging collective effort and deploying such insecticides as arsenical sprays against locusts.

Edmund Russell has highlighted the significance of the First World War in the co-evolution of war and the control of nature, from the mutually beneficial relationships developing between the military and economic entomologists to the cultural prevalence of conceptual connections between war on insects and war on people.[18] This conflict also served to strengthen conceptual connections between war and locusts in Australia and to render them more physically material. As early as November 1914, the *Maitland Weekly Mercury* wrote of the emerging forms of industrial warfare: 'Only machines ingeniously constructed to destroy men as locusts have to be destroyed when they sweep over fertile land . . . could carpet the earth with dead in this frightful way.'[19] Wartime developments in aviation gave rise to aerial deployment of agricultural pesticides; the US Army, for example, was involved in crop-dusting operations and companies in the 1920s.[20] Flamethrower and poison gas technology originally deployed in the First World War would soon be trialled against locusts in the Middle East and central Asia, and Australian farmers would advocate the use of such technologies locally.[21]

These overseas models of locust control were regularly brought to the attention of Australians in ways that maintained the military frame. In 1930, for example, the Australian press reported on a full-scale war against the locusts on the Sinai Peninsula, in which an army of 1000 humans equipped with six-wheel lorries and flamethrowers were fighting 'localised battles against the locust armies'. It was said that 'Highly tactical and strategic qualities are needed for coping with the plague of locusts in Egypt, because locusts display an uncanny mass intelligence', often sensing danger ahead. Unlike most armies, they had no leaders, except fliers which, it was said, 'resemble reconnoitring aeroplanes'.[22] As the mechanisation of war accelerated in the twentieth century with the development of tanks, aluminium aircraft and automated weaponry, the physical qualities of the locust – highly mobile, with a hard, armour-like exoskeleton – increasingly lent themselves to perception and description in military terms.[23]

Although the threat posed by locusts arose from their perceived excess, it was compounded by their sudden, enigmatic appearance in agricultural areas in large numbers. Deveson notes that the very first locust outbreaks in the 1870s were accompanied by speculation that locusts came from the 'vast uninhabited' interior.[24] In 1921, Russian entomologist Boris Uvarov developed an influential theory that at least some locust species had permanent breeding grounds in which they underwent phase changes and began their destructive migrations.[25] It is unclear whether this influenced New South Wales government entomologist Walter Froggatt's claim, publicised in 1921, that the locust 'breeds in the desert, or unoccupied land, and then flies to cultivated or fertile grassland'. Froggatt concluded, 'There will always be a large area of uncultivated or untilled land in Central Australia, where the plague locusts may breed; and we may expect this plague at any time in a very large portion of some of our richest lands'.[26] During an outbreak in 1928, Froggatt suggested that 'large armies of hungry locusts' emerged in the western districts of NSW before making their way south and east into agricultural areas.[27] Froggatt was writing at a time when transport and communication technologies were making the interior less forbidding: it was more than 20 years since Francis Birtles had ridden a bicycle across the continent and more than a decade since the two ends of the Trans-Australian Railway had met at Ooldea. Rev. John Flynn's Aerial Medical Service had just been established. Soon a new image of a breathtaking 'red centre' would join the older motif of the 'dead heart', reflecting Australians' increasing fascination with the aesthetics of the desert. Yet the interior remained enigmatic and challenging; its vastness and sparse population an ongoing cause for anxiety.

In 1934, when the next major locust outbreak occurred, Australia still lacked the capacity to tackle the locusts at their inland origin, so the military model was one of defending agricultural areas from the invading swarms. Newspapers provided a blow-by-blow account of the distribution of the swarms and the damage incurred as well as the success of countermeasures. During this outbreak, the main strategy for combating the advancing swarms was to mix arsenic with bran and lay the baits in their path in a pragmatic strategy that also mirrored the deployment of land mines during the First World War.[28] A special report for *Argus* conveyed the excitement of tackling the insects: 'An intense campaign of poisoning will be begun tomorrow morning, when the volunteers will rush to the area, taking with them, in motor-trucks, about five tons of poison, which will be mixed with bran and spread in front of the insects.'[29] The language of war was widespread in the reporting, describing the 'Uncultivated areas attacked', 'invading horde', and 'campaign of poisoning'. Farmers met 'to discuss plans for an attack on the swarms of grasshoppers'. However this language was not ubiquitous and was tempered by the more neutral language of natural disaster.

32 Andrea Gaynor

The Second World War: air power and chemical control

The Second World War played a key role in consolidating and materialising linkages between war on humans and war on insects, which was continued in the Cold War conflicts of the Korean War, Malayan Emergency and Vietnam War. The loss of HMS *Prince of Wales* and HMS *Repulse* to Japanese fighter planes off Malaya in December 1941 provided an early indicator of the importance of air power, which came to dominate the war in the Pacific. But there were airborne dangers other than Japanese aircraft. Although it was not widely publicised at the time, malaria caused more Australian casualties than wounds in the Pacific theatre, and the ability of Australian troops to continue fighting in Papua was solely due to the acquisition and deployment of anti-malarial drugs and mosquito control measures.[30]

Anti-malaria units were established within the Australian military, and in 1945, RAAF Beaufort planes also began to spray DDT in New Guinea, New Britain and Bougainville in order to protect troops.[31] Although DDT was ineffective against locusts, in the context of the broader significance of air power in the Pacific war, this activity certainly made an impression on Australian farmers.

In Australia in the 1940s, the insecticide of choice for locust control was BHC or benzene hexachloride, also known as Gammexane. It was one of the new organochlorine insecticides developed during the Second World War, inspired by the example of DDT. Gammexane is a potent neurotoxin and likely human carcinogen. It is also highly toxic to fish and bees and causes eggshell thinning in birds. An international ban on its agricultural use was implemented in 2009 under the Stockholm convention on Persistent Organic Pollutants.

In the spring of 1945, an RAAF aircraft equipped for DDT anti-mosquito spraying was used to treat a Rutherglen bug outbreak in northern Victoria. Attention then turned to the locusts which were unusually prevalent in the Victorian mallee that season. The equipment and techniques used for spraying mosquitoes during the Pacific war were found unsuitable for agricultural purposes, and the Commonwealth Scientific and Industrial Research Organisation (CSIRO) and RAAF worked together to modify the aircraft and technique to achieve better results. To find the best liquid carrier for the pesticide, they sought the assistance of the Chemical Warfare Section of the Munitions Supply Laboratories. Tests showed that diesel made the best and most cost-effective carrier solution. After a further process of field experimentation and modification, satisfactory results were achieved. The results were written up for an article in the *Journal of Agriculture, Victoria*, jointly authored by the Department of Agriculture senior entomologist and the RAAF flight lieutenant who led the operation.[32]

In 1946, a concentration of locust egg beds was again discovered in the Victorian mallee, and the Victorian Department of Agriculture approached the RAAF to see whether they could again assist in preventive spraying.[33] The RAAF immediately set about reconditioning and modifying more aircraft, and anti-grasshopper operations in the mallee using four RAAF planes commenced in October 1946.

The squadron leader reported that the work was 'highly successful and of great value to the agriculturalists. The modification which resulted from the tests should make a big improvement to our anti-mosquito technique should it be necessary to again undertake such work'.[34] He predicted that the spraying would continue for several weeks and noted that RAAF capacity to spray insecticides should also be maintained to protect personnel stationed in New Guinea and New Britain as well as those on exercises in remote island areas. When in November 1946 the Victorian Department of Agriculture asked for more resources to extend the spraying campaign, the RAAF replied that a manpower shortage made this impossible but proposed that Mustang aircraft could be used for spraying as part of air force pilot-training exercises.[35] Locust control was becoming yet more deeply entangled with military objectives.

In 1948, the NSW Department of Agriculture published a brochure on recent developments in grasshopper control in which they recommended the use of improved bran baits using Gammexane. However, they also noted that farmers were resistant to baiting, which they ascribed to 'widely publicised accounts of aircraft distribution of D.D.T. in the war-time malaria-control campaign'.[36] This had apparently given rise to a widespread belief that aerial spraying would be cheaper, easier and more effective than ground-based dispersal of poison to combat locusts.

In 1950, as another locust plague emerged in the mallee, the Victorian Department of Agriculture again sought the assistance of the RAAF. When told that they could not assist, the premier of Victoria, Jack McDonald, wrote to Prime Minister Robert Menzies to ask whether he could get the air force to cooperate.[37] The RAAF, however, really could not spare the aircraft but did provide two sets of spraying equipment as well as a tanker for insecticide, a radio vehicle and associated personnel. DC3 aircraft were provided by Qantas Empire Airways and Australian National Airways in an operation that materially as well as conceptually combined the civil and military.[38]

Towards surveillance and suppression

At this point, locust strategy still involved responding to imminent threats as they emerged; the focus was on defending agricultural areas, and there was no systematic strategy for forward surveillance and control. The latter approach was proposed at a conference of technical officers convened by the Council for Scientific and Industrial Research in May 1947. This meeting recommended that a trial control campaign, using a new strategy of 'outbreak suppression', should be carried out in central NSW as a joint undertaking of state and federal governments. The plan was delayed by lengthy consultations about the cost in 1947 and again in 1949.

The summer of 1952–3 saw a major locust outbreak starting in western NSW, which proceeded south. The Victorian Department of Agriculture coordinated the response described at the beginning of this chapter, 'attacking swarms in southern New South Wales to prevent the invasion of Victoria over the Murray

River'.[39] The campaign involved 29 days of constant aerial spraying of organo-chlorines, using both RAAF and TAA (Trans Australian Airlines) planes.[40]

One newspaper report on the event noted that 'hatchings safe from poison sprays often occur deep in the inland'.[41] However, this was no longer seen as an inevitability, and another conference was convened in 1954 to discuss the possibility of coordinated early control. There, Dr K. H. L. (Ken) Key, principal research officer with the Division of Entomology at CSIRO, said 'a campaign against the plague locust needed the same kind of organisation as a military campaign or that used in fire control'.[42] The head of the entomology division, Dr A. J. Nicholson, likewise suggested that what was needed was 'complete control over the organisation of the campaign on a quasi-military basis'.[43] As Edmund Russell has shown, entomologists did not resile from portraying nature as a battlefield in ways that helped to elevate the status of their profession and mobilise resources.[44] Ultimately, the conference recommended that a patrol officer be appointed and that a trial of 'outbreak suppression' be conducted as a joint Commonwealth-State undertaking, based on 'a highly-developed intelligence service' able to locate all swarms in or near the outbreak area.[45] This recommendation was then approved by the Australian Agricultural Council.[46]

This authorisation occurred at the end of a major plague, but it also took place in the context of a military conflict to the near north of Australia, the Malayan Emergency. The Malayan government had responded slowly to the threat posed by communist guerrillas, but in the early 1950s, conflict had escalated rapidly. In 1954, Australia was involved in a joint exercise called 'Operation Termite' (another invertebrate) in which a combined air and ground assault destroyed 181 communist camps. Further Australian troops were committed in October 1955.[47] This campaign offered a model for addressing the locust problem in Australia: pinpoint the enemy through careful surveillance and destroy them in a decisive coordinated joint action to prevent proliferation and counter-attack.

However, after the successes of 1954–5, Australian troops in Malaya were involved in a long mopping-up campaign, comprising extensive surveillance activities. Troops rarely encountered communists, leading to frustration and tension. In an ambush in early 1956, the Australians killed two communists but lost three of their own troops. This highlighted the difficulty of maintaining a controlled state space in a hostile environment.

In 1959, Sir Boris Uvarov, by then a highly influential international locust authority, visited Australia. Although impressed by the preliminary surveillance conducted in anticipation of the proposed trial, he cast doubt on its likely success in a limited form and instead proposed the creation of an interstate organisation that would undertake a coordinated response to locust outbreaks. Shortly after, the committee abandoned plans for the 'outbreak suppression' trial and instead recommended a policy of continual monitoring pending the establishment of an interstate locust organisation to lead monitoring and control efforts. Although this development clearly reflected Uvarov's intervention, it was also congruent with the wider strategic context: as Australians engaged in a drawn-out, frustrating and often fruitless campaign against an invisible and sparse enemy in the

Taking locust country 35

jungles of Malaya, in the absence of a major locust threat, enthusiasm diminished for a small-scale intervention that was unlikely to produce immediate and conclusive victory over the locust hordes. More locust control meetings were held during the 1960s, but the status quo was maintained in the absence of major locust activity, and it took another plague in 1973–4 to spur further action.

Making the unruly inland a state space

In the meantime, Australian troops were deployed in the jungles of Vietnam, engaged in 'search and destroy' missions against the Viet Cong. James Scott has characterised the widespread use of Agent Orange in Vietnam as one example of the 'unprecedented efforts to reclaim non-state space for the state' during that war: defoliating large sections of forest was intended to render it 'legible and safe' for government forces.[48] There are perhaps resonances here with the work of entomological researchers who, in the 1960s, were using regular transects and mark-recapture experiments to make the interior of Australia and its locust denizens known.[49]

After Vietnam, the incoming Australian Labor Party government in 1972 implemented the 'Defence of Australia' policy, focusing on defending continental Australia against external attack rather than on military objectives outside Australian territory. The emphasis here was on surveillance and agile local strike capability. This would lead to the establishment of constant patrols by units in the north of Australia as well as over-the-horizon radar. The patrols mirrored the Australian Agricultural Council's surveillance for locust outbreaks, while from the 1970s, entomological radar would be deployed in locust research and control operations.[50]

A major locust outbreak – the first for 20 years – occurred in 1973, affecting agricultural areas in New South Wales, Queensland, South Australia and Victoria. In October, the NSW government approached the Commonwealth government for assistance to combat the locusts. It responded by supplying aircraft, soldiers and vehicles for ground-to-air radio communications.[51] Sioux helicopters, used for reconnaissance in Vietnam, systematically searched parts of central NSW: locust bands were observed at close range, mapped and then sprayed from fixed-wing aircraft supplied by the army. Queensland also appealed to the Commonwealth government for assistance. In April 1974, the army was sent in with misting units mounted on Land Rovers to fight a 'locust war' over a 160-kilometre radius from Emerald.[52] By now, this was the conventional anti-locust strategy of defensive action against a hostile invader, implemented using actual military personnel and equipment.

At this time, there was also a convergence in organisational thinking between the military and agricultural planning. In 1973, convinced that military efforts in Vietnam were hindered by the division of the Australian military into three arms (army, air force, and navy), Secretary of the Department of Defence Arthur Tange recommended unification of the Australian defence forces. The amalgamation took place in 1976. Meanwhile, in 1974, the year after both the Tange

36 *Andrea Gaynor*

Report and the major locust outbreak, the Australian Plague Locust Commission (APLC) – first envisaged in the early 1950s – was established as a federal agency that could coordinate locust control and research.

When the APLC became operational in 1976, the organisational capacity to adopt Key's idea of 'outbreak suppression' was finally available, as was a military framework for it. Although continuing to defend the agricultural lands against invading locust armies, the APLC would coordinate surveillance and undertake rapid mobile strikes on swarming events in the arid locust heartland. This was akin to guerrilla warfare, and the Viet Cong had shown Australians the importance of environmental knowledge, surveillance, preparedness and mobility in maintaining control of territory. The 'outbreak suppression' strategy had gained significant support in Australia in the early 1950s, and arguably the absence of a major plague before 1973–4 explains the failure to implement it sooner; however, the broader context of changing paradigms of warfare and defence likely also played a role in legitimising, and operationalising, this strategy.

Even after the establishment of the APLC, state Departments of Agriculture remained responsible for locust outbreaks within their borders; their documents reflect the ongoing connections between contemporary warfare and locust response. A South Australian Agriculture Department report of 1977, for example, suggests the influence of the Vietnam experience in terms of both military strategy and public relations. It refers explicitly to 'search and destroy tasks' as well as to intensified surveillance in fringe local government areas and the arid zone. The report gives explicit attention to media liaison, noting that the department's senior entomologist fielded many media inquiries early in the campaign before a departmental media coordinator took control. The results were noted with satisfaction: 'considering the complexities of the campaign and the involvement with the total environment, in respect to the use of insecticides, the campaign overall received very little public criticism'. The report recommended the appointment of a media officer to handle media demands during future campaigns.[53]

Although conventional spraying also took place in major outbreak years, the surveillance and rapid-strike model continued to be the dominant approach to locusts in subsequent decades, as research extended understanding of the conditions under which locusts became gregarious and migrated from the arid interior. Increasingly sophisticated remote-sensing strategies were applied, including the establishment in 1999 of two fully automated insect monitoring radars connected via the phone network to the APLC, representing a low-cost, low-maintenance form of interior surveillance.[54]

Military discourse continued to shape approaches to locusts in the light of the September 11 attacks of 2001 and the Bali bombings in 2002. In December 2002, the face of warfare in Australia changed with the release of a three-month counterterrorism awareness campaign. The slogan was 'Be alert, not alarmed', and it sought to enrol all Australian civilians in the fight against terrorism by reporting suspicious activity to a central hotline.[55] As another major locust plague developed in 2004, the NSW Department of Agriculture released a brochure closely mirroring this language: 'Be alert, be aware, be active'. It encouraged farmers and graziers to observe and mark egg beds, monitor them and notify the local Rural Lands Protection Boards of locust activity on their land.[56] Securing landholder assistance had been a key problem for organisations seeking to control locusts, despite the passage of Noxious Insect Acts from the 1930s that required landholders to treat locust infestations on their properties. It is unsurprising, therefore, that in the early twenty-first century the same kind of language being used to mobilise the civilian population against the perceived terrorist threat was also used to mobilise landholders against the locust threat. The strategic shift evident here is from conscription to counter-insurgency.

Conclusion

Settler engagement with locusts in Australia has historically been shaped by the environment itself, as colonial pastoralism and agriculture unwittingly extended the environmental conditions that enabled locust excess. However, it has also owed much to entangled scientific and military networks of knowledge, technology, strategy and ideas within the broader context of anxieties over the inland. In settler colonial Australia, the biblical significance of locust plagues was stripped of part of its meaning: no longer a symbol of God's power, only the notion of locusts as a military opponent remained. Over time, settler Australians' perceptions of and responses to locusts co-evolved with engagement in warfare on humans. The First and Second World Wars developed scientific and technological capacity to respond to locust incursions into agricultural zones. In the case of the Second World War, counter-locust operations also developed military capacity in airborne and anti-malarial operations. In the wake of Australian involvement in conflicts in Malaya and Vietnam, military personnel and equipment were again deployed in response to large-scale swarming events. At this time, organisational capacity was developed in the form of the Australian Plague Locust Commission, which enabled coordinated surveillance and pre-emptive strikes on inland locust populations. As the military paradigm moved to a focus on the enemy within, landholder cooperation was sought in ways that mirrored Australian counter-terrorist strategy.

To control the locusts was not only to defend the occupied pastoral and agricultural territory but also to master the unruly inland so potently symbolised by the swarming excess of locusts this rebarbative territory unleashed upon the 'settled' districts at seemingly random intervals. Scientific knowledge and technology played a key role in making the inland a state space that was known, patrolled and amenable to central control. This also required a technological and organisational capacity that was developed in concert with military engagement, making use of the strategies, personnel and materials developed for human warfare. As such, the ongoing war on locusts highlights the entanglement of war on humans and war on nature as a key element of modernity.

38 *Andrea Gaynor*

Notes

1 This chapter is based on a seminar paper first presented at the Centre for the Study of the Inland, La Trobe University, 8 June 2016. For a recording and full transcript of the presentation, please see www.latrobe.edu.au/news/announcements/2016/the-war-on-locusts-in-inland-australia-1946-2010. I would like to thank audiences at that seminar and the Australian Historical Association conference in Ballarat for their feedback and encouragement. I would also like to thank Lara O'Sullivan for advice on Roman armies and Libby Robin, Nancy Cushing and Jodi Frawley for comments on an earlier version of this paper. Any errors or omissions are my own.

'Layout of the Big Battle', *Argus*, 25 November 1953, page 7; cited in Edward Deveson, 'Plagues and Players: An Environmental and Scientific History of Australia's Southern Locusts' (PhD diss., Australian National University, 2017), 309.

2 See, for example, S. E. Phang, *Roman Military Service: Ideologies of Discipline in the Late Republic and Early Principate* (Cambridge: Cambridge University Press, 2008); John McPhee, *The Control of Nature* (New York: Farrar, Straus, Giroux, 1989); Richard P. Tucker and Edmund Russell (eds.), *Natural Enemy, Natural Ally: Toward an Environmental History of Warfare* (Corvallis: Oregon State University Press, 2004); Chris Pearson, *Mobilizing Nature: The Environmental History of War and Militarization in Modern France* (Manchester: Manchester University Press, 2012).

3 Edmund Russell, *War and Nature: Fighting Humans and Insects with Chemicals from World War I to Silent Spring* (Cambridge: Cambridge University Press, 2001).

4 Geoffrey Bolton, *Spoils and Spoilers: Australians Make Their Environment 1788–1980* (Sydney: Allen & Unwin, 1981), p. 154; Luke Wong and Melanie Pearce, 'Ex-WWII Tanks Still Used as Paddock Bashers on Australian Farms', *ABC Central West*, www.abc.net.au/news/2016-11-19/tinkering-with-tanks-and-preserving-australian-farming-history/8017194 (accessed 9 October 2017).

5 C. Peloquin, 'Locust Swarms and the Spatial Techno-politics of the French Resistance in World War II', *Geoforum*, 49 (2013): 104.

6 John Thistle, *Resettling the Range: Animals, Ecologies and Human Communities in British Columbia* (Vancouver: UBC Press, 2014), 94ff; Deveson, 'Plagues and Players'; E. D. Deveson, 'The Search for a Solution to Australian Locust Outbreaks: How Developments in Ecology and Government Responses Influenced Scientific Research', *Historical Records of Australian Science*, 22 (2011): 1–31.

7 Scott, *Seeing Like a State: How Certain Schemes to Improve the Human Condition Have Failed* (New Haven: Yale University Press/Yale Agrarian Studies, 1998), 188.

8 Deveson, 'Plagues and Players', 37.

9 Agriculture Victoria, 'Australia Plague Locust Fact Sheet: Identification and Biology', http://agriculture.vic.gov.au/agriculture/pests-diseases-and-weeds/pest-insects-and-mites/plague-locusts/fact-sheet-identification-and-biology (accessed 8 December 2017).

10 Deveson, 'Plagues and Players', 17, 42.

11 Deveson, 'Plagues and Players', 72.

12 'The Locusts', *South Australian Register*, 5 November 1845, 2.

13 'The Locusts', *South Australian Register*, 5 November 1845, 2.

14 Deveson, 'Plagues and Players', 364.

15 Joel 2:4–2:7.

16 Joel 2:25.

17 See, for example, *Maitland Mercury and Hunter River General Advertiser*, 7 December 1844, 3.

18 Russell, *War and Nature*, 76–83.

19 'A War of Machines', *The Maitland Weekly Mercury*, 14 November 1914, 6, cited in Deveson, 'Plagues and Players', 223.

20 Russell, *War and Nature*, 79–80.

21 Deveson, 'Plagues and Players', 258.

22 'Conscripts Fight Locust Plague', *Daily Standard*, 24 April 1930, 1.

23 Note here the contrast with mouse irruptions. Although both mouse and locust irruptions were described as 'plagues', the locust discourse is highly militarised, while the mouse discourse is not. Katie Holmes, 'Mallee Mice' (paper presented at the Australian Historical Association Conference, Ballarat, Victoria, 8 July 2016).

24 Deveson, 'Plagues and Players', 359.

25 B. P. Uvarov, 'A Revision of the Genus Locusta (L.) (= Pachytylus Fieb.), with a New Theory as to the Periodicity and Migrations of Locusts', *Bulletin of Entomological Research*, 12 (1921), 135–63.

26 'A Wandering Plague', *The Advertiser*, 15 November 1921, 7.

27 Walter W. Froggatt, 'Locust or Grasshopper Plagues', *Sydney Morning Herald*, 1 December 1928, 1.

28 For an Australian example, see 'Innocuous Mines', *The Journal*, 21 January 1915, 1, in which land mines laid by the Germans to destroy Australian forces attacking the wireless station at Rabaul had failed to explode.

29 'Grasshopper Menace', *Argus*, 15 November 1934, 18.

30 Second World War Gallery, Australian War Memorial, viewed May 2016.

31 'Malaria and DDT', *Northern Miner*, 25 May 1945, 1; see also 'DDT and Malaria', *West Australian*, 26 November 1945, 4; 'Air Attack on Malaria', *Courier Mail*, 25 May 1945, 3. During the war, DDT and other pesticides were also used extensively in the Northern Territory to eradicate malaria: see Xavier La Canna, 'Curious Darwin: Why Is There no Malaria in Australia's Northern Capital?', *ABC News*, 26 September 2017, www.abc.net.au/news/2017-09-26/curious-darwin-why-is-there-no-malaria-northern-capital/8964984 (accessed 9 December 2017).

32 T. W. Hogan and H. W. Slape, 'Aerial Spraying for the Control of Agricultural Pests in Victoria', *Journal of Agriculture, Victoria*, 44 (1946): 553–8, 562.

33 National Archives of Australia (NAA), A705, 153/1/1304, Directorate of Operations – Department of Agriculture, Victoria – request for planes to spray mallee area with Gammexane.

34 NAA, A705, 153/1/1304.

35 NAA, A705, 153/1/1304.

36 S. L. Allman and J. A. Wright, *Grasshopper Control: Some Recent Developments* (Sydney: New South Wales Department of Agriculture, Entomological Branch, 1948), 2–3.

37 NAA, A705, 153/1/1304.

38 NAA, A705, 153/1/1304.

39 Grasshopper Control Conference and CSIRO, *Grasshopper Control Conference held at Canberra, A.C.T., May 1954* (Melbourne: Commonwealth Scientific and Industrial Research Organization, 1954), preface, 2.

40 Grasshopper Control Conference and CSIRO, *Grasshopper Control Conference held at Canberra*, 3.

41 'He Is Formally Called Pachytylus Australis', *West Australian*, 18 April 1953, 20.

42 Grasshopper Control Conference and CSIRO, *Grasshopper Control Conference held at Canberra*, 7.

43 Grasshopper Control Conference and CSIRO, *Grasshopper Control Conference held at Canberra*, 15.

44 Russell, *War on Nature*.

45 Grasshopper Control Conference and CSIRO, *Grasshopper Control Conference held at Canberra*, appendix G, 2.

46 The Australian Agricultural Council was established in 1935 as a body enabling Commonwealth and State government dialogue on primary production and primary products.

47 Conflicts 1945 to Today Gallery, Australian War Memorial, viewed May 2016.

40   *Andrea Gaynor*

48 Scott, *Seeing Like a State*, 188–9.
49 Deveson, 'The Search for a Solution to Australian Locust Outbreaks'.
50 V. Drake and R. Farrow, 'The Nocturnal Migration of the Australian Plague Locust, Chortoicetes terminifera (Walker) (Orthoptera: Acrididae): Quantitative Radar Observations of a Series of Northward Flights', *Bulletin of Entomological Research*, 73(4) (1983): 567–85, doi:10.1017/S0007485300009172.
51 Australian War Memorial, DPR/TV/1578, 'Army Assistance with NSW Locust Plague', 1973, www.awm.gov.au/collection/F04595/.
52 From John C. Blaxland, *The Australian Army from Whitlam to Howard* (Port Melbourne: Cambridge University Press, 2014), 38.
53 Department of Agriculture and Fisheries South Australia Agronomy Branch, *The Plague Locust Control Campaign – South Australia – 1976–77; Recommendations for the Future Control of the Plague Locust in South Australia*, Report no. 83 (Department of Agriculture and Fisheries, Adelaide, South Australia, 1977), 18, 31, 33.
54 V. Alistair Drake and Haikou Wang, 'Recognition and Characterization of Migratory Movements of Australian Plague Locusts, *Chortoicetes terminifera*, with an Insect Monitoring Radar', *Journal of Applied Remote Sensing*, 7(1) (2013): 075095–1–17.
55 Linda Morris, 'Be Alert, Not Alarmed – Grins Replace Guns on Anti-terrorism Ad', *Sydney Morning Herald*, 28 December 2002, www.smh.com.au/articles/2002/12/27/1040511177155.html (accessed 9 October 2017).
56 NSW Agriculture and Rural Lands Protection Boards, *Plague Locust: Be Alert, Be Aware, Be Active* (Orange: NSW Agriculture, 2004).

4 On the ant frontier
Ontological conflict with *Iridomyrmex humilis* in post-war Sydney

Adam Gall

Introduction: ant history, ontology, phenomenology

This chapter narrates the history of Argentine ants as domestic pests within urban and suburban space in post-World War II Sydney, Australia. Although pest control initiatives are hardly unusual in twentieth-century history, the Argentine ant eradication campaign was distinctive for its degree of publicity, the creation of a dedicated bureaucratic organ – the Argentine Ant Eradication Committee (AAEC) – and for its metropolitan, rather than rural, focus. Although ant pests, and particularly the Argentine ant, are historical actors whose actions are legible across multiple scales of time and space from the everyday to the depths of evolutionary time, the campaign itself ended but not because of the activities of ants. Instead, contradictions between public and bureaucratic practices of environmentalism, each dependent upon different assumptions about time and risk in relation to pesticide use, halted spraying. Once public support could no longer be mobilised by fears of the excessive numbers of ants and their threatening mobility, the persistence of organochlorines in soil and animals became a matter of greater concern. By focusing its narration on ants and the humans who sought to eradicate them across the post-World War II period, this chapter participates in a broader shift towards entangled, more-than-human accounts of past, present and future.[1]

The focus of this chapter has thematic precedents in environmental history, which has long wrestled with historiographic and theoretical problems raised by histories of so-called invasive species. In both global and Australian accounts, some introduced species are useful to colonisation, settlement or development, and others (or the same creatures at other times) become pests.[2] Pesticides, too, have been of interest as a category of pollution which has shaped contemporary environmental consciousness, particularly since Rachel Carson's *Silent Spring* appeared in 1962.[3] This suggests that although the Anthropocene may be synonymous with modern history,[4] its axiomatic expression – anthropogenic climate change brought about through an increasing density of atmospheric carbon and other greenhouse gases – is not the only example of a convergence of natural and human history in modernity. Argentine ants and human initiatives to control or

42 *Adam Gall*

destroy them are similarly implicated in questions of the relationship between narrative, historical time and deep time.

Argentine ants (now *Linepithema humile*, formerly *Iridomyrmex humilis*)[5] are small, dusty brown ants that originate "in lowland areas of the Paraná river drainage"[6] in northern Argentina. Since the late nineteenth century, these ants have acquired a global profile through their rapid expansion into urban and agricultural areas in South America and beyond. From multiple sites of (human-enabled) introduction, they now inhabit six continents and numerous subtropical islands and have achieved "ecological domination"[7] in many locations, displacing native species of ants as well as birds, mammals and other insects. Their destructive effects on agriculture have been acknowledged since the early twentieth century, although they are more widely recognised for their infestation of homes and gardens in urban and suburban areas. Contemporary ant ecology suggests a combination of ant qualities and environmental factors which has facilitated the rapid expansion of Argentine ant populations worldwide. When introduced beyond their native range – when subjected to a population bottleneck during transportation – the ants form single 'supercolonies', sometimes on an immense scale.[8] These expand gradually into promising terrain through incremental acquisition (rather than the independent dispersal of flying queen ants). Like other prominent invasive ant species (for example, the red imported fire ant), they have "generalist habits"[9] and are quick, effective and omnivorous foragers. Outside of their home distribution, they lack predators or intense competition from other ant species. They are successful in watered areas with a Mediterranean climate, particularly where there has been significant soil disturbance, tree removal or recent flooding. For these reasons, Argentine ants have responded favourably to suburban sprawl as well as to large-scale irrigation projects (for example, in California).[10]

Argentine ants' historical being in relation to humans can be understood in two ways. Ian Hacking's concept of historical ontology stresses that our categories, the formations of knowledge and power we assemble to make sense of the world, are themselves part of that world.[11] The concept of the "pest" as a category pertaining to the belonging or otherwise of certain groups of creatures can be understood in this way.[12] A more radically materialist version of this view can be found in Hobbins's account of arthropods in colonial Australia, particularly the red-back spider.[13] Arthropods, argues Hobbins, are conventionally constructed as "transhistorical objects".[14] This means that they are encountered and understood by humans as essentially unchanging and without qualities of agency or subjectivity.[15] But this construction itself has a history to which the behaviour and effects of arthropods contribute, producing change and themselves changing as they enter new relationships with humans, with new environments and with other species. The existence of Argentine ants as a pest species in Australia involves both senses of historical being: it is first generated in science and media at one remove, based in US experience, and then produced materially through everyday encounters and an eradication campaign in the Sydney basin. Specifically, it is firstly through mediated narratives and scientific accounts from elsewhere,

On the ant frontier   43

and then via interactions with humans within Australia, with technologies of eradication (such as pesticides and spraying techniques) and in further media representation (such as newspaper ads, television, campaign materials), that Argentine ants become pests.

Before moving on to the details of this history, our uncomfortable experience (or phenomenology) of ants – the fact that "ants get everywhere"[16] – must also be accounted for. Ants are mobile creatures in our knowledge systems: myrmecology (the study of ants) and entomology (the study of insects) bleed into other areas of knowledge, including linguistics, cybernetics, social psychology and studies of mass culture.[17] But ants sometimes act, too, to trouble our economically valued processes, our physical boundaries and our lived everyday embodiment. The ant as pest is experienced by humans in ways that prevent any sense of its belonging in our shared environments.[18] This phenomenology of infestation is ably captured by literary representation in Italo Calvino's mid-century tale "La formica argentina". In Calvino's story, a young family settles in a new town, and its members discover that their rented house, and the houses of all their neighbours, are beset by thousands of Argentine ants. Their home, which appears at first to be modest but solid, is exposed as "porous and honeycombed with cracks and holes"[19] by the ants' presence. Outdoors, "the insects formed an uninterrupted veil",[20] making practical activity virtually impossible. Their experience is offered as an allegory for capitalist exploitation: the central characters are working-class people, particularly vulnerable for their humble means and beholden to employers and landlords. But even as allegory, the choice of Argentine ants is a motivated one.

Calvino drew upon his own teenage experiences of Argentine ant infestation in San Remo, Italy, grounding literary allegory in this historical experience of infestation.[21] This experience of infestation lingers throughout the historical record. An account from American entomologist Wilmon Newell in 1908 gives authority to the ant's status as household pest, and the human war against them, with the following anecdote:

> In the case of my own residence, a new building, every square inch of surface in each room is regularly "patrolled" by the individual "scouts." No trunk, closet, book case, nor corner is left unexplored, and this despite the fact that since last spring I have waged constant warfare against them by destroying dozens of colonies with bisulphide of carbon.[22]

The first reports of Argentine ants in Australia, from 1939, also stress the experience of household infestation:

> Already the pest has caused so much trouble in the infested area [in the eastern suburbs of Melbourne] that some residents have actually been compelled to move. It has been impossible to keep the insects out of houses. They even invade beds. Babies have to be carefully watched, and in many cases cots and perambulators are stood in vessels containing water.[23]

44   Adam Gall

In Sydney, in 1950, an Auburn Council health inspector is reported as saying that "the ground is literally alive with ants" in certain suburbs.[24] Infestation is the immediate material version of "getting everywhere", and Argentine ant eradication is underwritten in the period I am examining by these human experiences of ant presence.

Given the proliferation of chemical control of pests from the early twentieth century, which intensified with the commercialisation of organochlorine pesticides after World War II,[25] it is perhaps not surprising that the twentieth-century history of Argentine ants is inseparable from the history of pesticides. We can see this from the earliest attention paid by economic entomologists, where chemical control is seen as the preferred means of control (rather than biological or cultural means). As I will discuss next, the ants' own living arrangements make them particularly susceptible to spraying. This association of Argentine ants and pesticides is evident in Australian applied entomology guidebooks, where all references to these ants are redacted because these passages also contained references to the banned chemical chlordane.[26] In what follows, these two dimensions of Argentine ant existence in Australia – a human-ant relationship of infestation as well as their (and our) imbrication with pesticides – change their relationship so that, by the early 1980s, the dangers of the latter come to eclipse lingering concern over the former.

An anticipated pest: economic entomology

In Australia, the ants had a mediated presence well in advance of their physical arrival. Australian newspapers reported on the Argentine ant infestation of Louisiana and elsewhere, narrating the intense campaign being waged against the ants by economic entomologists and farmers in the United States.[27] It was from this campaign that Argentine ants got their popular name and were categorised as a pest species with particular qualities. As an entomologist for the State Pest Crop Committee in Louisiana, Newell worked to promote interest and action against these ants, describing the ants and their activities but performatively shaping them as a pest species. Apart from his detailed anecdotes of domestic infestation, he was also the first to adopt and promote the name "Argentine ant" rather than using scientific nomenclature or local Louisiana designations, such as "crazy ant" and "New Orleans ant".[28] In opting for this designation, Newell was aware of Gustav Mayr's initial description of the species in Buenos Aires in 1868 and William Wheeler's view that its native range was in Brazil and Argentina, hypothesising its arrival in Louisiana with imported coffee beans.[29] Newell attributed to Argentine ants an "extreme hatred"[30] of other ant species that crossed their paths. The affective framing of these ant battles belied the politics of economic entomology as a populist discipline, shaping later encounters with Argentine ants as conflicts over being or existence itself.

Even the "purer" scientific discourse of myrmecology had a role in disseminating this pest characterisation in Australia. Touring Australia in 1914, Harvard's William Wheeler warned that authorities in Australia should "keep a careful watch [for] the Argentine ant, which was a great nuisance in California".[31] The ants were thus progressively folded into a meaningful set of discursive relationships with major scientific and governmental initiatives, particularly those of economic entomology and state and federal agricultural bureaucracies. Post-World War II, entomologists in Australian institutions, such as the Commonwealth Scientific and Industrial Research Organisation (CSIRO) and state Departments of Agriculture, cited this body of US scholarship and experimental work.[32]

Informed by expert testimony, Australian newspapers disseminated reports on "tropical" ants, including the Argentine ant, positioning them within an imagined exotic geography. In the absence of a defined local threat, reports posed ants as objects of curiosity as well as concern.[33] Through the 1920s and 1930s, public predictions were made of imminent arrival of the Argentine ants in Australia. As the Melbourne *Argus* predicted: "That [the Argentine ant] will spread to all the semi-tropical regions of the earth is practically assured".[34] The US experience thus prefaces the Australian post-World War II anti-Argentine ant campaign, ensuring vigilance which nevertheless did not prevent infestation. This discursive space, conditioned in the interface between science and media, awaited the arrival of Argentine ants.

Infestation and eradication: Argentine ants in Australia

Although Argentine ants appeared in Melbourne in 1939, it was not until the immediate post-war period, and the arrival of Argentine ants in Perth, Adelaide and Sydney, that the ant was figured as a clear and present menace and that calls for eradication were sounded in the press. An Argentine ant war was waged in Australia, roughly in parallel with the US fire ant wars, and overlapping the campaigns against locusts treated by Gaynor in this volume over a period from the early 1950s to the mid-1980s.[35] In Western Australia, the campaign became one of control and was legislated first through amendments to the Health Act of 1911 and then with dedicated legislation in Argentine Ant Act of 1954.[36] There was little state government intervention in Victoria until the 1970s, when inter-governmental initiatives to control the movement of ants to other states meant that port facilities had to be sprayed.[37] However, as Andrea Gaynor points out, in Victoria, "spraying was carried out by householders, private pest control operators, and where required by the [local] council".[38] Argentine ants were also understood and managed privately as household pests throughout Australia from this time onward.

In New South Wales, eradication was pioneered and advocated by federal and state entomologists. NSW Department of Agriculture entomologist Gordon Pasfield conducted spraying experiments in Sydney with chlordane solution in 1950. Later that year, he worked with CSIRO entomologist Tom Greaves to develop an application protocol for the pesticide mixture. Together, they determined it was to be "applied in a specially devised, open grid pattern".[39] This pattern appears in public information as well as in instructions later disseminated to fieldworkers.[40] When the 38th Meeting of the Australian Agricultural Council

46   *Adam Gall*

resolved to address the Argentine ant problem nationally, the CSIRO convened a Conference of Entomologists in Canberra from 24–25 June, 1952. The entomologists agreed that "the primary aim should be to remove this menace while this was still practicable".[41] The conference resolved to scale up the earlier experiments of Greaves and Pasfield and "to institute actual eradication campaigns in selected areas".[42]

The conference determined the "eradicability" of the Argentine ant based on five qualities the species was understood to possess: firstly, infesting ants were "numerous and very obvious";[43] secondly, their expansion was readily tracked and observed from initial points of infestation; thirdly, they did not produce flying swarms to initiate new colonies but moved to the boundaries of existing colonies; fourthly, individual nest treatment was not necessary because queens and workers moved around within the larger "mega-colonies" that were formed; and, finally, their nests were relatively shallow, making them susceptible to surface spray of organochlorine pesticides in solution. This eradicability was later inscribed in NSW legislation, with the assumption that the ants could be entirely removed. Thus, ants were encoded in necropolitical terms – that is, as unredeemable from a human perspective and thus killable and subject to proactive extermination – rather than the biopolitical register of control.[44] Eradication meant that human domestic space and ant environments were mutually exclusive.

Eradication was trialled in the Sydney basin, with a focus on its industrial heartland in the central west and on the Cumberland plain. Although infestation was already widespread in Western Australia, Sydney was selected by the conference because there "the infestation was isolated and still relatively small".[45] State government funding was secured from December 1952, with provision of expertise, as well as personnel and equipment, from the CSIRO. The ensuing campaign continued to focus on central western Sydney but was extended to many parts of the metropolitan area, as well as districts beyond Sydney's boundaries, including in the Illawarra region to the city's south.

The experimental campaign: 1952–1962

The campaign worked initially with CSIRO personnel and equipment, temporary contractors and university students doing spray and survey work during vacations in the southern summer months. Chlordane was the first chemical applied, but it was replaced with dieldrin for most applications after experience in Western Australia "had demonstrated its greater efficiency because of its longer residual effect".[46] Chlordane was retained where valuable stock was deemed to be at risk of poisoning from the spray. As with the anti-locust schemes, local newspapers narrated early events of the experimental campaign in military terms, evoking "a dramatic battle [. . .] being waged"[47] in Sydney. Protection of the Homebush abattoirs became an important early rationale for spraying, giving the program a relevance not only for those in immediately affected areas but also for anybody whose lamb chops and Sunday roasts came out of Homebush. The press celebrated the spraying of chlordane over entire suburbs,[48] and some 3590 acres were sprayed with either chlordane or dieldrin between 1952 and 1958.[49] Most of these areas remained Argentine ant-free in 1964. Subsequent infestations were attributable to reintroduction rather than to survival.[50]

From 1960, "a small, well-trained Unit"[51] was sought to continue work under the guidance of a committee (which would become the AAEC). An interim committee was set up to guide the establishment and operation of the unit and included Pasfield, representatives of NSW Departments of Agriculture and Local Government, and local council members nominated by the Local Government Association. Residents of affected areas requested further spraying of their own or their neighbours' properties, with such correspondence retained as evidence of public desire for ongoing government support.[52]

Eventually, the Argentine Ant Eradication Act of 1962 was passed to guarantee funds through money levied from selected local governments, accompanied by state funds. It also included coercive powers requiring landholders to clear land and grant access for clearing and spraying activities (though not to building interiors) wherever it was deemed necessary. The unit headquarters at Homebush – the geographical heart of the earlier experimental campaign – occupied facilities leased for a nominal fee from Strathfield Council. Recruiting and retaining technicians to inspect infestation sites and administer the sprays was a perpetual problem about which Pasfield was circumspect: "it should be remembered that a very special type of person is required for the meticulous work of eradication".[53] Such personnel who were hired required "no less than four months"[54] of training.

The Argentine Ant Eradication Committee: 1962–1985

Under the AAEC, the campaign developed into a routine pattern of inspection, land clearing (usually done by council workers or subcontractors engaged by local governments), then spraying of sites with dieldrin solution. According to detailed reports produced by J. T. Hamilton, the entomologist appointed to oversee the unit, activity tended to be concentrated on industrial estates, goods yards, suburban tips and dumps and their neighbouring residential areas. Particular sites presented difficulties for the unit's activities. Hamilton referred to "untidy properties" in Sydney's south[55] which hindered work. In Matraville, an infested area "contained a large market garden, which required careful spraying".[56] Disputes over ownership or jurisdiction, particularly in the marginal or in-between environments of suburban Sydney, also presented challenges. In the mid-1970s, an infestation at Underwood Road, in the Homebush Bay industrial and wetland area (which would later form the major site for the Sydney Olympics), was sprayed only after careful survey of maps to determine which parts of the site were privately owned and which were under the control of particular government agencies.[57]

There was a degree of sensitivity to work conducted around economically valued stock animals. Of an infested area in Rosehill, the site of a major horse-racing facility, Hamilton wrote that it "contained several properties with stables and these were treated very carefully with chlordane".[58] In 1964, spraying in South

48   *Adam Gall*

Granville "could not be completed because of the presence of a goat",[59] whose owner had been away on vacation. Unit workers occasionally came into harm's way when moving animals from areas to be sprayed. One Mr Keevil, a unit technician, "was slightly injured on the afternoon of 20th May [1965], when kicked in the nose by a sheep" at Stanwell Park, to the south of Sydney.[60] Handwritten notes suggest he "was out catching [the] sheep",[61] but it is unclear whether this was a routine activity or done to appease owners.

Committee records suggest some resistance, complaint and other negative responses. Some individuals sought to prevent the activities of the unit on their land, although it was more common for residents to complain about animal deaths and seek compensation. In 1965, the unit received a complaint from "a Mrs Proctor, 1 Kimberley Grove, Rosebery" that, at the beginning of that month, "her dog had been poisoned" during spraying. Mrs Proctor "was advised to have a post-mortem carried out on the animal".[62] An earlier complaint from a Collaroy couple had required more substantial action be taken by state bureaucrats and eventually compensation to be paid. Dr Ladd Loomis, a veterinarian at the University of Sydney, and his wife, Betty Ann Loomis, wrote letters requesting compensation for the deaths of four poodle puppies, poisoned, they said with dieldrin. Dr Loomis's letter keyed institutional authority by appearing on University of Sydney letterhead, expressing confidence in his conclusions about causality:

> I couldn't understand the illness in our four poodle pups until I heard the description of the convulsion caused by Dieldrin in dogs. Then the whole story fell into place.[63]

Hamilton investigated the site of spraying in Collaroy, and Department of Health officials independently verified the presence of dieldrin in tissue samples. Compensation was eventually paid, and Loomis published his investigations in the *Australian Veterinary Journal*, voicing concern over continued use of dieldrin in Australia.[64] Careful to manage public perceptions of its chemical products, Shell Chemical secured space in the same issue for a dissenting opinion through a letter to the editor.[65]

Although the Loomis's campaign implied perceived limits in pursuit of ant eradication measures, other correspondence tended in the opposite direction. Some constituents at Collaroy had called upon their local state representative to apply pressure to expedite sprayings in the area.[66] It is possible that this was the very spraying event that led to the deaths of the Loomis's puppies. Although a range of perspectives converged on the practical details of the unit's activities, for citizens, their representatives and government officials, the eradication of ants was prioritised over concern about pesticides.

Publicity, citizen science and the politics of scale

Infestation in such Victorian rural towns as Wangaratta and Sale led to "spot" survey work along major highways out of Sydney. Because such extra-metropolitan activity exceeded the unit's resources, publicity became an important aid to eradication. Early initiatives included "the display of Argentine ant colour leaflets in prominent places"[67] and the screening of a short documentary, *Ant Menace*, in rural NSW towns from January to June 1961. These methods allowed the campaign to expand the scale of eradication by enlisting locals to locate and poison ant nests beyond metropolitan boundaries.

Further cycles of publicity used a range of techniques and strategies to secure public assistance, even within metropolitan boundaries. Sometimes these appeals involved mascots or representative figures, most famously in the 1966–7 campaign "Trapper Tom" (played in the television ad by Australian celebrity Barry Crocker), complete with pith helmet, safari suit and magnifying glass.[68] Other examples included "El Argentino" (from the 1970–1 publicity campaign), a racialised cartoon of a "Latin" Argentine ant appearing in the comics pages of weekend newspapers and "the Antbeater", a character represented at public events by a campaign worker in a bespoke anteater costume. Pasfield himself appeared on the *Sydney Tonight* television program to talk about the eradication campaign and solicit public assistance.[69]

Each of these appeals involved ant samples, collected in vials or containers, being sent by participants to their local councils. Samples were then forwarded to the unit headquarters for identification, followed by site inspections. From at least 1966, children's participation was formalised through an Ant Hunter Club promotion, including badges and certificates distributed through local councils,[70] and at various times rewards were promised, with ant bounties being paid to schoolchildren as late as the 1980s.[71] This version of citizen science, which included enlistment and subjectification of primary-school-aged children as ant hunters, is not unlike an inverse or negative version of popular environmental campaigns of the early to mid-twentieth century.[72] As with nationalist articulations of the natural, the campaign keyed imperialist and racist discourses as well as a conception of the environment as subject to human interests and purposes (although in a way that uncannily echoed certain forms of ecological fieldwork). Publicity was also a major area in which the populist ontology of the Argentine ant as pest was secured throughout this period.

Popular environmentalism and the end of the campaign

Throughout the 1970s, the activities of the unit continued, gradually expanding to additional local government areas. In 1974, the act was amended to remove caps on state government contributions, although media campaigns became less spectacular in the more austere late 1970s and early 1980s. Contemporaneously, public use of organochlorine pesticides was curtailed by the government, with some substances being subject to much tighter control after the Pesticides Act of 1978. After reverting to the earlier chemical due to public perceptions about dieldrin, the Argentine Ant Eradication unit used chlordane solution in great quantities throughout this period.

50   *Adam Gall*

By the late 1970s, however, there was some friction with local government. In 1979, the committee fielded an inquiry from Concord Council expressing concern over "the loss of the Homebush Bay wetlands and any encroachment which could adversely affect it" and in particular the deaths of mangroves and other plants "due to the partial reclamation" which, in the council's view, had been done to combat Argentine ants.[73] Committee chairman A. L. Case was careful to assure the unit did not do reclamation work.[74] Public concern for wildlife and natural vegetation foreshadowed the events that would bring the campaign to an end only a few years later.

In the early 1980s, activists at West Lane Cove conducted a successful campaign against the unit's activities. Initially, the Lane Cove Council itself prevented spraying in West Lane Cove by refusing to clear land.[75] The committee applied further pressure, citing their authority to compel clearing under the act. Activists secured an order for an environmental impact assessment from the newly established state Land and Environment Court.[76] Ultimately, the court granted a further injunction against spraying in Lane Cove to Jozef Vissel (an activist and photographer),[77] who was working with other conservationists. Pending further expert and legal advice, the AAEC suspended its activities at that time not only in Lane Cove but also across all of Sydney.[78]

The act was later repealed, and the committee itself disbanded with little fanfare by the NSW government.[79] Liberal parliamentarian John Dowd spoke of this in parliament:

> In my electorate we have Argentine ants. Also we have people concerned about bushland – some people unkindly call them Greenies – who, on balance, would rather have the ants than destroy the bush, whereas there was a time when you got rid of the ants irrespective of the bush because the bush grew again and the ants were dangerous.[80]

Instead of "Greenies", the government's rationale for repeal emphasised the fact that "the stage has been reached where it can be said that the Argentine ant has been virtually completely eradicated from New South Wales".[81]

In early 1986, the last chairman of the AAEC took the opportunity to warn Sydney residents in the metropolitan press that there was "a strong possibility" that the Lane Cove bushland infestation could move into houses nearby and beyond.[82] With the end of the campaign and the repeal of the act, this eventuality would have represented an issue only for private homeowners who had already been denied access to dieldrin or chlordane (subject to total bans in NSW from 1986) and would fall well below the previous scale of activities of the campaign. The Lane Cove controversy represents the closure of this ant frontier.

Conclusion

The end of the campaign highlighted forms of environmentalism within "new Australia",[83] that growing portion of the population who valued proximity to indigenous vegetation and wildlife. In the context of transnational environmental movements, as well as activism elsewhere in the Australian context, the fact that sites affected by the unit's activities included bushland and wetlands was significant. However, it is clear from the examples of prominent campaigners in Lane Cove that it was the chlordane that was the immediate trigger for their activism: Josef Vissel mentioned having just read Carson's *Silent Spring* when the council had first sent notice of spraying in the area.[84] This was also a matter of concern in the earlier Loomis case, although the nascent green movement and new Land and Environment Court gave it social and institutional momentum.

Arguably, both the Argentine Ant Eradication Committee and these social movements were environmentalist in orientation: they both sought the best possible environment for the human inhabitants of Sydney. But, as Gaynor suggests, the mid-century modern environmentalism informing the eradication campaign was bereft of an ecological dimension.[85] The end of the campaign thus signals the supplanting of one form of environmentalism by another, the intervention in the metropolitan everyday of what Morton refers to as "the ecological thought".[86] Not only were Argentine ants no longer viewed as being present in excessive numbers but also there was an altered set of relationships with humans in this new ecological thinking which disrupted the response of treatment with organochlorine pesticides. Indeed, the notion of animal excess as a problem in any environment is dependent upon assumptions about whether the means used to deal with such problems – in this case, organochlorine pesticide – is itself excessive.

These pesticides also render ambiguous the closure of the ant frontier in Sydney. Dieldrin and chlordane, acknowledged as extremely dangerous by pharmacologists since at least the early 1950s, remain in ecosystems and in the fatty tissues of animal bodies,[87] giving them the status of historical actors with their own temporality. Organochlorine pesticides can be understood as agents of "slow violence", much less spectacular than that of sudden infestation.[88] The end of the Argentine Ant Eradication Committee was far from the end of this dimension of Argentine ant history.

It is also significant that Argentine ants themselves persist in Australia as well as in numerous sites beyond their native range all over the world. The supercolonies of Europe and Japan are spectacular examples of this persistence, studied and discussed by contemporary myrmecologists.[89] Sydney populations are more elusive, but the ecological consequences of Argentine ants in Victoria (where no systematic eradication campaign has been attempted) have been well documented.[90] Here further ambiguity is introduced: the ecological framing that led to the cessation of spraying returns to reconstitute Argentine ants as invasive species. In the ecological imaginary, a perception of ants existing in excessive numbers no longer stems primarily from their economic or experiential impacts on humans but on a different set of biocultural assumptions to do with biodiversity and "nativeness".[91]

52 Adam Gall

Notes

1 This phrasing is borrowed from cultural geography and recent writing in the environmental humanities. See Sarah Whatmore, 'Materialist Returns: Practising Cultural Geography in and for a More-Than-Human World', *Cultural Geographies*, 13.4 (2006): 600–9. See also, Donna Haraway, *Staying with the Trouble: Making Kin in the Chthulucene* (Durham: Duke University Press, 2016).

2 Alfred W. Crosby, *Ecological Imperialism: The Biological Expansion of Europe, 900–1900* (Cambridge: Cambridge University Press, 1986); Eric Rolls, *They All Ran Wild: The Story of Pests on the Land in Australia* (Sydney: Angus & Robertson, 1969).

3 Greg Garrard, 'Beginnings: Pollution', in *Ecocriticism* (New York: Routledge, 2004), 1–15.

4 Alison Bashford, 'The Anthropocene Is Modern History: Reflections on Climate and Australian Deep Time', *Australian Historical Studies*, 44.3 (2013): 341–9.

5 A change of scientific name was proposed in Steven Shattuck, 'Review of the Dolichoderine Ant Genus *Iridomyrmex* Mayr', *Journal of the Australian Entomological Society*, 31 (1992): 13–18. It is now widely accepted by myrmecologists. I retain the earlier name in this chapter to emphasise that the ants need to be understood differently as their relations to humans and environments change through time.

6 Alexander L. Wild, 'Taxonomy and Distribution of the Argentine Ant', *Annals of the Entomological Society of America*, 97.6 (2004): 1204. Wild also notes the difficulty of determining a precise native distribution because the species has often been confused with other, similar ants.

7 Valerie Vogel, Jes S. Pedersen, Tatiana Giraud, Michael J. B. Krieger and Laurent Keller, 'The Worldwide Expansion of the Argentine Ant', *Diversity and Distributions*, 16 (2010): 171.

8 N. D. Tsutsui, A. V. Suarez, D. A. Holway and T. J. Case, 'Reduced Genetic Variation and the Success of an Invasive Species', *Proceedings of the National Academy of Sciences of the United States of America*, 97 (2000): 5948–53.

9 Paul D. Krushelnycky, David A. Holway and Edward G. LeBrun, 'Invasion Processes and Causes of Success', in Lori Lach, Catherine Parr and Kirsti Abbott (eds.), *Ant Ecology* (Oxford: Oxford University Press, 2009), 255.

10 Krushelnycky et al., 'Invasion Processes', 245–60.

11 Ian Hacking, 'Historical Ontology', in *Historical Ontology* (Cambridge: Harvard University Press, 2002), 1–26.

12 Emily O'Gorman, 'Belonging', *Environmental Humanities*, 5 (2014): 283–6.

13 Peter Hobbins, 'Invasion Ontologies: Venom, Visibility and the Imagined Histories of Arthropods', in Jodi Frawley and Ian MacCalman (eds.), *Rethinking Invasion Ecologies from the Environmental Humanities* (New York: Routledge, 2013), 181–95.

14 Hobbins, 'Invasion Ontologies', 181.

15 This construction itself has a history and materiality in sites and forms of encounter from everyday life to the production of scientific knowledge. The ecological account of Argentine ants offered in the preceding paragraph itself suggests how much of the ants' current way of existing is a product of recent more-than-human history.

16 Charlotte Sleigh, *Six Legs Better: A Cultural History of Myrmecology* (Baltimore: Johns Hopkins University Press, 2007), 15–16.

17 Sleigh identifies these connections through the work of preeminent ant scientists Auguste Forel, William Wheeler and Edward Wilson.

18 See O'Gorman, 'Belonging'.

19 Italo Calvino, 'The Argentine Ant', in *Adam, One Afternoon and Other Stories*, trans. Archibald Colquhoun and Peggy Wright (London: Collins, 1957), 163.

20 Calvino, 'The Argentine Ant', 163.

21 Beno Weiss, *Understanding Italo Calvino* (Columbia: University of South Carolina Press, 1993), 68.

On the ant frontier 53

22 Wilmon Newell, 'Notes on the Habits of the Argentine or "New Orleans" Ant, Iridomyrmex Humilis Mayr', *Journal of Economic Entomology*, 1 (1908): 25.
23 'Melbourne Menaced by Argentine Insect Pest', *Hobart Mercury*, 30 October 1939, 3.
24 'Argentine Ants "By Billions"', *Sydney Morning Herald*, 8 June 1950, 1.
25 The canonical statement remains Carson's *Silent Spring*. For an Australian history of this alignment, see Andrea Gaynor, *Harvest of the Suburbs* (Cawley: University of Western Australia Press, 2006). Further international context on the preponderance of martial metaphors can be found in Sarah Jansen, 'Chemical-warfare Techniques for Insect Control', *Endeavour*, 24.1 (2000): 28–33. Jansen indicates that a "gap [. . .] emerged in about 1900 between ways of seeing insects and way of controlling them" (32) and that the techniques and language of chemical warfare offered a solution.
26 P. C. Hely, G. Pasfield and J. G. Gellatley, *Insect Pests of Fruits and Vegetables in New South Wales* (Clayton, Vic: Inkata, 1982). The altered edition is located in the University of Sydney library collection. In spite of the redaction, the original text remains visible when backlit.
27 For example, see 'Terrible Insect Pest,' *Evening News*, 28 November 1908, 3.
28 Newell, 'Notes'.
29 Discussed in Newell, 'Notes,' 22–5. A few years earlier, Wheeler had been prompted by the ants having "recently gained a foothold in the United States" to publish a brief note on their origins. See W. M. Wheeler, 'On Certain Tropical Ants Introduced into the United States', *Entomological News*, January 1906, 24.
30 Newell, 'Notes,' 34.
31 'Economic Entomology,' *Sydney Morning Herald*, 17 December 1914, 7.
32 For example, see Gordon Pasfield, 'Summary of Lectures' (Delivered at School of Instruction, Argentine Ant Eradication, for health inspectors and campaign personnel, 3–14 July 1961); Also, P. E. Madge and G. Caon, *Argentine Ant: An Historical Overview* (South Australia: Department of Agriculture, 1987).
33 'Tropical Ants', *Maryborough Chronicle*, 5 December 1913, n.p.
34 James Barrett, 'The Argentine Ant', *Argus*, 26 June 1926, 8.
35 Joshua Blu Buhs, *The Fire Ant Wars: Nature, Science, and Public Policy in Twentieth Century America* (Chicago: University of Chicago Press, 2004).
36 See Gaynor, *Harvest*, 147–9.
37 See Madge and Caon, *Argentine Ant*.
38 Gaynor, *Harvest*, 148.
39 Pasfield, 'Summary,' 31.
40 Tony Doogood dir., *The Argentine Ant* (CSIRO Film Unit, 1956), https://aso.gov.au/titles/documentaries/the-argentine-ant/; see also Tom Greaves, 'Notes for Spray Operators', appended to Pasfield, 'Summary', 1961.
41 Pasfield, 'Summary', 31.
42 Pasfield, 'Summary', 32.
43 Pasfield, 'Summary', 31.
44 Achille Mbembe, 'Necropolitics', *Public Culture*, 15.1 (2002): 11–40; Ghassan Hage, *Is Racism and Environmental Threat?* (London: Polity, 2017), 77–81.
45 Pasfield, 'Summary', 32.
46 Pasfield, 'Summary', 32.
47 'Argentine Ant May Cost Australia Millions', *West Wyalong Advocate*, 11 December 1952, 2.
48 'Scientists Begin War on Ants', *Sydney Morning Herald*, 29 November 1952, 4.
49 See Pasfield, 'Summary', 33.
50 J. T. Hamilton, 'Record of Areas Survey', 1 May 1964. Correspondence and working papers, Argentine Ant Eradication Committee, NRS 9677, 18/493.2.
51 Pasfield, 'Summary', 33.
52 D. Hayter, Letter to Mr Ferguson, 28 March 1962; and Frank Starkey, Letter to the Director, 26 April 1962. Correspondence and working papers, AAEC, 18/495.

54   *Adam Gall*

53 Pasfield, 'Summary', 34.
54 Pasfield, 'Summary', 34.
55 J. T. Hamilton, Report to AAEC, 22 February 1963 in Correspondence and working papers, AAEC, 18/493.2.
56 Hamilton, Report to AAEC, 16 October 1964.
57 Correspondence relating to Underwood Road, Homebush Bay site. Correspondence and working papers, AAEC, 18/496.
58 Hamilton, Report to AAEC, 20 August 1965.
59 Hamilton, Report to AAEC, 18 September 1964.
60 Hamilton, Report to AAEC, 17 June 1965.
61 Hamilton, Report to AAEC, 22 May 1965.
62 Hamilton, Report to AAEC, 17 September 1965.
63 Ladd N. Loomis, Letter to Chairman, Argentine Ant Eradication Committee, 18 November 1964.
64 Ladd N. Loomis, 'Dieldrin Poisoning in Four Puppies', *Australian Veterinary Journal*, 42 (January 1966): 25–7.
65 K. D. Coutts, 'Dieldrin Poisoning in Puppies', *Australian Veterinary Journal*, 42 (January 1966): 310–11.
66 Correspondence relating to treatment of Cliff Road, Collaroy, 18 January 1963 to 5 March 1964. Correspondence and working papers, AAEC, 18/495.
67 Pasfield, 'Summary', 34.
68 *Argentine Ants Advertisement* (Sydney: Eric Porter Productions, 1968), https://aso.gov.au/titles/ads/argentine-ants-advertisement/.
69 See 'Ant-Eater Design & Specification', Correspondence and working papers, AAEC, 18/495. *Sydney Tonight* aired on Sunday, 9 February 1969, on Channel Seven.
70 'Top Ten List of Ant Hunters', 14 March 1969. Correspondence and working papers, AAEC, 18/495; 'El Argentino is desperado', *Broadcaster*, 2 February 1971, 4.
71 Bob Branston, 'Argentine Ants Found at Chatswood', 23 March 1981. Correspondence and working papers, AAEC, 18/496.
72 See Libby Robin, *How a Continent Created a Nation* (Sydney: University of New South Wales Press, 2007).
73 G. Johnson, Letter to Secretary, AAEC, 20 December 1979. Correspondence and working papers, AAEC, 18/495.
74 It remains unclear whether private actors ever did reclamation work to control Argentine ants, although there are no references to this technique in public discussion during this period.
75 D. Lambley, Letter to Secretary, Lane Cove Municipal Council, 6 October 1981. Correspondence and working papers, AAEC, 18/496.
76 Roger Lembit, Letter to Secretary, AAEC, 13 December 1983. Correspondence and working papers, AAEC, 18/496.
77 Vissel was also a Holocaust survivor, an experience which may have given him insight into the interlinked representational and practical histories of the extermination of racialised human populations and the use of pesticide on arthropods. See Jansen, 'Chemical-warfare Techniques for Insect Control', 2000, as well as Edmund P Russell, '"Speaking of Annihilation"': Mobilizing for War Against Human and Insect Enemies, 1914–1945', *The Journal of American History*, 82.4 (March 1996): 1505–29.
78 Greg Roberts, 'Spray Ban Halts Ant Control Program', *Sydney Morning Herald*, 15 March 1985.
79 See Madge and Caon, *Argentine Ant*.
80 New South Wales Legislative Assembly, Parliamentary Debates, 26 November 1985, 10744.
81 New South Wales Legislative Council, Parliamentary Debates, 27 November 1985, 10871.

On the ant frontier   55

82 'Argentine Ant Threat to Lane Cove Homes', *Sydney Morning Herald*, 27 February 1986.
83 Stephen Pyne, *Burning Bush: A Fire History of Australia* (New York: Holt, 1991), 364.
84 Roberts, 'Spray Ban'.
85 Gaynor, *Harvest*.
86 Timothy Morton, *The Ecological Thought* (Cambridge: Harvard University Press, 2010), 1.
87 This was widely publicised from the time of Rachel Carson's *Silent Spring* (1962).
88 On the contrast between spectacular and "slow" environmental violence or injustice, see Rob Nixon, *Slow Violence and the Environmentalism of the Poor* (Harvard: Harvard University Press, 2011).
89 J. K. Wetterer, Alexander Wild, A. V. Suarez, Nuria Roura and X. Espadaler, 'Worldwide Spread of the Argentine Ant, *Linepithema humile*', *Myrmecological News*, 12 (2009): 187–94.
90 Lori Lach and Melissa Thomas, 'Invasive Ants in Australia: Documented and Potential Ecological Consequences', *Australian Journal of Entomology*, 47 (2008): 275–88.
91 See Lesley Head, 'Decentring 1788: Beyond Biotic Nativeness', *Geographical Research*, 50.2 (2012): 166–78; O'Gorman, 'Belonging'.

5 A swarm of sheep
Colonising the Esperance bioregion

Nicole Chalmer

Introduction

The Anglo/European colonisation of the Esperance bioregion was undertaken using a linked animal-human system that enabled the invasion and occupation of Aboriginal lands. It exemplifies Alfred Crosby's concept of ecological imperialism, where large numbers of domestic herbivores helped invading colonists take over new landscapes.[1] Elinor Melville's book, A *Plague of Sheep*, traces this process in Mexico in the sixteenth century when the Spanish claimed the land from Indigenous peoples with the help of sheep as biological co-invaders.[2] Similar mechanisms were used throughout much of the Australian frontal wave of invasion, as large herds of sheep and cattle helped colonists expand their range, with comparable environmental impacts on nature and Aboriginal peoples. The early Esperance bioregion pastoralists used their sheep swarms to invade the lands of the Nyungar and Ngadju Aboriginal peoples. Because they employed locally adaptive behaviours, including eco-shepherding learnt from Aboriginal people, their early environmental impacts were not as immediately devastating as elsewhere, but within decades, the cultural drive for economic growth and a lack of critical understanding about impacts of excess sheep stocking rates facilitated an ungulate eruption that contributed to the collapse of ecosystems and Aboriginal social ecological systems.

The Esperance bioregion

The Esperance bioregion is situated on the south-east coast and inland areas of Western Australia and includes the ancestral lands of Nyungar and Ngadju Aboriginal nations.[3] It provided a resource-patchy landscape demarcated by soil fertility. John Beard described the bioregion as featuring mallee heath and heath vegetation on relatively infertile sandy soils of the sandplain along the coast, with mallee eucalypts and woodland eucalypt species in the fertile soils to the north. There are mosaics of more fertile mallee soils in the southern sandplain, along rivers, around swamps and granite outcrops and along the boundaries of soil classification zones, which were important to plants, wildlife and Aboriginal food systems.[4]

Sandplain ecosystems are in the 700–400 millimetre rainfall belt, with plentiful fresh to brackish water. Until Aboriginal management ceased almost completely in the early nineteenth century, their burning regimes maintained many grassy mosaics for grassland species. Further north, the mallee-woodland ecosystems in the less than 400-millimetre rainfall zone feature better alkaline red to grey soils also with scattered grassland mosaics. Here water is scarce and impermanent, with most provided by large granite outcrop catchments, which fill Aboriginal enhanced rockholes (gnammas) and small dams, which were later enlarged by settlers.

Aboriginal landscapes

The Esperance bioregion encompassed Aboriginal social ecological systems developed by 40,000 to 60,000 years of Aboriginal land management and ecosystem co-evolution. Ecological geographers Ian Davidson-Hunt and Fikret Berkes describe social ecological systems (SES) as the co-evolving ecological relationships between people, their societies and nature within a defined boundary of space-time.[5] This concept is the basis for how people lived in the Esperance bioregion both pre- and post-colonialism.

Susan Prober et al. investigated the many ways Ngadju people ecologically managed their lands for food production. A complex and elegant system of fire use created and maintained mosaics of managed habitats for important animals and plants in ways that are still not fully understood. Periodically burning habitats was vital for plants, such as yams; for food animals, such as kangaroos, wallabies, smaller marsupials; and for birds, such as emus, bush turkeys and other grassland species. Larger trees were very often protected from fire, as they were a habitat 'city' for animals.[6]

Early shipboard explorers, including Bruny D'Entrecasteaux and Matthew Flinders, noted fires dotting the Esperance coastal landscapes. During his 1848–49 expedition to the region, Washington State surveyor John Septimus Roe observed that

> the coastal land appeared closely settled, with Aborigines numerous kangaroos and emus occurring together in this same country. There was much smoke from native fires and the occurrence of native huts was common.[7]

The sustainability of Aboriginal SES could be easily compromised by resource overexploitation, so the groups used various restraining approaches to prevent this. They managed people (themselves) with a wide range of cultural strategies, including combining mobility with sedentarism, deliberate birth control and a variety of plant- and animal-protecting totems.[8] As Johan Colding and Carl Folke discuss, these actions which were common among indigenous peoples, prevented the many possible fluctuations in ecosystems and animal and plant populations that could result from excessive human populations overexploiting

58   *Nicole Chalmer*

resources.[9] Nature/people interactions seemed designed to promote food abundance and biodiversity as the normal resilient state.

In the Esperance bioregion, it was the mosaics of grass and shrub lands created through these practices and designed to manage native herbivores that became the attractant for invasions by Anglo pastoralists with their sheep. The original native grasslands included tall warm-season perennial grasses, such as kangaroo grass (*Themeda triandra*), wallaby grass (*Austrodanthonia caespitosa*) and spear grasses (*Stipa eromophila; Austrostipa nitida*), and there were biannuals, such as windmill grass (*Chloris truncata*), edible herbs, including pigface (*Carpobrotus* spp.), and shrubs, such as bluebush (*Maireana* spp.) and saltbush (*Atriplex* spp.).[10]

Edward John Eyre was one of the few European explorers who recognised the prior land occupation by Aboriginal peoples, and he expressed deep concern about land alienation, displacement and impacts of European herbivores. He lamented that the country most suited for cultivation and grazing was also the most valued by Aboriginals for food production. The livestock impact was replicated throughout Australia and described by Sir Thomas Mitchell, who visited the NSW Bogan River valley first in 1335 and then in 1845. He was dismayed at the impacts of excessive livestock over these ten years, which had trampled the once beautiful springs, destroyed the surrounding wetland vegetation and eaten the valley bare so that 'hardly a blade of the once verdant grasses were to be seen'.[11]

Ungulate eruptions

When a species (this can include humans) invades or irrupts into a new range, with unlimited food and lack of predators, an eruption can occur. This means the population increases to peak abundance, crashes and then reaches a carrying capacity lower than its peak because resources have been overexploited and ecosystems damaged. In 1970, ecologist Graeme Caughly referred to this paradigm when related to rapidly increasing ungulate herbivore populations, such as sheep, as an 'Ungulate Eruption'. Eruptions are not necessarily accompanied by the paradigm of irruption, which refers to expansions of range, but such a population increase frequently occurs.[12] In his discussions of ecological imperialism, Crosby was describing these paradigms as they co-occurred. Invading colonists deliberately or inadvertently harnessed these features of animal behaviour and assisted irruptions and eruptions of domestic grazing animals to physically, psychologically and culturally claim lands from Aboriginal peoples.[13]

Melville documents how the Spanish claimed Mexico in the sixteenth century with an ungulate irruption and eruption. They disenfranchised Indigenous Mexican peoples with vast sheep herds that consumed Indigenous crops, grass fields and ecosystems and therefore culture. However, this eruption also affected the Spanish sheep farmers, as the severely degraded landscapes would no longer carry the previous numbers of sheep – and still cannot.[14] This pattern was mirrored in much of Australia as environmental destruction during initial eruptions of sheep in rangelands, especially around permanent water sources, has permanently reduced their carrying capacities to this day.[15]

In the Esperance bioregion, the human-facilitated swarm of sheep was initially an irruption with sheep moved throughout the landscape as the early Anglo pastoralists began taking over the Esperance bioregion and replacing Aboriginal SES with their own. The early relatively sustainable numbers and management practices were followed by an exponential eruption. Rica Erickson described the Dempster family building sheep numbers from the initial 518 in 1865 to 13,750 by 1875 and to over 30,000 by the 1890s.[16]

Sheep as landscape changers

Sheep are proactive agents, creating and mapping sheep landscapes with tracks that reflect their daily lives. As Michele Dominy concluded in New Zealand, they 'mediate the colonist's relationships to the [new] land'. In the Esperance bioregion, they also made the new landscapes navigable by developing pathways linking food and water resources and determining the tracks followed during mustering.[17]

Sheep have other behaviours that make them ideal colonising agents. They are social animals (especially Merinos) and can nearly double their numbers in a year on good forage when protected from predators. Huge flocks actively 'swarm' (irrupt) into new grazing areas looking for food, if allowed. It is worth exposing the myth of hard hooves at this juncture, for like most social herbivores, they tend to form discrete tracks linking food and water resources. But as numbers increase to excess, grazing, trampling and pressure upon the soil, as by any overstocked animal, whether ungulate, macropod or human, will damage it. Rangeland ecologist P. B. Mitchell asserts that the 'common sense' myth of hard hooves as the primary cause of soil compaction and therefore land degradation in semi-arid Australia is supported by little empirical evidence, but as an uncritical generalisation, it has become rife in scientific and popular literature. Accordingly, not enough attention is given to potentially more important factors in land degradation, such as the impact of excessive stocking rates, preferential grazing and animal behaviour.[18]

Sheep vigorously graze all palatable herbage within range, biting off forage with their teeth. Unlike tongue-grazing herbivores, such as cattle, they can graze to ground level and below by digging for roots and seeds, so they can appear healthy even when groundcover is largely gone and soil degradation is accelerating. When sheep are set stocked (left permanently on pastures) and not rotated (moved to new pasture before overgrazing, allowing perennial grasses/ shrubs to regenerate), preferential grazing by excess numbers can annihilate most palatable plants, especially perennial grasses and herbs, preventing seedling recruitment and baring ground. Colin Yates et al. and Andrew Burbidge et al. argue that such herbivore behaviours have deep ecological impacts. Ecosystems become dominated by widely spaced unpalatable plants and trees, and as perennial grasses, chenopod shrubs and herbs are eliminated, microclimates deteriorate

60   *Nicole Chalmer*

because evaporation increases significantly from bared ground. This starts a cycle of increasing aridity and topsoil loss as the ability of semi-arid land vegetation growth patterns to augment rainfall is reduced. Ground-dwelling animals, such as arthropods, small mammals, ground-nesting birds and reptiles, are particularly vulnerable to excessive grazing intensity damaging their habitats.[19]

In 1842, John Drummond described how sheep introduced seeds of European and Mediterranean annual grasses and weed species to Western Australia in their dung and wool, which then became naturalised. These included several cool-season annual grasses (*Bromus, Hordeum, Vulpia* spp.), forbs, such as capeweed (*Arctotheca calendula*), and annual legumes (*Trifolium* spp., *Medicago* spp.).[20] These plants, already co-adapted to withstand sheep grazing, can take over bare areas when native perennial species disappear. The landscape and ecosystems become annual based, which can lead to significant hydrological and habitat changes, with further aridification and drought.[21] Management practices that include conservative stocking levels and timely rotational grazing can limit environmental damage. Ultimately, the actions of people will decide the long-term impacts of grazing by sheep.

The pastoralists

The British form of pastoralism became an efficient colonising template with which to invade indigenous lands with domesticated herbivores. In the Esperance bioregion, sheep were also a form of capital that produced the income that maintained colonising enterprises by producing wool as a cash-paying export commodity.

As the agricultural lands around the original Swan River colony ran out, the colonial government of Western Australia developed a policy to increase colonial income and to consolidate land ownership and settlement by encouraging the pastoral industry to extend into the far reaches of the colony.[22] In the late 1850s, they offered generous terms, with leases of 20,000 to 100,000 acres granted to settlers, with the first four years rent-free. Under these terms, the Dempster brothers took up leases on the south coast and were the first of a wave of Anglo peoples to invade and settle the Esperance bioregion.[23]

The Dempster home farm was based at Northam-Toodyay, but with an erupting family of eight children, five of them sons, they needed to expand; they actively engaged in exploration to acquire new land. They first explored eastward from Northam in 1861 but were unimpressed by this region. It was during this journey that they came to appreciate the importance of granite outcrops as a source of water and feed.[24]

Perhaps due to glowing descriptions by colonial surveyor general J. S. Roe in 1848, an expedition was organised in 1863 to explore the south coast lands.[25] The party, led by Andrew Dempster, sailed from Albany eastwards, and after landing at Point Malcolm, travelled along the coast to Point Culver and then inland. In both areas, they found the scattered mosaics of grasslands and many large watered granite outcrops described by Roe. The region was deemed ideal

A *swarm of sheep*   61

and ready for sheep and cattle grazing.[26] Between them, the brothers eventually claimed 1.5 million acres (607,290 ha) from Stokes Inlet to Esperance Bay, including up to 20 Recherche islands close to the coast. As the leases were largely unfenced, the area exploited would have been very much larger.[27] During December 1864, about 518 wool sheep, 80 dual-purpose cattle (such as dairy shorthorns and Herefords) and 90 horses were overlanded to Esperance.[28] The operations established by 1865 at Esperance Bay were constrained by distance to markets so that sheep were primarily for wool and cattle for butter production as well as meat and milk for local consumption.[29] Being relatively non-perishable, wool and butter could be stored and survive long-distance transport. Each year a schooner was chartered to bring in supplies and to take the wool clip to market in Adelaide. In 1881, it was noted that sheep for the butcher were overlanded back to Perth.[30] A letter from relative Annie Gull, to another, Aunt Julia Barker, related that

> [after another lambing] . . . there are about 1500 from the 600 they started with. . . . Edward says the cattle are doing well, plenty of calves. It is so cool down there they can make butter all year round and someone in Albany is to take it all from them at the market price.[31]

The homestead at Esperance Bay was described as having good land for a field, a garden and plenty of water. Sheep were pastured around Esperance and Stokes Inlet to the west and further west at Fanny's Cove. Some of the islands were leased and sheep periodically boated to islands, including Middle, Cull and Woody Islands. By 1875, sheep numbers had risen to 13,750 and recorded as being overlanded to Fraser Range and Southern Hills about 240 kilometres north of Esperance Bay.[32]

Transhumance

To succeed in the Esperance bioregion, pastoralism needed to overcome several constraints, which included lands already occupied and managed by Aboriginal people and low in the types of soil nutrients required by domesticated ruminant herbivores adapted to the higher mineral soils of the geologically young northern hemisphere. Moving stock from coast to inland each year, as a form of transhumance to counter coastal nutritional deficiencies, became established. This Mediterranean system, researched by Fernand Braudel, traditionally involved taking livestock inland to the mountains and back every year. It improved production from sheep flocks, allowing pasture to rest, and was an accepted and ancient practice that 'offered fiscal resources which no state could ignore'.[33]

Transhumance was especially important in the ancient soils of the southwestern Australian coast and the Esperance sandplain, with low levels of macronutrients especially phosphorous and micronutrients, such as cobalt, copper and selenium.[34] Native plants and animals evolved with these low soil nutrients, unlike domestic ruminants which, without their required amounts of these nutrients, fail to grow, become emaciated and die.[35] The earlier settled west coast

62   Nicole Chalmer

colonists had found that for ruminant stock to thrive, they needed to spend part of the year inland on heavier soils away from the coast. According to F. A. R. Dempster, Andrew Dempster had experience of this 'coastiness', and even without understanding the basal cause, knew that the only cure was to take stock inland for a period each year. Very early on he had looked for suitable inland grazing land to combine with the coastal lands. In 1866, Frazer Range and Southern Hills about 240 kilometres north-east of Esperance Bay were decided upon.[36] Time spent on offshore islands was also a preventive measure, so those with fresh water and close to the mainland were leased. Middle, Cull and Woody Islands, fertilised by guano from the short-tailed shearwater (*Puffinus tenuirostris*) which nests all over the Archipelago, have fertile and mineral-rich soils compared to mainland coastal soils. Livestock grazed on them could be fattened within six to seven months.[37]

Thus, the Dempsters and later pastoral enterprises belonging to Campbell Taylor and the Dimer family were based on an annual transhumance from the summer coastal pastures to inland winter pastures and islands. Their ability to run large numbers of stock on inland pastures was further improved by sinking wells around the base of granite outcrops, damming water runoff from outcrops and enlarging existing Aboriginal gnammas and wells.[38]

Peter Spooner et al. have historical evidence that supports the use of Aboriginal traditional pathways by pastoralists as travelling stock routes (TSRs). The adoption of such pathways into a TSR system has likely occurred by 'passing on' of existing pathway knowledge by Aboriginal guides and trackers, settlers adopting tracks from observations of physical evidence and shared development of some TSRs from Aboriginal people working in the pastoral industry. Although this concept has not been explored in depth for the Esperance bioregion, it is likely that 'the Dempster track' and other tracks developed for transhumance had Aboriginal origins, as Aboriginal guides and shepherds were commonly included in explorations.[39] Overall, the outcome mirrored the Mediterranean transhumance systems, as it greatly improved production and therefore income (see Figure 5.1).[40]

In the Esperance bioregion, the ecological benefits of this annual movement of stock for mineral availability inadvertently provided a counterbalance to the erupting sheep herds' potential to cause significant environmental destruction. Its ongoing success was also linked to the inclusion of Aboriginal shepherds in the model, which I call Aboriginal eco-shepherding. Their grazing management skills, fire use and judgement allowed periods of rest and regeneration for the perennial grasses and shrubs both coastal and inland, as they moved sheep around the summer and winter pastures, within the larger annual transhumance pattern.

Aboriginal eco-shepherding: delaying a crash

In 1835, G. F. Moore recorded in his diary, 'the colony is now greatly in want of a few good practical shepherds. . . [and] It is surprising how much the condition of the flock depends on the goodness of the shepherd'.[41] Shepherding was a highly

Figure 5.1 Sheep flock moving inland from Israelite Bay, east of Esperance, circa 1890.
Source: In the possession of the author, unknown date and source.

skilled job, as shepherds needed to know how to manage sheep from lambing to shearing and also to learn about local conditions. As did Kimberley Tallbear's American Indians, for Aboriginal people to survive in the new monetary economy, they had to take on the extractivist practices of the invading colonial consumer front, and shepherding allowed them to do this whilst keeping connection to country.[42] Rica Erickson noted that sheep flocks managed by Aborigines did very well and attributed this to Aboriginal shepherds allowing the sheep to range more freely because they could use their tracking abilities to find them quickly for night penning.[43] It is likely that the reasons were far more complex than this and could be explained by eco-shepherding, where fire was used to regenerate pastures and sheep were moved consistently, as Karl Dimer (a pastoralist of mixed ancestry from the Israelite Bay region) explained, to prevent overgrazing.[44] With their long cultural experience and skills in managing kangaroos and other marsupial grazers, numbers of Aboriginal people became shepherds to survive the new order. They were documented by Dimer as highly skilled, using traditional (ecological) knowledge about location of the best grasses; avoidance of poisonous plants; how to follow thunderstorm rain that produced grass during dry years; when and where dingoes could be a problem; and when grasses and herbage needed a rest from grazing. Aboriginal shepherds also managed country with fire to regenerate grasses and to keep scrub under control for sheep grazing,

64   *Nicole Chalmer*

as they had done for kangaroos and other native animals.[45] In a letter to the *Eastern Districts Chronicle* in 1891, a 'Lady' (anonymous but probably Amy Baesjou) riding to Israelite Bay describes some encounters with Aboriginal shepherds using fire as a shepherding management tool:

> I see another native. Sheeptracks are everywhere around; he is evidently minding a flock. . . . [further on she has another encounter]. . . . A few miles further on in a thicket where they are burning bush, I encounter a third blackie, who is shepherding, accompanied by his wife and child.[46]

This experienced use of fire is likely to have contributed to the early sustainability of the Esperance bioregions pastoral system. When grazing country is not overstocked, there is sufficient grass residue to carry the fire needed to keep unpalatable woody weeds under control and to regenerate palatable grasses and herbs. These then need to be rested to allow root reserves to recover and sufficient seedlings to germinate. An overstocked ecosystem eventually becomes dominated by unpalatable plants, and as Colin Yates et al. explain, simply removing livestock has little impact because a new state of resilience has been reached that is very difficult to restore without major intervention.[47]

Impacts on Aboriginal SES

As pastoralists and their sheep encroached further, there were outbreaks of conflict as Aboriginal people attempted to keep their country and way of life. At Fraser Range, Aborigines made it clear that the Dempsters were not welcome, as noted in an 1870 diary entry: 'Sunday 7th June. Walk down to well in the flat. The natives have thrown in all the covering, platform, windless etc. They have also burned down all our huts'.[48] This immediate resistance to the Dempsters setting up Fraser Range for transhumance indicates that the impacts of pastoralism and sheep elsewhere was being communicated amongst Aboriginal groups.

Food stealing and sheep killing started taking place within 20 years of pastoralism. It likely reflected feelings towards the unfairness of pastoralists who ran sheep on Aboriginal land without recompense and the beginnings of native food shortages and hunger. Neville Green's research into Aboriginal prosecutions, spanning the period from 1831 to 1898, describes how during the 1880s and 1890s, the primary reason given for Aborigines on the south coast to appear before the Esperance and Albany courts was for sheep stealing. He cites frequent records of Aboriginals who were arrested for this, frequently at Esperance and Fraser Range by the Dempsters, tried in Albany and sent to Rottnest Island to serve sentences.[49] Incidents in police records for much of the Esperance district show that the transition from Aboriginal ownership of the land to European settlers was not peaceful – it could be described as a period of guerrilla war during the period from 1877 to the 1890s, with murders occurring on both sides.[50]

Moia Smith estimates that the original Aboriginal population in the southwest, south coast and Esperance bioregion was probably about 6,000 people.[51]

Within 10 to 20 years of the Dempsters and other pastoralists taking up vast areas of leasehold country, animal and plant food sources declined in abundance and vigour as sheep ate out the habitat. Hunger and malnutrition is likely to have played a role in the deaths of many Nyungar people from the severe measles outbreaks of 1883, as recorded by Emily Dempster, who wrote that she and Andrew nursed many sick people around Esperance Bay.[52] By 1900, Esperance police estimated there were only 300 full-blood Aboriginal people left in the Esperance district, compared to 420 Europeans, and by 1912, the Esperance Aboriginal population was reduced to 140 by further disease outbreaks.[53]

Disease in the 1880s and 1890s was also impacting marsupials. Ian Abbott's research supports an epizootic marsupial disease that wiped out over 90% of smaller marsupials in the Esperance bioregion (and the south-west), including possums, bettongs and burrowing bettongs – all important Aboriginal food animals and with essential ecosystem roles.[54] Esperance policeman Corporal McGlade in 1891 described the country as devoid of game and Aboriginal people as hard up.[55] At the same time, pastoralism intensified as more land was leased and sheep numbers dramatically increased. The two largest pastoralists, the Dempsters and Taylors, between them were eventually running at least 55,000 sheep from Esperance Bay to Thomas River. Combined with smaller holdings and uncollected statistics, the numbers may well have been higher. Colonial statistical records of the region that started in 1894 showed around 57,000 sheep, plus 1,000 or so cattle and domestic horses.[56]

For those Aboriginal people who were left, survival meant entry into the Anglo economy; for many, this was achieved by gaining employment in the sheep industry. Esperance Nyungar woman Annie Dabb related how her family survived because her great-grandfather Dabungoo (called Sambo by the Dempsters) became a trusted worker and shepherd for the Dempsters.[57] Anna Haebich relates that by 1902 when George Olivey, travelling inspector for the Aborigines Department in Western Australia, came to the Esperance district, he observed that most Aborigines worked on the Dempster family station as contract shepherds and shearers and were paid on average ten shillings per year, although much of this was retaken to pay for rations and consumables.[58] This employment was combined with limited traditional hunting and camping on the pastoral leases and unalienated Crown land. The need for further monetary income was met from dingo bounties and the sale of kangaroo and possum skins.[59]

When the Aborigines Act of 1905 was enacted, it severely limited the autonomy of those described as Aboriginal or 'half caste' in deciding where to work, or where to live and with whom. It effectively prevented Aboriginal people a dignified adaptation to living in Anglo SES whilst maintaining their own traditions. Encouraged to move into reserves and missions, few could now work as shepherds in the Esperance bioregion.[60] From being educated, comfortable and well off within their own SES, Aboriginal people became the uneducated poor and hungry of the new Anglo SES.

In 1905, another erupting species, rabbits, swept into the Esperance bioregion from NSW. As an overwhelming swarm, they moved in a wave from eastern to

66   Nicole Chalmer

Western Australia. An analysis by Brian Cooke et al. of rabbit-dingo ecosystem interactions in northern South Australia during the 1890s shows rabbits becoming the dominant grazers, having even greater ecosystem impacts than livestock.[61] Although there are few reports of this effect in the Esperance bioregion, pastoralist J. P. Brooks in 1927 laid all blame for his financial problems firmly with the rabbit invasion of 1905, when he claimed that 'On certain country where formerly I could run up to 2600 sheep in fair condition I now can only keep 500'.[62]

Rabbits saved many Aboriginal people, providing food as well as income from rabbit skins. Iris Burgoyne, a surviving Mirning elder (the Mirning bordered eastern Ngadju lands), tells how they did not care for rabbit meat but ate it because there was no choice, for by then kangaroos and possums were rare, and many of the preferred native mammals, such as boodies, woylies and bandicoots, were gone or disappearing.[63] She sadly explained how living in the dominant Anglo society was not easy, as it required people to forego traditional relationships with land and animals and to become complicit with the wasteful non-Aboriginal ways of exploitation.[64] Peter Gifford's referral to rabbits as being of primary importance to Aboriginals for food and economy throughout the early twentieth century suggests an underestimation of their importance in Anglo and Aboriginal SES change and warrants further study.[65]

The end of pastoralism

In the early years of the twentieth century, several coinciding shocks acted to weaken the Anglo pastoralist SES and led to its eventual demise, except in the eastern isolated parts of the Esperance bioregion. As the Dempsters prospered, the temptation or need to increase income seemed to override moderation as eventually a peak of around 35,000 sheep were shorn in the 1890s. This eruption likely moved the pastoral systems beyond a sustainable threshold regardless of transhumance and eco-shepherding, especially at Fraser Range and Southern Hills in the arid zone. Drought became more frequent as sheep and other livestock eliminated the drought-resistant perennial pastures, for as ex-pastoralist Geoff Grewar explained, dominant annual vegetation assemblages make droughts more frequent and severe and lower the livestock carrying capacity.[66]

During the last years of the nineteenth century, changes in government policy encouraged closer settlement of the Esperance bioregion. In the municipality of Esperance (1895), yeoman farms were developed, and the fertile land mosaics that were also the best coastal and mallee pastoral grazing country were fenced, drastically limiting extensive sheep grazing. The once influential Dempster pastoral company was dissolved in the early twentieth century, and coastal Esperance Bay station and inland Fraser Range station were separated. F. A. R. Dempster relates how William Dempster had 'prophesied ruin at Esperance as the separation of the two stations was a grave error because Esperance stock needed the change of herbage to keep them in good condition'.[67] Ending transhumance meant large numbers of stock could no longer be kept on the trace-element deficient sandplain, and they became confined to farms on fertile soil mosaics, such as those found at Dalyup River.

A swarm of sheep   67

In the eastern district, pastoralism continued successfully, but productivity declined from 1930 onwards, influenced by drying seasons, drought, and the loss of eco-shepherding and cheap labor when Aboriginal people moved into missions. Although fencing was being used by then, its efficacy was reduced by camel damage and the lack of cheap labor to maintain fences and shift sheep.[68] Without shepherds, a low labor set stocking system became the norm, leading to overgrazing and permanent rangeland damage.

Conclusion

The pastoral management system developed in the Esperance bioregion combined aspects of Aboriginal SES, such as mobility and fire use, with the need for transhumance to develop a system of grazing management that initially exhibited a high level of resilience and adaptation to the local conditions. Although there was early strong resistance from Aboriginal people, by the 1880s as sheep flocks erupted, the habitat destruction led to local flora and fauna food sources declining. Hunger and disease impacts meant that Aboriginal resistance could not be sustained, and the limited choices left meant that to survive they had to accept occupation of tribal lands and adapt as best they could.

Shepherding became a method for Aboriginal survival and integration into the invading Anglo SES.[69] Without their depth of knowledge for land, animal and ecosystem management which slowed the breakdown of existing ecosystems, it is unlikely that pastoralism could have succeeded so well. Over time Anglo pastoralism expanded with a developing a sheep eruption, and fundamental environmental impacts progressed. When land subdivision and fencing into smaller, more intensive farms began from the 1890s onwards, pastoralists lost their best sandplain and mallee country. Although pastoral SES continued in the eastern margins, it eventually declined as droughts became more frequent and Aboriginal eco-shepherding discontinued.

The Aboriginal role in the swarm of sheep, whether judged as compliant, complicit or compelled by the need for survival in a changed world, was crucial for transhumance and in mitigating the sheep eruption. Its use delayed the destructive effects of overgrazing on soils and landscapes as described by such writers such Eric Rolls, Neil Barr and John Cary as features of the initiation of pastoralism in eastern regions of Australia.[70]

Notes

1 Alfred Crosby, 'Ecological Imperialism: The Overseas Migration of Western Europeans as a Biological Phenomenon', in Donald Worster (ed.), *The Ends of the Earth: Perspectives on Modern Environmental History* (Cambridge: Cambridge University Press, 1989), 103–17.
2 Elinor Melville, A *Plague of Sheep: Environmental Consequences of the Conquest of Mexico* (Cambridge: Cambridge University Press, 1997).
3 Norman Tindale, *Aboriginal Tribes of Australia: Their Terrain, Environmental Controls, Distribution, Limits and Proper Names* (Adelaide: South Australian Museum, 1974).

68   *Nicole Chalmer*

4 John Beard, *Plant Life of Western Australia* (Sydney: Kangaroo Press Pty. Ltd., 1990).
5 Ian Davidson-Hunt and Fikret Berkes, 'Nature and Society through the Lens of Resilience: Towards a Human – in – Ecosystem Perspective', in *Navigating Social-Ecological Systems: Building Resilience for Complexity and Change* (Cambridge: Cambridge University Press, 2003). F. A. R. Dempster, Andrew Dempster Founder of Esperance and Muresk.
6 Susan M. Prober, Emma Yuen, Michael O'Connor and Les Schultz. *Ngadju kala: Ngadju Fire Knowledge and Contemporary Fire Management in the Great Western Woodlands* (Floreat, WA: CSIRO Ecosystem Sciences, 2013).
7 John Septimus Roe, 'Report on an Expedition to the South-Eastward of Perth, in Western Australia, between the Months of September 1848, and February 1849 under the Surveyor – General Mr. John Septimus Roe', *Journal of the Royal Geographical Society of London*, XXII (1849): 14–20.
8 Ethel Hassell and D. S. Davison, 'Notes on the Ethnology of the Wheelman Tribe of South-Western Australia', *Anthropos* (1936): 68. Hassell in 1831 describes totems called 'couberne' by the Wheelman tribe.
9 Johan Colding and Carl Folke, 'Social Taboos: "invisible" Systems of Local Resource Management and Biological Conservation', *Ecological Applications*, 11.2 (2001): 584–6.
10 Brendan Nicholas, 'Vegetation', in J. Platt, B. Nicholas, R. Short and S. Gee (eds.), *Esperance Region Catchment Planning Strategy* (Esperance: Esperance Land Conservation District Committee, 1996): 11–19; P. Moore, *A Guide to Plants of Inland Australia* (Chatswood: Reed New Holland, 2005).
11 E. J. Eyre, *Journals of Expeditions into Central Australia, and Overland from Adelaide to King George's Sound, in the Years 1840–1* (London: T. and W. Boone. 2v. 1845).
12 Graeme Caughly, 'Comments on Natural Regulation (What Constitutes a Real Wilderness?)', *Wildlife Society Bulletin*, 9 (1981): 232–4. Caughly distinguished between the dynamics of population eruptions and irruptions.
13 Crosby, *Ecological Imperialism*, 1989.
14 Melville, *A Plague of Sheep*, 1997.
15 Tony Brandis, *Rescuing the Rangelands* (Bentley: WA Department of Environment and Conservation, 2008).
16 Rica Erickson, *The Dempsters* (Nedlands: University of Western Australia Press, 1978).
17 Michelle Dominy, 'Hearing Grass, Thinking Grass: Postcolonialism and Ecology in Aotearoa – New Zealand', in D. Trigger and G. Griffiths (eds.), *Disputed Territories – Land, Culture and Identity in Settler Societies* (Hong Kong: Hong Kong University Press, 2003), 53–80.
18 P. B. Mitchell, 'Historical Perspectives on Some Vegetation and Soil Changes in Semi-Arid New South Wales', *Vegetatio*, 91, 1/2, Vegetation and Climate Interactions in Semi-arid Regions (Jan. 31, 1991): 175–9.
19 C. J. Yates et al., 'Grazing Effects on Plant Cover, Soil and Microclimate in Fragmented Woodlands in South-western Australia: Implications for Restoration', *Austral: Ecology*, 25.1 (2000): 36–47; A. Burbidge et al., 'Patterns in the Modern Decline of Western Australia's Vertebrate Fauna: Causes and Conservation Implications', *Biological Conservation*, 50.1 (1989): 143–98.
20 J. Drummond, 'Correspondence', *Inquirer*, 27 July 1842, 4; E. Wolfe (ed.), *Country Pasture/Forage Resource Profiles in Australia*.
21 Sarre, 'Slow Change on the Range', *Ecos*, 100 (1999): 44.
22 Erickson, *The Dempsters*, 1978.
23 Erickson, *The Dempsters*, 1978.
24 Leslie Brooker, *Expedition Eastward from Northam by the Dempster Brothers, Clarkson, Harper and Corell, July–August 1861* (Carlisle: Hesperian Press, 2006).

25 F. A. R. Dempster, *Andrew Dempster Founder of Esperance and Muresk* (F. A. R. Dempster, n.d.), 2–3.
26 Erickson, *The Dempsters*, 1978.
27 Dempster, n.d.
28 Erickson, *The Dempsters*, 1978; Dempster, n.d., 4; Mathew Tonts, R. Yarwood and R. O. Y Jones. 'Global Geographies of Innovation Diffusion: The Case of the Australian Cattle Industry', *The Geographical Journal*, 176.1 (2010): 90–104.
29 Tonts et al., 2010, 90–104. Old photographs from the period indicate merinos as the dominant breed, with infusions of dual-purpose sheep, such as the Lincoln. Esperance Museum Archives, Sheep. They also explain that English-based cattle breeds were far more dual purpose than today.
30 B. Rodgers, 'Transcription of Notes Used by Mrs. Rica Erickson for Her Book *The Dempsters*' (2001) Esperance Museum Archives, 425.
31 Erickson, *The Dempsters*, 1978, 83–4.
32 Erickson, *The Dempsters*, 1978; F. Ford, 'The Country Scene', *The Countryman*, n.d.
33 Fernand Braudel, *The Mediterranean and the Mediterranean World in the Age of Philip 11. Volumes 1 and 2* (London: Collins, 1972), 85–94.
34 Department of Agriculture and Food, Western Australia and GRDC, *Managing South Coast Sandplain Soils for Yield and Profit*, Bulletin 4773, (South Perth, October 2009): 17–19.
35 T. G. Hungerford. *Diseases of Livestock, 8th Edition* (Sydney: McGraw-Hill, 1975). Ruminant mammals use symbiotic microorganisms for the fermentation in the rumen and hindgut needed to break down plant cellulose. These need trace elements, especially cobalt, to make the vital B12 vitamin that animals need for growth and reproduction.
36 Dempster, n.d., 4; 'Pioneering Fraser Range', *The Western mail.* n.d. Esperance Museum Archives, 2066.
37 Erickson, *The Dempsters*, 1978.
38 Dempster, n.d. Gnammas are depressions enlarged with fire to flake the rock which is then chipped away.
39 P. G. Spooner, M. Firman and Yalmambirra. 'Origins of Travelling Stock Routes: 1. Connections to Indigenous Traditional Pathways', *The Rangeland Journal*, 32 (2010): 329–39.
40 Braudel, 1974, 85–94. Mineral requirements may also have been an unrecognised factor in Mediterranean transhumance.
41 G. F. Moore quoted in Rica Erickson, *Old Toodyay and Newcastle* (Toodyay: Toodyay Shire Council, 1974), Chapter 8, 62–8.
42 Kimberley TallBear, 'Shepard Krech's The Ecological Indian: One Indian's Perspective', *The Ecological Indian Review* (2000): 1–5.
43 Erickson, *Old Toodyay and Newcastle*, 63–4.
44 Karl Dimer, *Elsewhere Fine* (Bunbury: South West Printing and Publishing Co. Ltd., 1989). The book is about his family's life on Nanambinia Station north of Israelite Bay.
45 Dimer, *Elsewhere Fine*, 1989.
46 'Wood Notes from Western Australia', *Eastern Districts Chronicle*, 31 January 1891.
47 Yates et al., "Grazing Effects', 2000, 36–47.
48 Extract from diary of a Dempster brother at Fraser Range, 1870. Esperance Museum Archives, HS/694 DEM.
49 Neville Green, *Aborigines of the Albany Region 1821–1898: The Bicentennial Dictionary of Western Australia Vol.VI* (Nedlands: University of WA Press, 1989).
50 P. Gifford, *Black and White and in Between: Arthur Dimer and the Nullabor* (Carlisle: Hesperian Press, 2002), Chapter 2.
51 Moia Smith, *Recherché a L' Esperance: a Prehistory of the Esperance Region of South-Western Australia.* Doctoral thesis, University of Western Australia, 1993.

70 Nicole Chalmer

52 E. Cotton, *The Dempsters of Esperance Bay*, Esperance Museum Archives, 2029.
53 McGlade to Inspector T. Rowe, n.d. Feb. 1891, PRO WA, AN5/Esperance Museum Archives, 781, No.16, Esperance Police Station letter and report books, 1879–1893.
54 I. Abbott, 'Mammalian Faunal Collapse in Western Australia, 1875–1925: The Hypothesised Role of Epizootic Disease and a Conceptual Model of Its Origin, Introduction, Transmission, and Spread', *Australian Zoologist*, 33.4 (2006): 530–61.
55 McGlade to Inspector T. Rowe.
56 Bridges, 2004; Erickson, *The Dempsters*, 1978; Western Australian Year Books, Agriculture 1886–1904 (Perth: Government Statisticians Office, Government Printer.)
57 Annie Dabb, Nyungar Elder, interviewed by Nicole Chalmer, Esperance 19/01/2018.
58 Anna Haebich, *For Their Own Good: Aborigines and Government in the South-West of Western Australia 1900–1940* (Nedlands: University of WA Press 1998): 1–4.
59 Gifford, *Black and White and in Between*, 2002.
60 Aborigines Act, 1905, Western Australia; Haebich, 1998, 83–9.
61 Brian Cooke and R. C. Soriguer, 'Do Dingoes Protect Australia's Small Mammal Fauna from Introduced Mesopredators? Time to Consider History and Recent Events', *Food Web* (2016): 7–9.
62 Canberra, 'Our Pioneers' Gallery Fifty-three Years on the Frontier Mr. J. P. Brooks, of Balbania', *The Sunday Times*, 27 November 1927.
63 Gifford, 2002, 80–3; I. Burgoyne, *The Mirning – We Are the Whales* (Broom: Magabala Books, 2000).
64 Burgoyne, *The Mirning*, 2000, 6.
65 Gifford, *Black and White and in Between*, 2002, 46–7.
66 Geoff Grewar (retired pastoralist), interviewed by Nicole Chalmer, Coronet Hill, 20/08/2012.
67 Dempster, n.d.; Rodgers, 'Transcription of Notes Used by Mrs. Rica Erickson for Her Book *The Dempsters*', 2001; Australian Bureau of Statistics, 3; Western Australia, Year Book Australia (1911).
68 Dimer, *Elsewhere Fine*, 1989.
69 Pickard, 2008, 55–80; Gifford, *Black and White and in Between*, 2002, 46–7.
70 E. Rolls, 'Land of Grass: the Loss of Australia's Grasslands', *Australian Geographical Studies*, 37.3 (November 1999): 197–213; N. Barr and J. Cary, *Greening a Brown Land* (Melbourne: Palgrave MacMillan, 1992).

Part II

Abundance

Life hath its charms

"Learn to esteem life as it deserves; then thou art at the pinnacle of wisdom."

"Life hath its charms," so all things round us say;
The moon by night, the gorgeous sun by day,
The hills, the valleys, and, the silvery floods,
The rocks precipitous, the leafy woods;
All, all attest the great Creator's power,
And speak his goodness every changing hour.

"Life hath its charms;" the world is rich and fair,
The fields abundant, full of life and air;
Ten thousand flocks the verdant hills adorn,
The valleys glow with all-sustaining corn;
All things are ripe with pleasures made for man –
Great God! how good, how bountiful thy plan!
– Original Poetry, Australasian Chronicle
(Sydney), 24 April 1840, 2

6 Optimism unlimited
Prospects for the pearl-shell, bêche-de-mer and trochus industries on Australia's Great Barrier Reef, 1860–1940

Rohan Lloyd

In the early 1920s, the imagined futures of the pearl-shell, bêche-de-mer and trochus fisheries were promising, according to many of their exponents. In reality, the fisheries were frequently subject to resource depletion, issues surrounding its multi-ethnic labor force and shifting markets. A great deal of scholarship has sought to explain the complexities and problems of Australia's pearl-shell, bêche-de-mer and trochus fisheries.[1] Despite historically existing as distinct maritime enterprises, often with different bases, grounds and leaders, in histories of the Great Barrier Reef they are collated together and discussed as salient examples of settler Australia's misuse of the Reef.[2] Often overlooked, however, are the ways the fisheries were promoted to foster a perception of the Reef as a place of abundance. In this sense, historical perceptions of the Reef's marine resources closely resembled global trends.[3] Nonetheless, the imaginations of Reef exploiters did express themselves in novel ways.

This chapter considers how known histories of resource issues became marginalised within the romanticisation of the Reef's economic wealth. It does so by briefly addressing the pioneering period when ideas and rumours of the fisheries' potential to generate wealth drew government interest and regulation. It then considers a turbulent period wherein government concern for the fisheries resulted in three inquiries between 1890 and 1920. Finally, it examines the period from World War I to the 1940s when the idea of 'abundance' became particularly resilient, as writers recast the fisheries' histories and praised them as concrete examples of the Reef's potential abundance. By the 1950s, however, optimism about the future of the fishery had been sapped, and tourism replaced it as the Reef's primary economic activity. Nonetheless, this chapter shows that optimism remained despite legacies of resource depletion, labor issues and market difficulties. It argues that belief in the fisheries' abundance, expressed by fishermen, scientists, politicians and travel writers, embodied a confidence which was informed by a desire to ascribe a form of tangible value to the Reef.

Early days

Early accounts of the bêche-de-mer and pearl-shell fisheries celebrated them as a source of profit in a wild northern frontier. Bêche-de-mer was considered 'one of

74   *Rohan Lloyd*

the most curious incidents in commerce' because of its bizarre slug-like appearance and its value in China.[4] By the late 1870s, however, bêche-de-mer fishermen were venturing further afield to find stocks. Reports of conflict between fishermen and northern Indigenous peoples were common.[5] Yet despite the violence and hostilities, fishermen showed little inclination to restrain their expansion. Many believed that depleted beds along the coast meant it was necessary 'to push northward, and towards the coast of New Guinea' to allow the beds to replenish.[6] It was in the earliest years of the fisheries, when problems arose, that the notion of abundance emerged.

The pearl-shell fishery, although clouded in mystery, held a similar reputation. An 1879 pamphlet on the pearl-shell and bêche-de-mer fisheries sensationally described the early shellers as 'bold men', risking shipwreck and 'a fight for life against the ferocious and cannibal natives of the mainland, or of the islands'.[7] 'For their daring', the early shellers were rewarded with 'a rich gold reef, a veritable "jeweller's shop"'.[8] Rumours of resource depletion were dismissed as ploys by fishermen to discourage the competition.

With no oversight, policing and determining the fisheries' actual stocks and revenue was difficult. Indeed, even the Queensland colonial government was unaware. The only revenue the government received from pearl-shell, for instance, was the minimal amounts paid into the Thursday Island customs office. 'The greater part of the capital', Colonial Secretary Arthur Palmer proclaimed, 'belonged to New South Wales' where most of the fisherman and shellers were from.[9] The notion that Queensland's waters had a wealth in pearl-shell and bêche-de-mer pushed the colonial government to introduce legislation mainly aimed at collecting revenue: the Pearl Shell and Bêche-de-Mer Fishery Act of 1881.[10] The legislation initiated a more thorough recording of the fisheries' make-up and revenue, lifting the fog that had once clouded the industries. Nonetheless, the period before the 1880s would be remembered as a high time when abundance in shell and slug was real rather than imaginary.

Size limits and cultivation

By the end of the 1880s the bêche-de-mer and pearl-shell fisheries had enjoyed a brief boom before a bust cycle began. In 1890, it was suggested that the bêche-de-mer fishery was entering a remunerative period after production plummeted in 1887.[11] The pearl-shell fishery had seen yearly decreases in revenue, and by 1888, the total value of the industry had nearly halved despite high global demand. As shell beds became scarce, innovations were required. Full-dress deep-diving equipment was adopted as the shallow beds were depleted, and then schooner-based fleets or 'floating stations' were introduced. 'Floating stations' originated in the Torres Strait in the mid-1880s, but as beds were depleted, the embryotic stations migrated to north-west Australia.[12] When the fleets returned, at the end of the 1880s, the Queensland government had appointed an oyster expert, William Saville-Kent, as commissioner of fisheries.

Almost immediately, Saville-Kent raised concerns for both fisheries. He believed the bêche-de-mer fishery required better policing to protect the largely Indigenous labor force, as well as better resource management, but his own limited understanding of the slug precluded him from making specific recommendations.[13] Saville-Kent was, however, better acquainted with the pearl-shell fishery. It was, he asserted, suffering from extensive depletion caused by the 'indiscriminate collection' of young shell and the 'considerable depletion' of fishing grounds.[14] At Thursday Island, Saville-Kent claimed he had consulted with 'members of the trade', described as 'leading boat owners', and achieved consensus on recommendations to introduce an internal size limit of six inches and, possibly, the closing of grounds. Finally, Saville-Kent, on the basis of his own experiments, recommended provisions to encourage cultivation initiatives.[15] The provisions included granting cultivation leases over foreshore areas and exempting cultivators from the size restrictions. The Queensland government incorporated many of Saville-Kent's recommendations into its 1891 amendment of the Pearl Shell and Beche-de-Mer Fishery Act

Protests from within the fishery emerged immediately. The size-limit restrictions were blamed for the decline in yields.[16] Others contested the restrictions' effectiveness because the shell would be opened, measured and, if it was too small, discarded back into the ocean to perish.[17] Many denied that Saville-Kent had been as consultative as he had claimed and called it 'legislation in the dark'.[18] Some smaller shellers – especially those who operated from shore stations – accused Saville-Kent of exclusively consulting larger fleet owners. They claimed the legislation placed the industry in the hands of a few leaseholders who could remove unlimited amounts of shell to transfer to their 'cultivation' grounds. The 'cultivation' provisions, which were positioned as preservationist measures, were, according to critics, leading to greater denudation of beds. A letter from a number of shellers protested that a single large operator, James Clark, was removing huge quantities of undersized shell and transferring it to a leased area in Friday Island Passage. They foresaw the loss of an industry that provided '200 divers and 1200 seamen of their present means of livelihood'.[19] They ended their protest by reminding the government of the legacy of the fishery as having 'grown of itself without any subsidy direct or indirect from the government'.[20]

The debates on the cultivation regulations stoked flames of animosity within the industry held between the larger and smaller operators. As Steve Mullins has argued, the floating station system introduced a 'formidable competition for what was now, only too apparently, an exhaustible resource', and the cultivation measures strengthened divisions between the two groups.[21] The shore-based operators contended that cultivation was destroying not only the beds but also the community and identity of the fishery itself. The problems in the industry, while in need of some reform, could be addressed by modest, industry-informed regulations.[22] Their protests were hardly a denial of resource depletion, but this issue was marginalised in their defence of an idealised practice of shelling.

76   Rohan Lloyd

In contrast, the fleet operators owned their monikers as 'capitalists' and denigrated the shore-based shellers by referring to them as 'storemen'. They argued that cultivation initiatives were both scientifically sanctioned and would protect the fishery's future.[23] James Clark, whose fleets and cultivation leases made him the largest operator in the Torres Strait, attracted scorn from within the fishery. Clark wrote that he was endeavouring to work 'in a more modern, economical, and profitable way', and those who joined him 'need not be afraid of the future'.[24] Cultivators found some support from the *Brisbane Courier* that claimed: 'Our motto of "Advance Australia!" demands that the cultivators be granted a free hand'. Repealing the provisions would, they suggested, 'roll back the wheel of progress'.[25]

The majority of shellers perceived their fishery to be one which would be best run without government intrusion. Concerns of limited resources were dismissed, and cultivation was considered a capitalist initiative that threatened to unsettle the fisheries' existence. Eventually, in 1896, the size limit was reduced from the six-inch internal measurement to a five-inch internal and six-inch external measurement. The government also removed the previous exemption for 'cultivators', effectively extinguishing the incentive to continue cultivation initiatives. Nonetheless, the government announced it would hold a commission of inquiry into the fishery the following year. The next season, however, witnessed a record catch and an additional 100 vessels in the Torres Strait.

The 1897 commission made clear the industry's attitude towards notions of resource depletion. The lone voice of concern at the commission was George Bennett, the Thursday Island sub-collector and Queensland's inspector of fisheries. Bennett cautioned that the size-limit reduction led to more young shell being fished which would cause imminent problems for the fishery.[26] Bennett was unequivocal that if nothing was done to limit this overfishing, then the majority of boats would cease working within five years.[27] Shellers, however, both large and small, received Bennett's prophesising with indifference.[28] Many endorsed the need for the fishery to be better managed, not by a scientist but by a floating inspector equipped with 'a hardy sailing vessel, a practical knowledge of the industry and a reputation that commands confidence'.[29]

The Great Barrier Reef

Although Saville-Kent did not assist in implementing his recommendations or participate in the 1897 commission, his presence was still felt. In 1895, he published *The Great Barrier Reef: Its Products and Potentialities*. Its colourful illustrations and photographs allowed for a new appreciation of the Reef's aesthetics. Yet accompanying the vivid depictions was a promotion of 'the harvest-field, rich from both a commercial and a scientific standpoint, that this Queensland possession constitutes'.[30] The book's final chapters evoked notions of abundance which, in time, proved resilient among promoters of the Reef. Reef fish, Saville-Kent declared, presented 'almost unlimited possibilities of profitable development'. Sharks, rays and skates were 'almost unlimited', and the Reef possessed 'literally a mine of wealth' of coral for lime and ornamental purposes. The pearl-shell fishery was 'capable of unlimited development', especially if cultivation methods were adopted'.[31] He believed the establishment of a marine biological station could aid the Reef's economic development, and the Reef's development would progress, hand-in-hand, with the growth of Reef science.

Significantly, the book linked the pearl-shell and bêche-de-mer fisheries and their economic viability with the Reef's value. The *Brisbane Courier* praised Saville-Kent for confirming the Reef as 'one of Queensland's most valuable assets', rich in 'intrinsic beauty' and of 'considerable direct monetary importance'.[32] Shellers had refuted claims that the fisheries suffered from resource depletion; booms and busts were part of the fisheries cycle, and the beds would continue to produce wealth. By 1900, perceptions of the Reef were underpinned by an entangled valuing of its natural and economic virtues. The most profitable and identifiable economic pursuits on the Reef – the ones with a history of profits and perceived insulation from resource depletion – were the pearl-shell and bêche-de-mer fisheries.

Post-federation blues

The fisheries did not evade controversy for long. In 1901, James Tosh, Queensland's new fisheries expert, and George Bennett issued alarming reports on the state of the fisheries. Tosh claimed the pearl-shell fishery was at 'a critical stage', the shell was becoming more scarce and 'year by year the boats have ventured further afield'.[33] Both men suggested closing grounds seasonally or, in some localities, closing them permanently.[34] Tosh called for the reintroduction of the six-inch limit and the reduction in the number of licenses and boats engaged in the fishery.

The bêche-de-mer fishery was also under a cloud of concern. Bennett reported that the industry, comprising eleven licensed vessels at the time, was in the beginnings of a revival. Slugs were making their appearances near Darnley and Murray Island and along the Barrier Reef.[35] Bennett warned, however, that pearling vessels were 'being fitted and licensed' for gathering bêche-de-mer. He encouraged more stringent regulations to ensure that abuses within the industry, principally of labor, did not take place. He added that no provision for regulating the fisheries stock at the time existed and suggested that steps be taken 'to ensure the permanency of the industry in case of its revival on a large scale'.[36] He accepted that patrolling the fisheries would be expensive, but without proper oversight, the various conservation recommendations were 'worse than useless'.[37]

These concerns prompted a second inquiry. In 1908, a Royal Commission was established to inquire into the working of the fisheries. The commission, of which Bennett was a member, concluded that the depletion of the pearl-shell grounds was caused by a 'belief that the supply was inexhaustible', the introduction of floating stations, an excessive number of vessels, the broad employment of highly skilled 'Asiatic divers', the absence of a scheme for the periodic closure of grounds and the reduction in size of the exportable shell. On bêche-de-mer, the

78 Rohan Lloyd

commission concluded that the industry had reached its 'zenith' in 1907 and that grounds had been fished bare from New Guinea to Lady Elliot Island at the southern end of the Reef. They recommended that the fishery be closed for two years by prohibiting the exportation of bêche-de-mer from all Queensland ports.[38]

One witness whose evidence contradicted the commission's report was James Clark. Clark's enterprise had become the most successful pearl-shelling operation in the Australian industry.[39] Clark told the commission that a principal reason for the reduction in the yearly take of pearl-shell was poor weather; 'Weather', Clark asserted, 'provides all the protection that the beds need'.[40] Clark believed, however, that the increase in boats on the grounds had contributed to depletion. To solve this issue, Clark offered to rent the entire Torres Strait fishing ground from the government for £5,000 a year.[41] Ceding control of an entire fishery to a single enterprise seemed, however, untenable.[42] Moreover, Clark's unpopularity had inspired regulations designed to prevent his re-entry into the Torres Strait fishery after he left to establish his enterprise in Aru in 1905. As Mullins argued, the 1908 commission, which recommended further legislation prohibiting Clark's re-entry, was the 'practical expression' of a pervasive and insistent 'pro-small owner, anti-monopoly theme' in the public discourse about pearl-shelling in the late nineteenth and early twentieth century.[43] Apart from the marginalisation of the floating stations, little change was made which would have an impact upon resource management.

Develop the Reef

The fishery continued to be plagued by resource and labor issues, the latter of which was the subject of another Royal Commission in 1913. Additionally, the value of pearl-shell received competition from a new product. The trochus fishery, which sought the coned-shaped trochus shell for its internal nacre, expanded rapidly in the interwar period with grounds along the Reef and into the Torres Strait, despite the lower quality of the shell. Additionally, the trochus fishery, along with the bêche-de-mer and pearl-shelling industry, continued to be dominated by non-white labor. The continued prevalence and success of Asian workers within the fisheries was a particularly vexing issue, especially for the Commonwealth that was eager to bleach Australia, particularly its northern regions.

Importantly, the fisheries were perceived as essential contributors to the Reef's value. Proponents of development remained optimistic in the fisheries' abilities to provide large profits and fuel northern development.[44] Japanese and Chinese fishermen were presented as competition to white shellers and an affront to 'white' Australia. Their presence in the fisheries was depicted as profit stealing, a threat to national sovereignty and a symptom of southern neglect of the north. Edmund Banfield accused the Queensland and federal governments of rejecting the fisheries while Japan and China benefited.[45] Banfield envisioned scientists guiding the fisheries' development and praised the establishment of a 'Special Corresponding Investigating Committee' within the Advisory Council of Science and Industry

Optimism unlimited 79

to consider the 'economic possibilities and development of the tropical waters of Australia'.[46] The implications for the Reef were clear to Banfield. The Reef 'is a great national asset' and 'its potential wealth must be ascertained and dealt with in a conservative spirit . . . for the advantage of Australians'.[47]

Banfield contributed to a broad criticism of the lack of development of the Reef's wealth and its plundering by 'indiscriminate resource raiders'. A response to Banfield's piece on the trochus fishery, entitled 'Raiders of the Reef', asserted the government only became aware of the Reef's existence 'when some luckless ship hit it too hard'. The article continued:

> As [Banfield] says the trade in marine produce is practically in the hands of Chinese and Japanese. Buttons made in Japan from trochus are the clothes of patriotic Australians, people who mouth such phrases as "Australia for Australians: support local industries etc. etc" . . . Personally, I have spent half my life in the North and I share [Banfield's] optimism. But – and this is the rub – it seems a case of "all are for the party and none for state." In the hurly-burly of politics and the wild unscrupulous scramble for place and power, the claims of the North can go bang.[48]

For those connected with the politics of North Queensland, the Reef figured as an important economic resource to be exploited – albeit conservatively. Within this notion, the proper development of the trochus, pearl-shell and bêche-de-mer fisheries could only be realised by white-Australian fishermen and scientists. The commentary spoke not only to anxieties of an empty north and the associated threats to Australia's resource sovereignty but also to a faith in Western science to reveal and effectively exploit the Reef's untapped economic potential. Rarely did commentary on the need to investigate the fisheries emphasise the depletion of resources as a result of 'white' shellers.

Scientists were happy to embrace the faith placed in them. The notion that Reef industries, particularly the three fisheries, would develop alongside greater investment in Queensland's marine science gained considerable momentum in the early twentieth century. Enthusiasm grew for the establishment of a research station along the Reef, which would assist in revealing the Reef's economic resources. Indeed, a major rationale behind the establishment of the Great Barrier Reef Committee (GBRC) in 1922 was as a research body to determine the Reef's economic products.[49] For early twentieth-century scientists, the most readily identifiable economic products from the Reef were pearl-shell, bêche-de-mer and trochus, and the GBRC considered it their priority to ensure 'others' did not 'use them in an unlicensed and uncontrolled manner'.[50]

The prospects of the fisheries also became linked to the development of other Reef industries. After World War I, all three fisheries were used to pique public interest in the Reef, and they routinely featured in the promotion of Reef tourism. In 1923, a Queensland Government Intelligence and Tourist Bureau (QGITB) brochure promoted the Reef as 'the scene of several important industries which may under good management attain larger dimensions'. The brochure depicted the pearl-shell fishery as one with a history of innovation and riches where the diver 'walks about the seafloor, picking up what shell he finds'. The account, however, was not completely celebratory and acknowledged that beds had become 'exhausted by over-fishing', but the fleets 'give them time to recover by moving to another district'. It also signalled that in the previous year the crop from Queensland had reached only four tons but added, with a hint to the future, 'the crop has frequently exceeded 1000 tons'.[51]

Similar promotional material featured in novels, too. Writing under the pseudonym Frank Reid, Alexander Vennard produced the short story *Toilers of the Reef: A Tale of the Pearling Fleet*. In *Toilers*, Melbourne schoolboy Vernon Sinclair visits his family in Cape York. Vernon's uncle, a pearler, begins the story aboard 'his sturdy fishing luggers . . . on the fringe of the Great Barrier Reef, searching for the valuable mother-of-pearl shell'.[52] Eventually, Vernon joins his uncle and is placed in a diving suit and dropped into the water to see for himself the 'gardens of the sea'. Images supplied by the QGITB helped create a perception of abundance. Decks of schooners were covered with large shells, and the pearling fleet was photographed from a hill in Thursday Island with boats moored well out to the horizon (for an example of the former, see Figure 6.1). Abundance, hard work and settlement were the themes often attached to the three fisheries. They embodied a sense of romantic pioneering and were perceived as a vehicle through which the Reef's and the north's development could progress. Resource depletion was rarely entertained in promotional or popular literature.

Figure 6.1 Opening pearl shells on Thursday Island, 10 February 1907, postcard.
Source: State Library of Victoria, H38424.

Interest in the Reef grew significantly in the early 1930s. Scientists, journalists and popular authors travelled along the Reef and promoted the Reef's beauty and wealth. The three fisheries received romanticised appraisals despite their histories of resource depletion and labor issues. The marine biologist Charles Yonge commented that the pearl-shell industry had settled into 'an orderly collection from the bed of the sea of an important raw material of commerce'.[53] Most believed science would ensure the commercial success of the fisheries. Reef tourist pioneer Monty Embury envisioned the return of cultivation and asserted that 'scientists will lead the way to something of value commercially'.[54] Theodore Roughley, the superintendent of New South Wales Fisheries, called pearl-shell the 'richest treasure' on the Reef and believed the fishery was heading for 'prosperous days'.[55] He warned, however, that the trochus fishery would face serious depletion unless restrictions were introduced.[56] Despite the introduction of a 2.5-inch size limit in 1931, Department of Harbours and Marine reports from 1936 suggested the trochus supplies were becoming scarce. Optimism in the future of the industries, however, remained, and a feeling that the fisheries would produce good yearly harvests prevailed.

This optimism, however, and the links with the Reef soon faded. With greater publicity of the Reef came broader development of its tourist industry. By World War II, tourism was the major economic contribution of the Reef. After the war, images of shellers drowning in shell were replaced with travellers walking across reefs and hooking marlins. More importantly, romanticised imagery and descriptions of shellers and bêche-de-mer fishermen became largely absent, except in the few passages devoted to the Reef's history. Following the war, the absence of celebration of the productivity of the three fisheries was stark. During the war, the pearling beds had been closed; when the beds reopened, prices for pearl-shell were high, and the Torres Strait beds were well populated with shell. One would imagine that these maritime industries presented fertile ground for those interested in promoting the development of the Reef.

There was, however, apprehension about the fisheries' abilities to be both profitable and sustainable. The emergence of plastics had rendered the use of pearl-shell and trochus for buttons largely redundant. Technological and industrial improvements would have to take place, too. Most of the pearling luggers had been requisitioned during the war, and many had been damaged or lost and therefore needed to be replaced. Additionally, the fisheries' conditions and wages would need to change to meet post-war standards. A fourth inquiry, headed by H. C. Coombs, then the director-general of the Department of Post-War Reconstruction, was conducted into the pearl-shell fisheries of north Australia in 1946. Like earlier commissions, the inquiry endorsed regulations that could halt the fisheries' contraction. Yet while earlier reports allowed the shellers' appeals to the past to dictate the future, Coombs used the fisheries' history as evidence of their malfunction. The fisheries, he stated, had been marked 'by a frequency of Commissions and investigations, which indicates that there must be many problems in the development and normal conduct of the fishery'.[57]

Conclusion

Coombs pointed to the fisheries' figures, its booms and busts, as signs of the fisheries' 'major epochs'. The regulation of the fisheries, or the management of its resources, became hindered by an enduring belief in the ability of the fishermen to produce the level of wealth which had once, only in rumour, been furnished in the fisheries' early days. This optimism fuelled opposition to change, and regulatory intrusion was viewed as an affront to the fisheries' pioneering spirit. From 1895 to 1940, the three fisheries were recast as symbols of the Reef's untapped wealth. Collectively, these depictions of the fisheries in association with the Reef helped foster a seemingly erroneous idea: that the Reef's size denotes abundance and resilience to human interference.

Notes

1 See, for instance, John Bach, 'The Political Economy of Pearlshelling', *The Economic History Review*, 14.1 (1961); 'The Pearlshelling Industry and the "White Australia" Policy,' *Historical Studies*, 10.38 (1962); Regina Ganter, *The Pearl-Shellers of Torres Strait: Resource Use, Development and Decline, 1860s–1960s* (Melbourne: Melbourne University Press, 1994); Steve Mullins, 'From Ti to Dobo: The 1905 Departure of the Torres Strait Pearl-Shelling Fleets to Aru, Netherlands East Indies,' *The Great Circle*, 19.1 (1997); 'To Break "the Trinity" or "Wipe out the Smaller Fry": The Australian Pearl Shell Convention of 1913,' *Journal for Maritime Research*, 7.1 (2005); Julia Martínez and Adrian Vickers, *The Pearl Frontier: Indonesian Labor and Indigenous Encounters in Australia's Northern Trading Network* (Honolulu: University of Hawai'i Press, 2015).

2 See, for instance, James Bowen and Margarita Bowen, *The Great Barrier Reef: History, Science, Heritage* (Cambridge: Cambridge University Press, 2002); Iain McCalman, *The Reef: A Passionate History* (Melbourne: Penguin, 2013); Ben Daley, *The Great Barrier Reef: an Environmental History* (London: Earthscan from Routledge, 2014).

3 See, for instance, Callum Roberts, *The Unnatural History of the Sea* (Washington, DC: Island Press, 2007) and Arthur McEvoy, *The Fisherman's Problem: Ecology and Law in the California Fisheries 1850–1980* (Cambridge: Cambridge University Press, 1986).

4 E. Thorne, *The Queen of the Colonies or Queensland as I Knew It* (London: Sampson Low, Marston, Searle & Rivington, 1876), 245.

5 See, for instance, 'Another Massacre at Green Island', *The Telegraph*, 29 August 1873, 3; 'The Dangers of Beche-de-Mer Fishing', *South Australian Advertiser*, 27 November 1879, 7.

6 'The Bêche-de-Mer Industry', *Brisbane Courier* (*Courier*), 31 October, 1882, 6.

7 Pearl Shell, Beche-De-Mer and Dugong, ed. *International Exhibition, Rise and Progress of Queensland Industries* (Brisbane: s. n, 1880), 1.

8 Pearl Shell, Beche-De-Mer and Dugong.

9 Hansard, 26 July 1881, Legislative Assembly, 186.

10 Trochus was included in 1931.

11 William Saville-Kent, 'Bêche-De-Mer and Pearl-Shell Fisheries of Northern Queensland', in William Saville-Kent (ed.), *Fisheries of Queensland, 1889–1905* (Brisbane: Government Printer, 1889–1905), 4.

12 Mullins, 'To Break "the Trinity"', 219–20.

13 Saville-Kent, 'Bêche-De-Mer and Pearl-Shell Fisheries of Northern Queensland', in *Fisheries*, 1–6.

14 Saville-Kent, 'Pearl and Pearl-Shell Fisheries of Northern Queensland', in Ibid., 2, 10.

Optimism unlimited   83

15 Saville-Kent, 'Progress Report on Pearl-Shell Fisheries', in Ibid., 1.
16 Queensland State Archive (QSA), SRS 6232 General Correspondence, ID951318, Treasury Department general correspondence – Pearl shell and beche-de-mer fisheries, extract of letter from George Smith's to E.B. Forrest, 3 April 1892, 2.
17 QSA, SRS 6232, ID951318, Petition from pearlers to the Legislative Assembly of Queensland, January 1893, 3.
18 Letter-to-the-Editor, Pearlshell, 'The Pearlshell Industry', *Courier*, 25 May 1894, 7.
19 'Pearlshell Cultivation Question', *Courier*, 27 November 1893, 6.
20 'Pearlshell Cultivation Question'.
21 Mullins, 'To Break "the Trinity"', 222–3.
22 See, for instance, 'The Pearlshell Fishery', *Courier*, 21 December 1893, 6; Letter-to-the-Editor, 'The Pearlshell Industry', *Courier*, 9 November 1894, 2; QSA, SRS 6232, ID951318, Petition to Hugh M. Nelson, 22 March 1894.
23 See, for instance, QSA, SRS 6232, ID951318, Letter James Clark to Colonial Treasurer, 4 December 1893 and Letter-to-the-Editor, James Clark, 'The Pearlshell Fisheries', *Courier*, 17 November 1893, 7.
24 Letter to the Editor, James Clark, 'The Pearlshell Industry', *Courier*, 13 October 1894, 6.
25 'Pearlshell Controversy', *Courier*, 26 November 1894, 4.
26 J. Hamilton et al., 'Report Together with Minutes of Evidence and Proceedings, of the Commission Appointed to Inquire into the General Working of the Laws Regulating the Pearl-Shell and Bêche-De-Mer Fisheries in the Colony,' QVP (Brisbane: Government Printer, 1897), 1319.
27 Ibid., 1320.
28 Ibid., 1305, 1332 and 1342.
29 Ibid., xxxiiii–iv.
30 W. Saville-Kent, *The Great Barrier Reef of Australia: Its Products and Potentialities* (London: W. H. Allen, 1893), ix.
31 Saville-Kent, *The Great Barrier Reef of Australia*, 317.
32 'The Great Barrier Reef', *Courier*, 31 October 1893, 6.
33 QSA, SRS16785 Batch Files, ID315197 Treasury Department batch file – Royal Commission – Pearl-Shell and Beche-de-Mer, 'Report on the Marine Department for the Year 1900–1901', 29.
34 Ibid., 29–30.
35 Ibid., 13.
36 Ibid.
37 Ibid.
38 H. A. C. Douglas J. Mackay and G. H. Bennett, *Report Together with the Minutes of Proceedings, Minutes of Evidence Taken before the Commission, and Appendices of the Royal Commission Appointed to Inquire into the Working of the Pearl-Shell and Beche-De-Mer Industries*, ed. John Mackay (Brisbane: Government Printer, 1908), LXXIII–IV.
39 Mullins, 'To Break "the Trinity"', 222.
40 J. Mackay, *Royal Commission Report*, 28.
41 J. Mackay, *Royal Commission Report*, 30.
42 Mullins, 'From Ti to Dobo', 36.
43 Mullins, 'To Break "the Trinity"', 236.
44 See, for instance, 'Barrier Reef Industries', *Worker*, 17 May 1917, 17; 'The Great Barrier Reef', *Queenslander*, 30 April 1921, 38.
45 Edmund Banfield, 'Rural Homilies', *Townsville Daily Bulletin*, 12 April 1917, 7.
46 Edmund Banfield, 'Rural Homilies', *Northern Miner*, 7 February 1917, 7.
47 Banfield, 'Rural Homilies'.
48 'Raiders of the Reef', *Townsville Daily Bulletin*, 19 April 1917, 3.
49 Rohan Lloyd, '"Wealth of the reef": The Entanglement of Economic and Environmental Values in Early Twentieth Century Representations of the Great Barrier Reef', *Melbourne Historical Journal*, 43.1 (2015): 52–4.

84   *Rohan Lloyd*

50 H. C. Richards, 'Problems of the Great Barrier Reef', *Queensland Geographical Journal* 36/37 (1922): 52.
51 Queensland Government Intelligence and Tourist Bureau, *The Great Barrier Reef of Australia: A Popular Account of Its General Nature* (Brisbane: QGITB, 1923).
52 Frank Reid, *Toilers of the Reef* (Melbourne: Whitcombe and Tombs, 1922), 5.
53 Charles Yonge, *A Year on the Great Barrier Reef: The Story of Corals and of the Greatest of Their Creations* (London: Putnam, 1930), 167; see also Vance Palmer, 'Trochus and Beche-de-Mer Fishing', *Walkabout* (August 1935): 44–6.
54 E. M. Embury, *The Great Barrier Reef* (Sydney: The Shakespeare Head Press, 1933), 5.
55 T. C. Roughley, *Wonders of the Great Barrier Reef* (Sydney: Angus Robertson, 1936), 231.
56 Roughley, *Wonders of the Great Barrier Reef*, 237–42.
57 Northern Australia Development Committee, *Pearl Shell, Beche-de-Mer and Trochus Industry of Northern Australia* (Sydney: Government Printer, 1946), 1.

7 Swamplands
Human-animal relationships in place

Emily O'Gorman

Toowoomba, a city in south-eastern inland Queensland, Australia, is built on swamps. The swamps have been central to the history of this city. From the mid-nineteenth century, European colonists sought to control and contain them as a source of disease and damaging floods while also being reliant on their aquifers for water supply. This chapter takes up one part of this history, examining the ways in which animals were entangled in colonists' relationships with the swamps as a source of disease. The first section provides background on the town being built on the swamps and engages with European colonists' views of the swamps as a changeable space and source of disease from 1840 to 1900. A range of interacting factors, pathogens, and organisms, including animals but also aquifers, vegetation, and bacteria, shaped colonists' views of the swamps and of the spread of disease in the period, the latter underpinning their efforts to control the swamps, including through drainage works. The second section focuses on a particular kind of animal, mosquitoes, examining the eradication campaigns conducted from 1900 to 1940. These insects were targeted as potential vectors of disease and underpinned further attempts to control the swamps. At the same time, the lives of mosquitoes were shaped by the actions of people in Toowoomba, who had co-created ideal breeding grounds in the swamps and then sought to eradicate these insects from the town.[1]

Through this history, the persistence of initially British-led colonial imperatives to control the swamps as a source of disease and the entanglement of animals within these becomes evident. Across these periods, dominant Western scientific understandings of the relationships between animals and human disease changed significantly, from miasma to germ theory to mosquito-borne diseases. In charting these changes, this chapter draws out the roles and agency of a variety of domesticated animals and their dead bodies, and then the mosquitoes, all present in abundance in the swamps. By focusing on the swamps, this chapter also aims to show the value of situating human-animal relationships within wider sets of shifting relationships in order to more fully examine the co-creation of places by animals.

The chapter draws on archival and newspaper sources and attempts to highlight evidence of non-human animal agencies within them. These sources represent particular human concerns, and colonial ideologies and power relationships

86   Emily O'Gorman

are distinctly evident, at times with meagre information about other humans or about individual animals or even the kinds of animals in question. If we accept that humans are always in relation, we can nevertheless view these sources as emerging out of entangled more-than-human worlds and containing traces of animal agency. We can even view these archives as in some sense co-created or shaped by the animals they describe.[2]

A town built on swamps: colonisation, disease outbreaks, and animals, 1840s to 1900

In the 1850s, within a context of pastoral expansion by European colonists, violence between Aboriginal peoples and these colonists, disease, and dispossession, a small colonial settlement was established at a set of swamps in Giabal Country.[3] The swamps run through and permeate volcanic basalt soils, which formed 27 to 19 million years ago. A series of violent volcanic eruptions likely formed this part of a mountain range, now known as the Great Dividing Range, creating multi-layered lava fields that covered over sandstone. The swamps are located at the top of an escarpment of this range and have supported and been shaped by many animals, plants, and people with dynamic histories. Aboriginal people have lived in and around this region for thousands of years, with archaeological dating of human remains placing people in the area 10,000 years ago; but the human history is probably much older, with human occupation of the continent now dated to at least 60,000 years ago.

In 2002, a heritage report tried to reconstruct the swamplands terrain of the early nineteenth century, conjuring a landscape that was quite varied, in places containing open eucalypt forests, and along parts of the watercourses River Red Gum, with cumbudgi reeds growing in the deeper waterholes. The swamps themselves, fed by underground springs and rainfall, formed a combination of watercourses, lagoons, and marshy areas and supported an abundance of freshwater fish, yabbies, water birds, and other animals. Aboriginal burning regimes shaped the swamp landscapes, parts of which were likely burned fairly regularly. Although part of the Country of Giabal people, many Indigenous groups have camped and hunted at the swamps, especially during the periods of large gatherings at the nearby Bunya Mountains. For these gatherings, which happened every two to three years, people would travel from up to 250 kilometres away for ceremony, trade, and meetings, which centred on bunya nut harvests. The swamps, located on the pathway to Bunya Mountains, provided an opportunity to rest, exchange information, hunt such animals as ducks, and catch fish.[4]

The history of Toowoomba as a township is deeply steeped in British colonial pioneer narratives of pastoral expansion, a period of violence and upheaval for Aboriginal people across eastern Australia but often narrated in heroic terms by European colonists.[5] These pastoralists initiated a period of intense frontier violence in the region. The pastoralists came from the south, bringing with them sheep and cattle to establish illegal stations that the colonial government then legitimised through surveys. Towns soon followed to service the needs of the stations.[6] In the late 1840s, the swamps, located just eight kilometres away from the colonial settlement of Drayton, were being used by colonists for timber supply, thatching, and as a "camping ground for passing drays".[7] In the 1840s, Aboriginal people were also present in the swamplands, hunting waterfowl and undertaking other activities.[8]

As Drayton's population expanded and water supply ran low, colonists began to look for an alternative site for their businesses, and in 1850, the Queensland government surveyor James Charles Burnett laid out town allotments at "The Swamp", as it became known to colonists. The strict grid pattern placed the centre of the town in the heart of the swamplands, nestled in the crook of East and West Swamps, as they were later called. Where these swamps met, they joined in one large swamp, which became known to colonists as "the main swamp". This large swamp then drained into a watercourse called Gowrie Creek (see Figure 7.1).

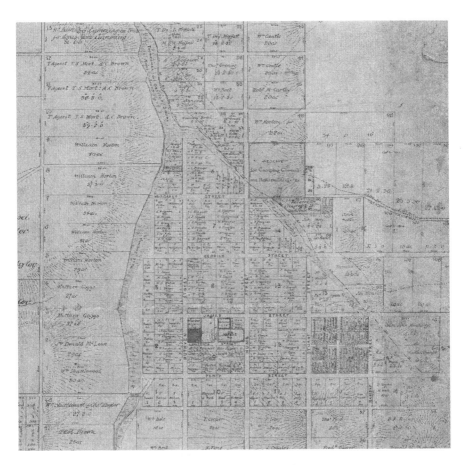

Figure 7.1 Detail of a map from 1857 showing Toowoomba swamps.

Source: Plan of Toowoomba at Drayton Swamp, Parish of Drayton, County of Aubigny showing the lands recently measured for sale, circa 1/1/1857 – circa 31/12/1857, Department of Natural Resources and Mines, Qld 2017. Queensland State Archives Item ID714269, Map.

88   *Emily O'Gorman*

Increasingly, colonists moved their businesses from Drayton towards the better-watered swamps.[9] By 1855, the population of Toowoomba was 84 and Drayton was 61.[10]

Although The Swamp – also called Drayton Swamp and Toowoomba Swamp – possessed resources that colonists needed, they also associated it with negative meanings. For example, colonial traveller and entrepreneur Nehmiah Bartley, recounting his journey through the area in July 1854, called it "green and oozy" and quickly continued on to "old Drayton".[11] In Britain in the mid-nineteenth century, swamps were seen as sources of disease and of danger more generally and were often associated with spiritual elements.[12] The name of The Swamp was officially changed to Toowoomba in 1857–8 to shed these kinds of negative connotations. In fact, the rise of the term "wetlands" in Australia and many countries from the 1960s can be understood as a part of a re-evaluation and subsequent "rebranding" of watery areas so as to emphasise their importance as a habitat to birds and other biota.[13] The etymology of "Toowoomba" is still contested but is most likely derived from a Giabal word for the swamps.[14] As more people bought land and moved to the swamps, the area eclipsed Drayton as a business and population centre and was incorporated as a municipality in 1860, with Drayton eventually becoming one of its suburbs. By that year, the population of the Darling Downs, as the wider region became called, included 7,000 colonists, 1.5 million sheep, and 140,000 cattle.[15]

An advantage that Toowoomba had over Drayton was its closer proximity to the new Toll Bar Road, completed in 1855. This road became a key traffic route linking the Darling Downs with colonial settlements east of the mountain range (primarily Ipswich and Brisbane) so that Toowoomba became a main watering place for horses and cattle en route with bullock drays and herds of livestock driven through the town.[16] People in the town likely also kept horses, cattle, dairy cows, pigs, and other domestic animals.[17] With greater numbers of people, new industries, and concentrations of new kinds of animals, the swamps changed character, too. Trees were felled for building material. Cattle and horses grazed and drank at various points along the swamps, which had become Crown land, and were treated as a kind of common by residents, stockmen, and dray drivers. Their hooves would have created muddy bogs and, along with colonists' land clearing, facilitated erosion. At the same time, some colonists who owned or rented property created gardens along the edges of the swamps in an effort to "improve" the land.[18]

The swamps continued to grow in size, encroaching further into the adjacent blocks and in one case expanded to "within eighteen feet of a man's house".[19] The shallow channels were also used to dispose of waste, including animal carcasses, rotting vegetation – seemingly including swamp plants like reeds along with dumped vegetable waste – and slop water, which combined to form "noxious exhalations", understood as miasmic vapours that were thought to cause disease.[20] Swamps were already often associated with disease-causing miasmas, but colonists' use of the swamps as dumping grounds exacerbated their miasmatic qualities. In particular, the rotting flesh of animal carcasses was blamed for combining in putrefaction with other organic matter to create deadly vapours. Animal remains were part of a mess of organic matter that in its putrefaction caused disease.

Residents traced outbreaks of scarlet fever and diphtheria to the swamps, and in the mid-1860s, the Toowoomba Council began to lobby the new Queensland government for permission and funding to drain them for sanitary reasons and to "reclaim" some of the swampy ground.[21] However, the council was unsuccessful, and its campaign to drain the swamps was ultimately drawn out over nine years, stalled by a range of legal and financial complications. Essentially, although the swamps were Crown land, the government would not pay for the works, so the Toowoomba Council needed to first gain legal control of the swamps and then make arrangements to borrow money from the Queensland government for the works. Over this period, the council and the town's ratepayers continued to see the "noxious exhalations" from the swamps as an ongoing source of disease, especially deadly outbreaks of typhoid and diphtheria.[22] It was not until 1874 that the council gained legal control of the swamps and funds for the drainage work. These began the same year and were completed by 1875.[23]

People's activities brought new diseases and increased the area of the swamps. Yet the animals had agency here, too. Their behaviour and biology helped to shape the swamps. There is little detail given about the animals that grazed the swamps, although horses and cattle were amongst them. There is even less information about the identities of the dead animals, but they may have included the inedible elements of horses, cattle, pigs, and other domestic animals. Their eating habits and size, their fleshy decomposition, and the various animals and microbes their decomposing bodies attracted shaped the character of the swamps.

Surface water drainage aimed to address the visual and olfactory issues of rotting organic matter. However, as typhoid and diphtheria outbreaks continued, the townspeople began to turn their attention underground, to the aquifers that lay beneath the swamps' surfaces. In the late 1870s, the close proximity of wells to cesspits stirred suspicion among some residents, including medical practitioners, that contaminated sewage was leaking into the aquifers that were tapped by wells, the water from which was a significant source of drinking water in the town. Towards the end of the nineteenth century, a different theory of epidemic disease transmission began to gather support amongst the medical professions in Europe and colonies like Australia, as more people began to draw the connection between sewage-contaminated drinking water and ill health. Importantly, these connections were made during the cholera epidemics in London in 1854 and 1866 and then in Hamburg in 1892.[24] In many ways, the public health responses in Toowoomba to typhoid and dysentery in the 1870s and 1890s chart this shifting approach to disease, from miasmatic to germ theory. Yet they also show that the miasmatic theory was still influential in this period and often ascribed to by medical professionals and others in tandem with germ theory. Although many of the discussions centred on cesspits, animals, especially pigs, were also entangled in the council's public health responses to disease outbreaks in the later decades of the nineteenth century.

90 Emily O'Gorman

Following another typhoid outbreak in 1878, a commission was assembled by the council to report on reasons for ongoing outbreaks of disease. In May of that year, the commissioners reported their findings, which were published in a local newspaper. The committee focused on "the relative situations of the (wells and pits) [which] make it imperative that there should be a connection between them, and it cannot be otherwise".[25] However, they also described "overflowing cesspits, filthy pig-styes, dirty poultry houses, offensive middens, sometimes dry but more frequently wet and consisting of every possible kind of refuse, putrifying accumulations of fruit and vegetables, ill-kept drains, and stagnant slop water and slime". All of this, the commissioners asserted, fostered "disease and death", which "might most naturally be expected" in the town. The comments of the commissioners – three white males in professional positions of power in the town – resonate with arguments by a growing middle class in other cities in Australia and Britain for slum clearance, based on the view that the lower classes had poor sanitary conditions.[26] The commissioners made ten recommendations, including replacing cesspits with the dry earth system and using reservoir or rainwater instead of well water. They also recommended "[t]he banishment of all pigs within the municipality" and "[t]he supervision of Chinamen's gardens".[27]

The removal of pigs from the municipality aimed to address two issues: the transmission of typhoid and hog cholera from pigs to people and the offensive material associated with the feeding of pigs. The commissioners wrote that the feed often consisted of "animal or vegetable refuse and scraps" that if uneaten by the pigs was "left to decay just where they have been cast", creating strong smells, long associated with disease.[28] Piggeries were water intensive and located near the swamps, contributing to an understanding that these areas were generally unhealthy.[29] The poor also often reared pigs, and thus this recommendation pathologised the practices of a particular group of people as well as animals. Excluding pigs from the municipality would significantly impact this group, who would need to change their practices or move to the outskirts of the town.

The other socially stigmatised group that was singled out was the Chinese market gardeners. As with many towns and cities in Australia at this time, the Chinese market gardens in Toowoomba were an essential source of fresh fruits and vegetables. By the 1870s, there were many Chinese market gardens along the East and West Swamps, particularly towards their junction north of James Street.[30] Their horticultural practices included the use of a range of animal manure, including that of pigs, as fertiliser.[31] The recommendations regarding pigs and the monitoring of Chinese market gardens may well then have been linked, although the commissioners' allegations of the use of human excrement as fertiliser in the gardens was a key focus in their report. The commissioners recommended that the council "prohibit the further establishment of these gardens in such close proximity to thickly populated portions of the town".[32] At this time, anti-Chinese feeling was increasing amongst those of European descent in many parts of Queensland, and more broadly in Australia, and the sanitary conditions of the market gardens became subsumed within broader ideologies of race.[33] These recommendations for disease prevention aimed to refigure human and

Swamplands 91

non-human relations, including the exclusion of particular people and animals from the town. These kinds of sanitary practices were part of a hygiene-focused colonialism, racism and classism through which colonial authorities sought to establish social power and environmental control.[34]

In response to the typhoid epidemic of 1878, the council moved to establish a reticulated water supply, which was completed in 1880.[35] The earth closet system was introduced and gradually extended.[36] However, the condition of the swamps, including the state of the drains constructed in 1874, was still cause for complaint by residents.[37] Animals and their relationships with the swamps also continued to be a source of concern for the spread of disease. However, in the early twentieth century, the focus of public health shifted to mosquitoes.

Vectors: mosquitoes and the swamps, 1900–1940

In the 1890s, scientific proof of the life cycle of the malaria parasites and the role of mosquitoes as vectors in transmitting that disease to humans saw a surge in research into possible diseases spread to humans and other animals by mosquitoes. In the twentieth century, mosquito elimination became a key aspect of public health campaigns. The link between disease and mosquitoes changed people's relationships with mosquitoes and with watery places in which the insects bred.[38] In Toowoomba, it led to renewed efforts to drain and otherwise control the swamps. Such approaches were evident in many places, but in Australia, Toowoomba's specific strategies became a model that was adopted by other towns and cities. The success of the Toowoomba Council in destroying mosquitoes was largely attributed to a local physician, Dr Thomas Price, labelled "The Mosquito King".

From 1912, Price advocated for a mosquito survey of the city by the state government. Toowoomba, like other places in Queensland, experienced outbreaks of bubonic plague traced to rats and fleas and of mosquito-borne diseases, such as dengue fever.[39] These animals thrived in close proximity with humans, and public health campaigns aimed to eliminate their favoured habitats, which were often places co-created with, but neglected by, humans. Like Toowoomba's swamps, these were often seen as dirty places that troubled the firm boundaries many people tried to establish between humans (and human-controlled places) and "nature".[40]

In early 1914, local businesses joined Price's call, urging that "steps . . . be taken to combat the present mosquito pest", and in 1915, the Queensland government agreed to a mosquito survey of Toowoomba. This was undertaken by L. E. Cooling from the Department of Public Health. Cooling found that the most common mosquito was *Culex fatigans* (now called *Culex quinquefasciatus*), a carrier of filarial, a parasitic worm; and the next most abundant, *Stegomyia fasciata* (now seen as part of the *Aedes* genus), could carry yellow and dengue fever. Both species of mosquitoes fed on birds and mammals, including humans, and during feeding could transmit diseases. Cooling surveyed the mosquitoes in September and noted that although "the mosquito nuisance at present is slight . . . a different

92 Emily O'Gorman

state of affairs must exist in the summertime" [December to February], when the mosquitoes bred in greater numbers as higher temperatures were needed for larvae to hatch.[41]

The swamps featured in Cooling's survey and his descriptions reveal not only the way mosquitoes inhabited these places but also the broader changes to the swamps that had fostered mosquito breeding sites. When reporting on Culex breeding places, he wrote: "Toowoomba is traversed by what are locally called swamps. . . . A 'drawn-out cesspool' is perhaps the most applicable name for it receives the whole town sewage and storm water in what may be termed from a sanitary engineer's point of view 'the combined system'". In dry weather "crude sewage" filled the watercourses, "in which larvae of *culex fatigans* delight to breed". He thought that "these sewage streamlets are the principal mosquito breeding place of Toowoomba". The East and West Swamps, after receiving local waste, fed into Gowrie Creek, which Cooling described as "really a slowly moving body of town sewage". After leaving the town, this creek gathered waste from several factories, where butter, milk, and bacon were produced. At the points at which this waste entered the creek, Cooling described a putrid stench and ideal Culex mosquito breeding grounds, where many of the larvae were present. The factory waste provided a nutrient-rich growing environment for the larvae. Cooling described the "streamlets" of the East and West Swamps as silted with mud and debris where cattle and horses wandered, creating more mosquito breeding places with their hoof prints.[42] People's relationships with the swamps, as grazing grounds and places of waste disposal, along with the behaviour and characteristics of the animals that grazed there, had helped to shape ideal breeding places for mosquitoes, "as if for them".[43]

Cooling's report on his Stegomyia survey reveals another aspect of the town. Although the water supply was "pipe borne", people still supplemented this with well water, which was "lifted to elevated storage-cisterns through the agency of windmills". In these cisterns or water tanks, which were uncovered or partially covered, he found *Stegomyia fasciata* larvae. They were also in rainwater tanks and likely in the street cisterns for public use and water-logged gutters. Cooling recommended a range of "temporary measures". His first recommendation was "rough canalisation" to deepen the "streamlets" and to clear them of vegetation "so as to give the sewage a clear run". This was not only for mosquito prevention, he noted, but also for "general sanitary benefit". Second, he recommended oiling "[a]ll stagnant and moderately running water" with a crude petroleum oil or kerosene-based spray once a week. Ultimately, however, Cooling argued that what was required for "Toowoomba mosquito reduction is a sewage scheme", which would need to be constructed for more thorough and permanent results. A sewerage system that conveyed waste in pipes began to be built in the centre of Toowoomba in the 1920s, gradually being extended into other parts of the city. In addition, Cooling recommended that the reservoirs should "be stocked with some mosquito larvivorous fish", such as native crimson-spotted sunfish (*Melanotaenia duboulayi*) or carp gudgeon (*Hypseleotris* spp.), which were already present at the headwaters of the West Swamp. He further recommended that all tins at the Newtown rubbish tip be buried and the ground be levelled to stop the pooling of water. Further, tanks should be screened and wells boarded over.[44]

As a result of Cooling's survey and recommendations, a Toowoomba Rat and Mosquito Board was established in 1916–7 under the Queensland Rat and Mosquito Prevention and Destruction Act of 1916. This act aimed to establish control and eradication measures for these two animals, both then seen as significant threats to public health. At the same time, Toowoomba's Council boundaries were redrawn and the City of Greater Toowoomba created. At these elections, Price campaigned for a seat on a platform of health, especially mosquito control to combat typhoid and dengue, arguing that the cost of treating these diseases was more than the cost of preventing them. So central was mosquito eradication to his campaign that his rivals derided him as "The Mosquito King".[45] However, his message of vector control, disseminated through advertisements in theatres and film reels in public meetings, convinced many. He was successful in the election, being appointed chairman of the Health Committee and then elected mayor in 1918. Price established systematic programs of mosquito eradication for Toowoomba. The council regularly oiled the swamps and water bodies or sprayed with them with distillate and removed vegetation. Screening tanks became compulsory, with fines for breaches of this and a range of other regulations. These were enforced in house-to-house inspections.[46] The council also established an education campaign, the wartime expense of which was justified by Price as important in maintaining healthy citizens.[47]

Following the Australian state governments' monitoring of returning soldiers for malaria, and with one case identified in Toowoomba in 1920, the Queensland government urged the council to put into effect mosquito eradication regulations "without delay" in case of an outbreak. The city inspector – often a person with public health experience – was already making regular reports on the mosquito and other work. In one report made in 1920, he notified the council that he had discovered the larvae of *Anopheles* mosquitoes, which could transmit malaria from an infected human to other humans. He wrote that "seeing that there are some malaria patients in the town it is essential that we keep this species under control".[48] A case of dengue, spread by *Aedes aegypti*, was also reported in 1921. With so many mosquitoes being identified as vectors in Toowoomba, and more and more species being linked to disease transmission by scientists, mosquito elimination campaigns targeted all mosquitoes as a precaution.

The city inspector reports reveal a ramping up of efforts to contain the swamps. This included patrolling the border between the swamps and their animals, as hoofed animals were banned from walking in parks and areas like the swamps so that their hoof marks did not create mosquito-breeding places. This also aimed to mitigate the spread of ticks, and the council impounded unattended animals and fined owners in breach.[49] The city inspector oversaw a series of incremental drainage works that aimed to further remove moisture from the swamps.[50] Another border that was patrolled was between the town and its animals – for instance, the "bird proofing" of houses to limit peoples' exposure to disease-carrying lice.

94   *Emily O'Gorman*

All these regulations and drainage works again refigured a range of human and non-human relationships.

Animals participated in this refiguring in sometimes unexpected ways. For instance, fluctuations in mosquito behaviour and numbers, influenced by a range of factors, including rainfall and temperature, made eradication programs difficult to implement in a consistent way.[51] These dynamics in mosquito behaviour meant that inspectors had to adjust their efforts and behaviours accordingly. It also meant that mosquito numbers could rise quite suddenly. Toowoomba's reputation as "free from mosquitoes" supported its claim as a healthy place to visit. However, in 1938–9, mosquito numbers increased significantly, described by one resident as "hoards". Residents urged the council to increase its efforts to suppress the "pest", reporting on the location of "infestations".[52]

In 1920, in a paper to the Australasian Medical Association held in Brisbane, Price advocated for mosquito eradication and prevention to be undertaken more systematically throughout Queensland, as many towns were "badly infested". As in his Toowoomba campaign, Price justified the need for action in terms of the relative costs: prevention was cheaper to the state than the diseases, which could become endemic, as with malaria in parts of north and north-west Queensland and filaria in Brisbane, and create epidemics as with a dengue outbreak in 1904; and "yellow fever was an ever threatening menace".[53] He ended with a series of recommendations, which was essentially that the process he developed in Toowoomba be adopted all over the state.

In 1923, the Hookworm Campaign employed Ronald Hamlyn-Harris to undertake a mosquito survey of the Darling Downs, focusing on the mosquito-transmitted parasites of filaria and malaria. This was part of a broader set of public health activities undertaken by this organisation targeting parasites. In his report, Hamlyn-Harris singled out the practices in Toowoomba as being the best in the region at preventing mosquito breeding. He wrote, "Situated as it is on what was once a swamp of considerable size, Toowoomba lends itself particularly to mosquito breeding – and though Toowoomba is now practically free from this pest it is only by constraint and vigilance that the City can keep this enviable position". Despite his enthusiasm for the processes of eradication of mosquitoes in Toowoomba, Hamlyn-Harris found *Culex quinquefasciatus* near the centre of the town and *Stegomyia aegypti* "in defective tanks a mile or more out of town". He also warned that the hydrology of the East Swamp, fed by springs and "scoured out" by storm water to form pools, created conditions for *Culex quinquefasciatus* to breed if left unattended. The water holes would need to be continually filled in and sprayed with oil. Hamlyn-Harris also found *Anopholes* breeding in part of the East Swamp, and here troughs, depressions, and "low lying paddocks would soon become infested unless cleaned and oiled weekly". He praised the drainage work that had turned a part of the swamps "so wet and bogy no cattle could graze on it" into a paddock through spade-cut drains, which were also oiled. Outside the city limits, mosquitoes were abundant, indicating both the success of the city in reducing mosquito numbers and the danger to humans in these areas, albeit being less populated. He concluded his report on Toowoomba by stating, "The responsible members of the Toowoomba city council are to be congratulated upon their work and its results".[54]

Toowoomba soon gained a growing reputation as being free from mosquitoes and from dengue fever. This was fuelled, in part, by newspaper reports of the city's success, which detailed the methods the council used, including regular removal of any receptacles that gathered water, tarring over holes in the streets, screening tanks, clearing vegetation from watercourses and weekly treatment with oil, and extensive swamp drainage, perhaps aided by the relative wealth of the council located within a booming pastoral district. Although Toowoomba had already undertaken a significant amount of swamp drainage, the mosquito campaign motivated further efforts and, as one newspaper reported, the council set out to concrete a section of swamp channel each year, filling in the neighbouring swampland as it went. Gradually, the swamps became concrete channels. From the mid-1920s to the mid-1940s, local councils had workers available for these kinds of projects from employment programs during the Depression. A number of councils from around Queensland and New South Wales, including inland places like Quirindi and more coastal areas like Maitland, wrote to the Toowoomba Council for further advice and details on the methods it had used to eradicate this "pest". Toowoomba became an exemplar for mosquito eradication, and the methods used by the council were implemented elsewhere. The city inspector's reports distilled some of the principles that underpinned these efforts into slogans: "No water, no mosquitoes"; "No mosquitoes, no dengue".[55]

The new focus on insects, particularly mosquitoes, as vectors of disease renewed efforts to drain swamps in many towns and cities in Australia. In the 1930s, Queensland government regulations for "mosquito prevention and destruction" in fact required that all swamps and other water bodies on public or private land that, in the opinion of the local authority, might breed mosquitoes, be "effectively treated" with oil to asphyxiate the larvae and prevent adult mosquitoes from laying eggs, or drained. The outbreak of World War II, far from directing attention away from mosquito eradication, refocused attention on it locally, nationally, and internationally.[56] The techniques and approaches changed significantly during and after World War II, including the use of DDT to spray mosquito breeding places like swamps.

The swamps have deeply shaped the history of Toowoomba. Attempts to control and contain the swamps as a source of disease were ongoing from the period of British-led colonisation in the nineteenth century through to the mid-twentieth century and beyond. A range of animals became entangled in residents' understandings of the swamps and their changing views about these places as sources of disease. From 1840 to 1900, a variety of domestic animals helped to change the shape and character of the swamps. Early in this period, the combination of rotting animal carcasses with other organic matter in the swamps was understood by colonists as contributing to deadly miasmas. Later excrement, along with pigs and other animals, were seen as producing germs and miasmas, and wealthy colonists used sanitary measures to exclude particular animals, as well as some people, such as poor European colonists and Chinese gardeners, from the town. From

96 Emily O'Gorman

1900, mosquitoes, vectors of disease to humans, significantly shaped people's relationships with the swamps and became the targets of sustained elimination campaigns. Colonists had created ideal breeding conditions for mosquitoes that they now sought to contain. Mosquitoes both shaped human relationships with the swamps and were shaped by them, as efforts to control the swamps became efforts to eliminate these insects. These animals were part of wider sets of shifting relationships, which included a range of humans and non-humans, and participated in co-creating the changing swamplands of Toowoomba.

Notes

1 Many thanks to James Beattie and Thom van Dooren for our valuable discussions about this work and to Jodi Frawley and Nancy Cushing for their very helpful comments. The members of the Toowoomba Historical Society helped to track down some important information, particularly Peter Cullen. This research was funded by the Australian Research Council (DP160103152). Timothy Mitchell, *Rule of Experts: Egypt, Techno-politics, Modernity* (Berkeley: University of California Press, 2002), 19–53; Anna Tsing, 'Others without History: Organisms as Agility-shifting Actors in the Trajectory of Capital', Eric Wolf lecture, Austrian Academy of Sciences, October 2016.

2 My approach here has particularly been influenced by the following work: Donna Haraway, *When Species Meet* (Minneapolis: University of Minnesota Press, 2008); Anna Tsing, *The Mushroom at the End of the World: On the Possibility of Life in Capitalist Ruins* (Princeton: Princeton University Press, 2015); Etienne Benson, 'Animal Writes: Historiography, Disciplinarity, and the Animal Trace,' in L. Kalof and G. M. Montgomery (eds.), *Making Animal Meaning* (East Lansing: Michigan State University Press, 2011), 3–16.

3 Maurice French, *Conflict on the Condamine: Aborigines and the European Invasion: a History of the Darling Downs Frontier* (Toowoomba: Darling Downs Institute Press, 1989); Maurice French, *Toowoomba: A Sense of History: 1840–2008* (Toowoomba: University of Southern Queensland, 2009), 29–39.

4 Archaeo, 'An Assessment of Cultural Heritage Values Associated with Gowrie Creek Waterways', Toowoomba City Council, 2002, 17–29; French, *Conflict on the Condamine*.

5 Marion Diamond, 'The Myth of Patrick Leslie', *Queensland History Journal*, 20.11 (August 2009): 606–17; L. J. Jay, 'Pioneer Settlement on the Darling Downs, Scottish Geographical Magazine', 73.1 (1957): 35–49, doi: 10.1080/00369225708735667; Thos. Mathewson, 'Personal Reminiscences of '53', *Journal of the Royal Historical Society of Queensland*, 1.2 (1916): 96–8; Thomas Hall, 'The Early History of Warwick District and Pioneers of the Darling Downs', n.p., 1925.

6 French, *Conflict on the Condamine*.

7 *Queenslander*, 3 July 1869, 3; French, *Toowoomba*, 29–39.

8 *Toowoomba Chronicle and Darling Downs Gazette*, 21 July 1962, Toowoomba Historical Society Collection; see also Peter Cullen, *Toowoomba's Story in Brief* (Toowoomba: Toowoomba Historical Society, 2009), 6.

9 French, *Toowoomba*, 29–39; French, *Conflict on the Condamine*, 122; Cullen, *Toowoomba's Story*.

10 Benjamin Glennie Diary, John Oxley Library, OM67–25, State Library of Queensland, Australia, 23.

11 Nehemiah Bartley, *Opal and Agates; or, Scenes Under the Southern Cross and The Magelhans: Being Memories of Fifty Years of Australia and Polynesia* (Brisbane: Gordan and Gotch, 1892), 114.

12 Rod Giblet, *Postmodern Wetlands: Culture, History, Ecology* (Edinburgh: Edinburgh University Press, 1996), 1–4; James Beattie, *Empire and Environmental Anxiety: Health, Science, Art and Conservation in South Asia and Australasia, 1800–1920* (London: Springer, 2011), 42–3.

13 Emily O'Gorman, 'Bird Migration, Wetlands, and Global Environmental Crisis', forthcoming; National Research Council, *Wetlands: Characteristics and Boundaries* (Washington, DC: National Academies Press, 1995), 43.

14 French, *Conflict on the Condamine*, 122–31.

15 French, *Toowoomba*, 2, 40.

16 *Courier*, 31 May 1862, 4.

17 Andrea Gaynor, *Harvest of the Suburbs: An Environmental History of Growing Food in Australian Cities* (Crawley: University of Western Australia Press, 2006), 19.

18 Tom Griffiths, *Forests of Ash: An Environmental History* (Cambridge: Cambridge University Press, 2001), 40–2.

19 *Darling Downs Gazette and General Advertiser*, July 1, 1865, 3.

20 Correspondence, briefs, maps, and associated papers relating to the acquisition of swamp reserves at Toowoomba, 1900–1915, Crown Solicitor, 36/3424, Queensland State Archives (QSA); Warwick Anderson, 'Excremental Colonialism: Public Health and the Poetics of Pollution', *Critical Inquiry*, 21.3 (1995): 640–69, 644; Beattie, *Empire and Environmental Anxiety*, 42–3; Stephen Halliday, 'Death and Miasma in Victorian London: An Obstinate Belief', *BMJ: British Medical Journal*, 323.7327 (2001): 1469–71.

21 *Darling Downs Gazette and General Advertiser*, 1 July 1865, 3.

22 Correspondence . . . swamp reserves. QSA.

23 *Toowoomba Chronicle and Queensland Advertiser*, 4 April 1874, 2; Correspondence . . . swamp reserves. QSA.

24 Halliday, 'Death and Miasma in Victorian London', 1470–1; Stephen Halliday, *The Great Stink of London: Sir Joseph Bazalgete and the Cleansing of the Victorian Capital* (Stroud: Sutton Publishers, 1999); A. S. Wohl, *Endangered Lives: Public Health in Victorian Britain* (London: Methuen, 1984); Anderson, 'Excremental Colonialism', 642.

25 *Toowoomba Chronicle and Darling Downs General Advertiser*, 11 May 1878, 3.

26 James Alfred Yelling, *Slums and Slum Clearance in Victorian London* (London: Routledge, 2012).

27 *Toowoomba Chronicle and Darling Downs General Advertiser*, 11 May 1878, 3.

28 *Toowoomba Chronicle and Darling Downs General Advertiser*, 11 May 1878, 3.

29 Joanna Boileau, *Chinese Market Gardening in Australia and New Zealand: Gardens of Prosperity* (London: Palgrave Macmillan, 2017), 192–3.

30 Anne Fisher, 'The Forgotten Pioneers: The Chinese in Southern Inland Queensland (1848 to circa. 1914)' (master's dissertation, University of Southern Queensland, 1995), 38–52; Boileau, *Chinese Market Gardening in Australia and New Zealand*, 11; James Beattie, 'Dragons Abroad: Chinese Migration and Environmental Change in Australasia', in Christof Mauch, Ruth Morgan and Emily O'Gorman (eds.), *Visions of Australia: Environments in History* (Munich: RCC Perspectives, Transformations in Environment and Society, 2017), 59–70; James Beattie, 'Chinese Resource Frontiers, Environmental Change, and Entrepreneurship in the Pacific, 1790s–1920s', in Edward Melillo and Ryan Jones (eds.), *Migrant Ecologies in the Pacific* (Honolulu: Hawai'i University Press, 2018).

31 Boileau, *Chinese Market Gardening in Australia and New Zealand*, 192–3.

32 *Toowoomba Chronicle and Darling Downs General Advertiser*, 11 May 1878, 3.

33 Raymond Evans, Kay Saunders and Kathryn Cronin, *Race Relations in Colonial Queensland: A History of Exclusion, Exploitation and Extermination*, third edition (St. Lucia: University of Queensland Press, 1993), 235–318.

34 Anderson, 'Excremental Colonialism', 643.

35 *Darling Downs Gazette and General Advertiser*, 21 July 1880, 3; Cullen, *A Short History*, 19.

36 *Darling Downs Gazette*, 27 November 1895, 5.
37 *Darling Downs Gazette*, 4 April 1894, 3; *Darling Downs Gazette*, 29 September 1894, 5; *Darling Downs Gazette*, 5 September 1894, 4.
38 Emily O'Gorman, 'Imagined Ecologies: A More-Than-Human History of Malaria in the Murrumbidgee Irrigation Area, New South Wales, Australia, 1919–45', *Environmental History*, 22.3 (2017): 486–514.
39 John Howard Lidgett Cumpston and Frank McCallum, *The History of Plague in Australia, 1900–1925* (Melbourne: Commonwealth Government of Australia, 1926); Peter H. Curson and Kevin McCracken, *Plague in Sydney: The Anatomy of an Epidemic* (Sydney: UNSW Press, 1989); J. Burton Cleland, Burton Bradley and W. McDonald, 'Dengue Fever in Australia', *Epidemiology & Infection*, 16.4 (1918): 317–418.
40 O'Gorman, 'Imagined Ecologies'.
41 Rat and Mosquito Destruction, Toowoomba City Council, 1918–1949, Box 12, Books 3 and 4, 18980, Queensland State Archives.
42 Rat and Mosquito Destruction, Toowoomba City Council.
43 Tsing, 'Others Without History'. This was not an uncommon occurrence, for example see John McNeill, *Mosquito Empires: Ecology and War in the Greater Caribbean, 1620–1914* (Cambridge: Cambridge University Press, 2010).
44 Rat and Mosquito Destruction, Toowoomba City Council.
45 Bob Dansie, 'Dr Thomas Price – The Mosquito King', unpublished, Toowoomba Historical Society Collection; *Warwick Daily News*, 1 December 1922, 5.
46 Dansie, 'Dr Thomas Price – The Mosquito King'; Rat and Mosquito Destruction, Toowoomba City Council.
47 Dansie, 'Dr Thomas Price – The Mosquito King'; Rat and Mosquito Destruction. Toowoomba City Council; *Darling Downs Gazette*, 26 August 1920, 3.
48 Rat and Mosquito Destruction, Toowoomba City Council.
49 *Queensland Government Gazette*, 30 April 1932, 1643; Rat and Mosquito Destruction, Toowoomba City Council.
50 Rat and Mosquito Destruction, Toowoomba City Council.
51 See also, McNeill, *Mosquito Empires*.
52 Rat and Mosquito Destruction, Toowoomba City Council.
53 *Darling Downs Gazette*, 26 August 1920, 3.
54 Rat and Mosquito Destruction, Toowoomba City Council.
55 Rat and Mosquito Destruction, Toowoomba City Council.
56 Rat and Mosquito Destruction, Toowoomba City Council; O'Gorman, 'Imagined Ecologies'.

8 'Pain for Animals, Profit for People'

The campaign against live sheep exports, 1974–1986

Gonzalo Villanueva

Australian animals, notes sociologist Adrian Franklin, have always been represented in enigmatic, complex ways, which are entangled with the construction of national identity and values. They are inscribed in our moral, social, and cultural affairs.[1] In twentieth-century Australian suburbia, productive animals, such as livestock, occupied diverse positions within the imaginative geography, shaped by class location, gender, discourses of modernity, and the animals themselves.[2] In Australia, sheep have historically been at the heart of rural economic progress and Australian identity, captured in the aphorism 'riding on the sheep's back'.

In the 1970s and 1980s, two social movements – the meat workers' union and the animal movement – united to fiercely contest the existence of the lucrative live animal export trade. The meat workers were anxious about the impact of the trade on their quickly declining job opportunities. Animal activists were concerned with protecting the welfare of sheep. Both social movements, for completely different reasons, sought to permanently abolish the lucrative trade by making animals count through mobilisations, public displays, and performances. In this way, the abundant numbers of sheep used in this live export trade came sharply into view as a matter of concern.

Through public displays of worthiness, unity, numbers, and commitment, social movements like the labor and animal movement activate 'democracy-promoting processes', widening the issues under public debate and shaping the decisions and actions taken by government.[3] In advancing their claims, social movements in Australian history have combined a mixture of disruption, symbolism, politics, and theatre. Whether it was anti-war protests, women's and gay liberation, Aboriginal rights, or conservation, the 1960s and 1970s are rich with examples of disruptive actions by social movements. According to Sean Scalmer, these 'political gimmicks' appeared as intrusions into public life, cultivating attention and publicity through their performances.[4] They were important resources that shaped Australian politics and activism.[5] In general, the Australian political system has tended to recognise, legitimise, and incorporate the issues and identities demanded by the 'new' and 'old' social movements, even though the process has been marked by compromise and containment.[6] Trade unions, much like political parties, were both supporters and opponents of social movements. For instance, in the 1970s, the New South Wales Builders Laborers' Federation allied with

100   *Gonzalo Villanueva*

environmentalists to enact 'green bans' to obstruct property development, conserve urban heritage, and protect the environment.[7]

The campaign to end live sheep exports represents a modern instance of the politicisation of sheep and the struggle over the lives of animals. Throughout the 1970s, meat workers, who saw sheep as a resource whose exploitation was thwarted because they were exported to a foreign market, contested the issue of live sheep exports. In order to protect local jobs, the Australasian Meat Industry Employees' Union (AMIEU) confronted the government and the rural sector on economic terms. In their escalating industrial dispute, meat workers used pickets and blockades to militantly disrupt the trade. Lacking wider support for their cause, the union's dispute reached an impasse. In the late 1970s, a new actor emerged: the animal movement. For animal activists, the sheep possessed their own interests that needed to be defended and protected. Their focus was on the sheep's condition. Because the trade caused pain and suffering, activists contested the trade on the issue of animal welfare. In the pursuit of animal rights, they used a range of tactics, including lobbying governments for reform. During this time, they found long-standing allies in the Australian Democrats. Through their interactions, both movements influenced the political agenda. However, by the 1980s, the meat worker's economic arguments were, I argue, eclipsed by the debate around animal welfare. Despite various achievements along the way, neither social movement could claim the ultimate victory: the ban on live sheep exports.

'The Quest to Protect Our Jobs': the union

Although the export of live animals in Australia originated in the colonial period,[8] the modern trade developed in the early 1960s, when Australia commenced trade with the Middle East. A booming oil economy and a strong preference for fresh meat, or 'hot meat', facilitated the development of the industry. Countries that imported live animals were predominately Islamic, and the killing and consumption of sheep were considered *halal* and therefore permissible. Initially, two carriers had the capacity to transport 6,000 sheep to ports in the Persian Gulf. By 1970, the largest carrier, the *Cormoran*, had the capacity to carry 28,000 sheep. In the mid-1970s, ships able to transport 50,000 animals were coming into existence.[9] As the trade developed, livestock carrier ships were specifically built, techniques were improved, and organisational skills evolved to handle the immense number of sheep. By 1980, the largest ship, the *Al Qurain*, was able to carry 92,000 sheep to the Middle East for slaughter.[10] Overall, the industry was divided into many sectors and operated through a mixture of Australian and Middle Eastern companies and stakeholders.

For several years, the export of live animals developed unopposed. However, this all changed in early 1974. Concerned about the impact of the trade on the livelihood of Australian abattoir workers, delegates from the West Australian branch of the AMIEU raised the issue at the federal executive meeting.[11] Established in 1906, the AMIEU had a militant history, underpinned by socialist,

'Pain for Animals, Profit for People'   101

working-class values. It supported the anti-war cause, Aboriginal rights, equal pay for women, and opposed nuclear testing, among many other things.[12] In a bid to protect jobs, the union adopted a position against the export of live sheep for slaughter. Although the AMIEU did not call for the trade's immediate abolition, it embraced several criteria under which the trade should be restricted. The union insisted on a ratio system, that for every live sheep exported, 15 must be locally slaughtered for export (this ratio would later be reduced to 2:1). They demanded that the compensatory ratio quickly 'increase by one hundred per cent'. After 1 July 1976, the union ambitiously demanded that 'the export of live sheep for slaughter shall cease'.[13] Similar principles applied to other exported animals: lambs, goats, and cattle. The campaign was led by AMIEU President Jack Sparks, who, in 1963, was elected president of the Victorian branch and in a few years rose to be federal president. The industrial campaign against the trade did not unfold smoothly; rather, it unleashed a series of confrontations.

After a few years of isolated pickets around Australia, in April 1978 the cycle of industrial action intensified. For years, the AMIEU's demand for a 2:1 ratio was disregarded as unfeasible by exporters, who had been increasing their sales and expanding their market. Due to a lack of progress, the union systematically picketed ports in Adelaide, Fremantle, and Albany, preventing about 100,000 sheep from being loaded and shipped. In Adelaide, farmers retaliated by withholding the supply of livestock to abattoirs and demonstrated in the streets, disrupting peak-hour traffic. The lack of livestock meant that hundreds of slaughtermen began losing their jobs.[14] Prime Minister Malcolm Fraser declared that his government would do everything it could to stop the union's industrial action.[15] With a defiant union resisting a federal court order prohibiting the picket lines in Adelaide and the looming threat of a nationwide meat workers' strike, Australian Council of Trade Unions (ACTU) President Bob Hawke negotiated with the government and the AMIEU, trying to produce a resolution.[16] Hawke and the government proposed a truce, whereby the picket lines would be lifted and legal action against the union would be suspended. The AMIEU leadership rejected the 'vague' proposal, as it did not include a compensation ratio.[17] Furthermore, the Waterside Workers Federation (WWF) launched a stoppage to protest against farmers who had secretly loaded sheep. Hawke, who said that the jobs of wharfies needed to be protected, supported the action.[18]

After a bitter three-week dispute, stalled negotiations, repressed pickets, arrests, scab labor, and confrontations, a compromise was reached. Hawke had somehow convinced the AMIEU to lift its ban and end its picket. Farmers agreed to withdraw from the ports, which in turn appeased the WWF. The federal government also agreed to drop its injunction against the union. Although the finer details of the truce were not immediately clear, it is apparent that the AMIEU leadership were persuaded by a promise of serious negotiations in the near future over its fundamental grievances. Hawke was certainly relieved that an agreement 'over a dispute which threatened to escalate into serious proportions' had been reached.[19] However, further action by the AMIEU threatened to unravel Hawke's armistice.

102   *Gonzalo Villanueva*

Despite lifting the picket lines, on Tuesday, 11 April 1978, the AMIEU called on its 45,000 members to execute a 'National stoppage' of all meat works. The strike had not been ruled out as part of the deal that Hawke had fiercely won.[20] Hawke saw little value in the performance and desperately tried to separate the stoppage from the export issue. The four-day strike began on Wednesday at midnight. In case of any public concern, the *Sydney Morning Herald* reassured its readers that 'Sydney butchers will have adequate supplies of meat' over the weekend.[21] When the strike had ended and normality resumed, the AMIEU declared to its members: 'we are satisfied that [the] stoppage was a great success. We state that we will support further stoppages if they are necessary in the quest to protect our jobs'.[22]

The AMIEU did not define how the stoppage was a 'great success'. At the very least, they achieved some bargaining power ahead of a meeting of key stakeholders, which had been arranged as part of Hawke's truce. From the meeting, an inquiry emerged that was to be headed by the Federal Bureau of Agricultural Economics, during which there were to be no bans, no legal action, and a continuation of live exports.[23] The Miller report was released in July, and one of the findings was that 'the net effect of the live sheep trade has been to generate greater income and more jobs' in Australia.[24] The AMIEU rejected the 'controversial' report and announced plans for future industrial action.[25] In the following years, the Bureau of Agricultural Economics continued its research and maintained similar conclusions.[26] Such reports were effective counterarguments against the union's claims.

Throughout the 1970s, the union's militant actions, rather than galvanising a wider support base, alienated parts of the community and produced no positive media coverage.[27] 'Ordinary Australians', wrote the editors of the *Sydney Morning Herald*, were 'sick and tired of the arbitrary exercise of trade-union power' and were more sympathetic with the farmers during the ordeal. The demands of the meat workers were 'remarkably shortsighted'.[28] Furthermore, the union lacked the crucial support from the wider labor movement and the ACTU. Groups like the Australian Workers' Union, one of the nation's largest unions and home to many pastoralists and agricultural workers, had declared its 'emphatic opposition' to the AMIEU's demands.[29] In the context of droughts and low commodity prices, the live sheep export market provided, in the words of the prime minister, 'a ray of light and hope for sheep growers'.[30] The AMIEU also faced a dearth of support from the Australian Labor Party, even during the progressive Whitlam Labor Government years, 1972–75.

Naturally, the AMIEU lamented the state of affairs. In December 1979, frustrated by the 'totally oblivious' government and ACTU, Jack Sparks felt that the union were the 'victims of incompetency and complete disregard'.[31] Nevertheless, they were determined to turn the momentum in their favour. Further industrial actions continued throughout 1979; wharfies stopped work in solidarity, having, as one politician denounced, taken up 'the cudgels on behalf of other unionists'.[32] But perhaps the next great confrontation emerged in Victoria in 1980.

'Pain for Animals, Profit for People' 103

Throughout April and May 1980, meat workers held militant pickets in Portland, Victoria. In April, about 200 workers obstructed the wharf, preventing thousands of sheep from being loaded onto livestock carriers. Truck drivers who defied the picket lines were threatened and served with a black ban from delivering to Australian slaughterhouses.[33] On 12 May, the AMIEU mobilised to prevent sheep from travelling on the *Al Qurain*, which was to transport 92,000 sheep to Kuwait.[34] They blockaded two roads that led to the port. More than 100 police cleared the path and escorted the trucks through. After 12 hours of skirmishes and blockades, by evening, mounted police approached, and, to avoid violence, Sparks urged the meat workers to disband, which they begrudgingly did. The following day, approximately 5,000 Victorian meat workers across 30 facilities went on a 24-hour strike.[35] Reflecting on the Portland action, Wally Curran, state secretary of the AMIEU, believed they were 'achieving success'.[36] This was once again an upbeat assessment, particularly when contrasted with Curran's earlier remarks about the state of the campaign.[37]

The events in Portland received wide media coverage. But, as before, the media were critical and unsympathetic to the meat workers' grievances. *The Canberra Times* viewed the AMIEU's position as 'an extremely simplistic view', arguing that the trade had a net economic benefit throughout 'country towns, and through transport, handling, selling and retailing of farm goods and farm inputs'.[38] Melbourne's liberal newspaper, *The Age*, held a similar position, noting that the 'meat workers are being obstinate':

> For the sake of 100 or so jobs, in an already ailing industry, they are willing to jeopardise a thriving and apparently rewarding industry that has generated a net gain in job opportunities.[39]

The editor's position was unambiguous; they concluded the union's campaign was unjustifiable. However, another matter, previously unmentioned, came to the attention of *The Age* and the general public, and that was the problem of animal cruelty.

'Pain for Animals, Profit for People': the animal movement

Concerned for the well-being and rights of animals, the animal movement emerged in the mid-1970s during a lively period of women's, gay, and black liberation. A central figure was the young Australian moral philosopher Peter Singer and his 1975 book, *Animal Liberation*, which inspired and politicised a new generation of ordinary people who wanted to do something for animals. Singer's unemotional and unrhetorical moral arguments, his descriptions of intensive farms and animal experimentation, and his appeal for vegetarianism provided the ideological foundations for mobilisation and action.[40] Between 1976 and 1980, 'Animal Liberation' groups were founded in Sydney, Melbourne, Brisbane, and Canberra. Animal Liberation ambitiously aimed to 'abolish man's speciesist attitude toward animals'.[41] Seeking to challenge the politics and culture of

104   *Gonzalo Villanueva*

animal exploitation, they broadly campaigned on issues around intensive farming, animal experimentation, animals in sport and entertainment, and wildlife conservation. By 1980, Animal Liberation, other smaller animal welfare societies (not including the RSPCA), and conservation groups banded together to form the Australian Federation of Animal Societies, which would unite the diverse positions of the movement and be its national voice.

The movement campaigned against live exports because of how it affected animals. In Australia, animals selected for export travelled between 15 to 30 hours by trucks to ports. Livestock carriers were overcrowded, like an intensive farm, and meant that animals suffered from a range of health problems: hypocalcaemia, acidosis, heat stress, trauma, and pulmonary failure. Sea voyages lasted several weeks, and mortality numbers were often in the thousands. Awaiting the sheep was ritual slaughter, where their throats were slit while they were fully conscious, leaving them to slowly and painfully bleed to death.[42]

In Portland in 1980, unionists were joined by a handful of members from Australia's fledging animal movement. Animal activists, which included Christine Townend and Patty Mark, founders of Animal Liberation in Sydney and Melbourne, carried placards which read: 'Pain for Animals, Profit for People', 'Stop Live Export', and 'Peacefull Co-Existence Not Painfull Export [sic]'. In Portland, over a public address system, Sparks introduced Townend and Mark to the crowd. The animal liberationists explained to the mass of workers, many of them male unionists who were a bit confused by these women carrying placards about animals, that they were united in a common struggle: to ban live animal exports. That statement was warmly received.[43] At the same time, the president of the recently federated Royal Society for the Prevention of Cruelty to Animals (RSPCA), Australia, Hugh Wirth, inspected sheep being loaded on the *Al Qurain*. Wirth, a veterinarian, believed the welfare of the animals was poor and in need of improvement. He concluded the sheep were unfit for a long sea voyage. *The Age* noted this and thought it was an argument worthy of further consideration but believed it was a 'separate issue and should not be used to cloud the economic arguments about the trade'.[44]

'A Very Serious Matter': Parliament

Against a backdrop of recent controversies – including a consignment of horses found to be unfit for export, the death of 40,000 sheep on the *Farid Fares* vessel, which caught fire at sea, and the dispute in Portland – questions about the trade were once again being asked in federal parliament. On 13 May 1980, Liberal Member of Parliament (MP) Peter Falconer asked Peter Nixon, Minister for Primary Industry, about the measures being taken to ensure the welfare of the sheep.[45] Traditionally, politicians had either supported or denounced the union's campaign, but concern for the welfare of animals was noticeably absent. Falconer had previously referred to the AMIEU as 'an arrogant, pompous mob of industrial blackmailers!'[46] However, Falconer's question signified the beginning of a new theme in the debate – the emergence of an animal welfare discourse,

'*Pain for Animals, Profit for People*' 105

one that would carry through to the present. Nixon responded to Falconer by recognising the 'considerable public comment on this trade'. Nixon allayed any doubts about the viability of the trade, stating that the government was 'most concerned to ensure the highest possible standards for the welfare of all live animals that are exported'. The government supported the continuation of the trade provided 'steps are taken to protect animals from suffering and undue stress'.[47] Despite the opposition welcoming Nixon's statements, other politicians were not satisfied.

The Australian Democrats were vocal critics of the government on a number of issues, including matters around the exploitation of animals and more specifically the export of live animals. Founded in 1977, the centrist party was led by the charismatic Don Chipp, a seven-time coalition minister who resigned from the Liberal Party as it became increasingly hostile to moderate liberals.[48] The new party welcomed social activists from various causes, including the animal liberationist Christine Townend, who played a significant role in designing the party's animal rights policy. In this area, the goal of the Democrats was to present an 'advanced and enlightened policy on animal welfare'.[49] With five senators elected in 1980, the Democrats had established themselves as a third force in Australian politics. By May 1980, they swiftly moved to establish the first senate inquiry into animal welfare.

In September 1982, Victoria's AMIEU temporarily suspended its industrial dispute. With looming elections in March of the following year, when Bob Hawke's Labor Party would claim victory, the AMIEU leadership accepted the ACTU's recommendation to cease industrial action against live sheep exports. The deal would last until March and was ostensibly designed to allow an agreement reached with the Australian government to contribute to a market fund for the expansion of sheep-meat markets in the Middle East.[50] With a Labor government, the AMIEU were willing to 'see if the dispute can be handled by political means'. However, the union still held the position that it was essential to stop 'all live exports out of Victoria and other States'.[51]

Although a motion to create the Senate Committee on Animal Welfare (the senate committee) initially struggled to pass the senate floor, due in large part to political inertia, it was eventually established in 1983. This was due to the persistence of the Democrats and the tireless lobbying efforts of animal activists. Among its terms of reference, the senate committee would investigate live animal exports.[52]

Between 1985 and 1991, the senate committee delivered 11 reports on various aspects of animal use and welfare.[53] Queensland Senator George Georges chaired the senate committee between 1983 and 1987. Once described as an 'urban guerrilla', Georges was a Labor politician from the Left faction and had a reputation for progressive politics. He was sympathetic to the animal cause. He had the delicate task of balancing the inquiries' terms of reference with the considerable concerns of all stakeholders, including the rural sector, the animal movement, and the union.[54] To this end, Georges fulfilled his duty, which earned him the respect and appreciation of his peers and rivals.[55] Although members would come

106 *Gonzalo Villanueva*

and go, and Georges would eventually defect from the Labor Party and lose his seat, the senate committee appears to have mostly worked in harmony.

In August 1985, the senate committee's report entitled *Export of Live Sheep from Australia* was released. It was a detailed examination of the structure of the industry: selection of the sheep; road and rail transportation; feedlots; nutrition and feed; embarkation; conditions aboard sheep carriers; and conditions in importing countries, such as the Middle East. The senate committee reported that

> if a decision were to be made on the future of the trade purely on animal welfare grounds, there is enough evidence to stop the trade. The trade is, in many respects, inimical to good animal welfare, and it is not in the interests of the animal to be transported to the Middle East for slaughter.[56]

This was an extraordinary acknowledgement and validated the criticisms of those who had been concerned about the well-being of animals. However, the senate committee also agreed that the trade's future could not only be judged on animal welfare grounds but also that it 'cannot be divorced from economic and other considerations'. Although it acknowledged that the trade should be terminated in the future, it concluded that the trade should continue for some years and provided a number of recommendations to improve animal welfare.[57] Despite its terms of reference, which were solely concerned with 'the question of animal welfare', the senate committee had prioritised the economic interests of the export industry above the interests of the sheep. One could only imagine the disappointment of animal activists and the union that the report had not recommended phasing out the trade.

The report's ambivalent conclusion, particularly the point about the future of the trade, caused some misunderstanding and dismay. The senate committee's report and recommendations, which, as Georges described, was 'Delphic' in style, resulted in varied, confused news articles. The *Sydney Morning Herald* reported that 'MPs want an end to sheep shipping'.[58] At a press conference, the media asked Georges about the likely time frame of phasing out the trade. He answered that 'if a decision were made', then 'it would take five to seven years'. This only fuelled speculation and uncertainty, which outraged the National Farmers Federation.[59] In Parliament on 21 August 1985, Georges emphasised that his personal view was misrepresented and was made to appear as though it was the senate committee's recommendation.[60] This ultimately reassured vexed stakeholders.

The Hawke Labor government accepted the general conclusions of the report and adopted several of its recommendations, which included improving the provision of animal care throughout the industry.[61] These reforms were designed to reduce but not eliminate animal suffering and death; future mobilisations would re-contest these issues. Ultimately, the establishment and those who had a vested economic interest in the trade welcomed the senate committee's report. In 1986–87, the livestock export industry in Australia grew to assume the position as the world's leader, with the Middle East being the largest and most valuable market.[62]

Conclusion

Throughout the 1970s and 1980s, sheep were contested, political animals. In 1974, in order to protect local abattoir jobs, the AMIEU initiated a long-lasting campaign to end the export of live sheep. A series of militant pickets and blockades unfolded across ports in Australia. On a number of occasions, the industrial dispute escalated into violent clashes with police. It alarmed the ACTU, the government, and the rural sector, but it also brought them to the negotiating table. Despite their efforts, the union failed to secure wider support from the Labor movement and the public. They were effectively isolated. By the late 1970s, the animal movement began contesting the politics and culture of animal exploitation in general and specifically targeted the export of live sheep. By focusing on the welfare of animals, animal activists animated a campaign that had become largely stagnate, where the economic arguments of the union had been either disproven or dismissed. New opportunities became available with the rise of the Australian Democrats. They secured the establishment of the Senate Committee on Animal Welfare, a body that became an important avenue for investigating and debating animal protection. Although the senate committee's *Export of Live Sheep from Australia* report did not recommend phasing out the trade, it delivered some improvements in animal welfare. However, the economic and political interests that upheld live sheep exports proved impossible to overthrow; only reforms that did not upset the economic order were warmly received. Similar to the experiences of other social movements, the state contained the live animal exports campaign and integrated its more palatable, least radical, demands.

The AMIEU and animal movement continued their campaign and their informal alliance. Employed and unemployed meat workers sustained pickets throughout the mid- to late 1980s, although none seem to have reached the heights of confrontation displayed in the earlier stages of the campaign. In 1983, due to declining prospects for mutton and wool, and an increase in the number of sheep exported to 7.3 million that year, the *Meatworker* lamented 'the lowest sheep kill for over thirty years'.[63] In 1985, Georges predicted that calls to abolish the export industry based on animal welfare grounds would persist and that the industry should be wary of them. 'Any major disaster at sea in this trade would lead to an increase of pressure to stop the trade', Georges said.[64] Georges did not foresee the challenge that Lyn White of Animals Australia and her novel transnational investigations in the 2000s and 2010s would pose. With her graphic first-hand video footage of animal suffering on ships in marketplaces and slaughterhouses in the Middle East and Southeast Asia and through prominent media coverage, Lyn White would once again draw Australia's attention to the plight of exported animals and revive a campaign that sought to end the trade.[65]

Notes

1 Adrian Franklin, *Animal Nation: The True Story of Animals and Australia* (Sydney: University of New South Wales Press, 2006), Chapter 1.
2 Andrea Gaynor, 'Animal Agendas: Conflict over Productive Animals in Twentieth-Century Australian Cities', *Society and Animals*, 15 (2007): 29–42.

108   *Gonzalo Villanueva*

3 Charles Tilly, *Social Movements, 1768–2004* (Boulder: Paradigm Publishers, 2004), 140–3.
4 Sean Scalmer, *Dissent Events: Protest, the Media and the Political Gimmick in Australia* (Sydney: UNSW Press, 2002), 6.
5 Scalmer, *Dissent Events*, 10.
6 Sean Scalmer, 'The History of Social Movements in Australia', in Stefan Berger and Holger Nehring (eds.), *Towards a Comparative Global History of Social Movements* (Basingstoke: Palgrave Macmillan, 2016).
7 Meredith Burgmann and Verity Burgmann, *Green Bans, Red Union: Environmental Activism and the New South Wales Builders Laborers' Federation* (Sydney: UNSW Press, 1998).
8 Nancy Cushing, '"Few Commodities Are More Hazardous": Australian Live Animal Export, 1788–1880', *Environment and History* (2018), forthcoming, doi:10.3197/0967 34018X15137949591954.
9 Senate Select Committee on Animal Welfare, *Export of Live Sheep from Australia: Report by the Senate Select Committee on Animal Welfare* (Canberra: Australian Government Publishing Service, 1985), 3–4.
10 Australian Bureau of Animal Health, *Sea Transport of Sheep* (Canberra: Australian Government Publishing Service, 1981), 1.
11 'Export of Livestock', *AMIEU Victorian Branch Newsletter*, 14.2 (10 April 1974): 1–2.
12 A. E. Davies, *The Meat Workers Unite* (Annandale: Union Printing Pty, 1974), 253–68.
13 AMIEU, 'Minutes of the Federal Executive Meeting Held at the Teachers' Federation Building on Thursday 15th August, 1974 at 11 A.m' 15 August 1974, Box 1, AMIEU, University of Melbourne Archives.
14 Land Editor, 'Farmers Retaliate to Ban by Meat Workers', *Sydney Morning Herald*, 31 March 1978.
15 'Fraser Backs WA over Ban', *Sydney Morning Herald*, 27 March 1978; Land Editor, 'Protest over Export Ban', *Sydney Morning Herald*, 4 April 1978.
16 'Talks to Ease Chances of Conflict on Sheep Bans', *Sydney Morning Herald*, 1 April 1978.
17 'Plan to End Sheep Ban Rejected', *Sydney Morning Herald*, 5 April 1978.
18 'Ports to Halt Today in Sheep Dispute', *Sydney Morning Herald*, 11 April 1978.
19 'Union Lifts Ban on Sheep Export', *Sydney Morning Herald*, 12 April 1978.
20 'Committee of Management Bulletin', 28 April 1978, Box 62, AMIEU, University of Melbourne Archives.
21 'Meat Workers Begin Nation-Wide Strike', *Sydney Morning Herald*, 13 April 1978.
22 'Committee of Management Bulletin'.
23 'Truce in Live Sheep Export Dispute', *Sydney Morning Herald*, 20 April 1978.
24 Report cited by Anthony Street, *Commonwealth Parliamentary Debate, House of Representatives*, 23 August 1978, 612.
25 'Meat Union Acts to Resume Export Pickets', *Canberra Times*, 11 August 1978.
26 Bureau of Agricultural Economics, Canberra, *Australian Live Sheep Exports* (Canberra: Australian Government Publishing Service, 1983), 7–9.
27 Majorie Jerrard, 'Building Alliances to Protect Jobs: The AMIEU's Response to Live Animal Export', in Donna Buttigieg et al. (eds.), *Trade Unions in the Community: Values, Issues, Shared Interests and Alliances* (Heidelberg: Heidelberg Press, 2007), 189.
28 'Threat to Trade', *Sydney Morning Herald*, 12 April 1978.
29 Keith Martin, 'AWU Opposes Ban on Live Sheep Trade', *Sydney Morning Herald*, 31 January 1979.
30 Malcolm Fraser, *Commonwealth Parliamentary Debate, House of Representatives*, 4 April 1978, 901.
31 Jack Sparks, 'Export of Jobs', *Meat Employees' Journal*, December 1979, 6.

'Pain for Animals, Profit for People' 109

32 Alan Cadman, *Commonwealth Parliamentary Debate*, *House of Representatives*, 22 August 1979, 482.
33 'Truck Drivers Face Black Ban over Sheep Row', *The Age*, 17 April 1980.
34 Mark Brolly, 'Unionists Move to Stop Sheep Shipment', *The Age*, 12 May 1980.
35 Mark Brolly, 'Meat Workers Strike Today over Export of Live Sheep', *The Age*, 13 May 1980.
36 Wally Curran, 'State Secretary Reports. Export of Livesheep', *Meat Employees' Journal*, no. 3 (1980): 1.
37 Wally Curran, 'The Live Sheep Issue', *Meat Employees' Journal*, no. 2 (1980): 3–4.
38 'Exporting Live Sheep', *Canberra Times*, 15 May 1980.
39 Editorial Opinion, 'The Live Sheep Row Goes On', *The Age*, 13 May 1980.
40 Gonzalo Villanueva, '"The Bible" of the Animal Movement: Peter Singer and Animal Liberation, 1970–1976', *History Australia* 13, no. 3 (2016): 399–414.
41 'What Is Animal Liberation?', *Animal Liberation Newsletter*, n.d.
42 Senate Select Committee on Animal Welfare, *Export of Live Sheep from Australia: Report by the Senate Select Committee on Animal Welfare* (Canberra: Australian Government Publishing Service, 1985), 39–100.
43 Christine Townend, *A Voice for Animals: How Animal Liberation Grew in Australia* (Kenthurst: Kangaroo Press, 1981), 81–95.
44 Editorial Opinion, 'The Live Sheep Row Goes On'.
45 Peter Falconer, *Commonwealth Parliamentary Debate*, *House of Representatives*, 13 May 1980, 2600.
46 Peter Falconer, *Commonwealth Parliamentary Debate*.
47 Peter Nixon, 'Statement by the Minister for Primary Industry', *Commonwealth Parliamentary Debate*, *House of Representatives*, 13 May 1980, 2600–03.
48 John Warhurst, '1977: Don Chipp's New Party', in John Warhurst (ed.), *Keeping the Bastards Honest: The Australian Democrats' First Twenty Years* (St Leonards: Allen & Unwin, 1997), 49.
49 Don Chipp, *Commonwealth Parliamentary Debate*, *Senate*, 25 March 1982.
50 'Sheep Export Ban Off', *Canberra Times*, 2 September 1982.
51 'Live Sheep Campaign', *Meat Employees' Journal*, July 1985, 2–3.
52 Don Chipp, *Commonwealth Parliamentary Debate*, *Senate*, 1 April 1981, 965.
53 See Parliament of Australia, 'Significant Reports' n.d., www.aph.gov.au/Parliamentary_Business/Committees/Senate/Significant_Reports (accessed 30 July 2014).
54 George Georges, *Commonwealth Parliamentary Debate*, *Senate*, 5 October 1984, 1328.
55 D. B Scott, *Commonwealth Parliamentary Debate*, *Senate*, 30 May 1985, 2854.
56 Senate Select Committee on Animal Welfare, *Export of Live Sheep from Australia*, xiii.
57 Senate Select Committee on Animal Welfare, xiii
58 Rod Frail, 'MPs Want an End to Sheep Shipping', *Sydney Morning Herald*, 15 August 1985.
59 George Georges, *Commonwealth Parliamentary Debate*, *Senate*, 21 August 1985, 114.
60 Georges, *Commonwealth Parliamentary Debate*, *Senate*.
61 Don Grimes, *Commonwealth Parliamentary Debate*, *Senate*, 11 February 1986, 6–10.
62 'AMLC Annual Report July 86–June 87', *Australian Meat and Live Stock Corporation*, June 1987.
63 'More Live Exports More on the Dole', *The Meatworker*, 13.6 (October 1984): 4.
64 George Georges, *Commonwealth Parliamentary Debate*, *Senate*, 21 August 1985: 118.
65 Gonzalo Villanueva, *A Transnational History of the Australian Animal Movement, 1970–2015* (London: Palgrave Macmillan, 2018), Chapter 7.

Part III

Equilibrium

The Ento(M)-usician

Piano player. Hands agonised into
Deftness,

By ten you'd almost
Charmed an octave

(While I was chasing insects
With a salvaged net,

Suckling the nectar out of
Wildflowers). In a

Pool of light
You press needles
Into *Apollo*.

You explain:
The wings are clad
In scales of dye,

I observe:
The proboscis quavering
Beneath your weight.

Another day,
We listen to Liszt's études in the kitchen;
You palpate the tune
Across my rib cage.

You tell me:
My right hand's too stiff
For these studies

112   *Equilibrium*

As I disrobe grapefruits for the salad,
Divest the flesh
Of seeds and rind.
In summer, we drive South.

In valleys that antler
Seaward,
Through fists of granite
And nimble scrub,

You hunt *Lepidoptera*,
Circling flowers in legato,

Conquering with ease
The woman in the tent –
Your fervid prey.

Though there was

An evening in the Wimmera
When the cicadas,
Quelling the earth with their staccato
Spared a moth its genus

And I bunched wild grass
Up in specimen jars marked
Antipodea atralba, Ogyris subterrestris.
                              – Emma Carmody

9 "Cunning, intractable, destructive animals"

Pigs as co-colonisers in the Hunter Valley of New South Wales, 1840–1860

Nancy Cushing

The colonial transformations of the Australian landscape were primarily engineered by and for non-human animals raised for meat and wool. The most important of these – numerically, economically and on the plate – were sheep and cattle, but other introduced species were also part of this process. Leading them was the pig. After arriving with the First Fleet in 1788, pig populations rose to a point considered desirable amongst the settler-colonists, consistent with their supplementary rather than central role in the British-derived diet and the economy. This sense of sufficient but not excessive numbers did not prevent pigs from being seen as troublesome animals. As self-directed omnivores, they drew public censure, governmental regulation and direct punishment. Although these measures ensured that pigs were largely held in equilibrium in the streets, houses, gardens and cultivators' plots, regulation of their exploits outside the fences was negligible, with the effect that pigs became unintended but effective settler-colonial allies in disrupting existing ecologies to the detriment of native species and Indigenous peoples. The number of pigs which was acceptable to settler-colonists was excessive by other measures.

In keeping with their lesser status amongst domesticates, pigs were long overlooked by historians, although this has begun to be addressed in the past decade. Taking a global perspective, Brett Mizelle asserts that pigs were "structurally and symbolically significant in the making of human society and culture".[1] Mark Essig's study of the pig in the United States demonstrates its centrality to that nation's foundations and its nineteenth-century modernisation.[2] In Australia, the sheep and cattle which sit squarely at the centre of popular accounts of the colonial period overshadow pigs. Both agricultural historians and those studying the cultural and environmental impact of introduced species, including Adrian Franklin and Eric Rolls, have maintained the focus on the most numerous ungulates.[3]

The general emphasis on sheep and cattle in Australian historiography reflects not only their numerical dominance but also their significant contributions to the colonial economy and the social standing of those who owned them. Like sheep and cattle, pigs were part of the foundational array of livestock brought to Australia, most of them purchased at the Cape of Good Hope, in 1788.[4]

114 Nancy Cushing

Although many species struggled, pigs settled in so well that they outnumbered all other types of livestock except sheep in 1801.[5] By mid-century, however, pigs had lost this dominance and were vastly exceeded in number by sheep, cattle and horses in New South Wales, not rising above 80 000, whereas there were 13 million sheep in the colony by 1850. As in the Middle East, where pigs are not only overlooked but also demonised, the hot, dry, open environment of Australian inland plains did not suit pigs, and they earned no place in the dominant pastoral narratives of the "big man's frontier".[6] An artefact of their marginality survives in the printed form used in the mid-1840s for the recording the Returns of the Colony of NSW. In the absence of a dedicated column in which to record pigs, the heading "goats" was crossed out and "pigs" written in by hand.[7] Between 1840 and 1860, Cumberland County, which included the main centre of the human population in Sydney and an area of small-scale agricultural settlement along the Hawkesbury-Nepean system, had the greatest number of pigs in the colony, fluctuating between 10 000 and 11 600.[8]

Being few, it is perhaps not surprising that historians have overlooked pigs, but when deliberately made a subject of inquiry, pigs are very rewarding because of their well-documented "experientially meaningful and actively authored" actions.[9] Although the agency of animals can be difficult to capture because of the human-centredness of many historical records, pigs in urban and peri-urban environments are a welcome exception. Pigs produced events and effects that mattered, to use Nance's definition of agency, and their deliberate actions drew attention and documentation.[10] Lisa Ford identified the decision of a hungry sow to enter the wrong person's property in Sydney in 1795 as the trigger for what she called one of the most important legal decisions ever handed down in the colony of NSW.[11] This case preceded the first newspaper, but from the time the *Sydney Gazette* appeared in 1803, Michael Connor found that pigs were newspaper stars, consistently written about as independent entities within the nascent urban society that had to be planned around like other wayward neighbours.[12] In pursuing their own ends, pigs could counter human intentions and challenge human assumptions of supremacy.[13] They were capable of acting on their individual tastes and preferences and, being known for these traits, were permitted, even encouraged, to look after their own best interests.

Pigs gained this distinctive positioning through a long history of relations with humans based on mutual advantage. Like wolves, they chose domestication rather than having had it forced upon them.[14] Central to this process was their preferred diet. Unlike sheep and cattle, pigs are not ruminants and cannot live on high cellulose fodder. They are omnivores who eat a wide range of plants and animal foods, including those that are unappealing to or indigestible by humans, and the buried roots, tubers and fungi which are inaccessible to many other animals. Pigs were drawn to human settlements by the leftovers from the foods with which humans provided themselves, and humans viewed the pigs as useful scavengers and food banks. Pigs were allowed to roam freely in many settings, feeding on what they could find. With their capacity to produce litters of eight or more young after four months' gestation, from a human perspective, pigs constituted

"*Cunning, intractable, destructive animals*"   115

a constantly renewing and readily divisible resource that converted food energy to meat more efficiently than cattle or sheep.[15] Pigs and humans lived together in a variety of functional and often very close relationships in places as diverse as China and Papua New Guinea, but in the west, whether in English medieval towns or New York City in the early nineteenth century, pigs gained a reputation as troublesome animals.[16] As local authorities struggled to address pig-based conflict, the pigs' ultimate recourse was to stretch or even break ties with humans, entering a free-living state and resuming fully independent lives. At some 23 million, these "feral" pigs now outnumber domestic pigs in Australia, giving them a central place in debates over how to manage invasive species.[17]

This chapter is the first to draw attention to the wider role of pigs in the Australian colonial project. Its focus is on their presence in the Hunter Valley of New South Wales in the mid-nineteenth century, where they were seen as both an asset and as "most cunning, intractable, destructive animals".[18] This tension between the two guises of pigs created a sense within the settler colonial culture that they were in equilibrium, and those who spoke against them did not call for reductions in their numbers but for containment to curtail their damage to crops, property and settlers themselves, preferably behind stoutly built pig-proof fences. What was overlooked was the other aspect of their destructiveness, that which took place outside of the fences, in the fertile swamps and gullies of the region. There, from the perspective of the existing ecology and the Indigenous people who relied upon it, any number of pigs was excessive.

Pigs in Australia's Hunter Valley

As settler-colonists expanded their occupation of Aboriginal lands beyond the Sydney basin, pigs were a helpful ally. The valley of the Hunter River, located north of Sydney and running from the port at Newcastle north-west some 130 kilometres, then east and north, was attractive to capitalist settlers seeking land for agriculture and pastoralism, with water transport to the main market at Sydney.[19] It was opened to settlement after the closure of the Newcastle penal settlement at the river mouth in 1822 and was then quickly occupied by prosperous settlers who obtained sizeable blocks through grant and purchase.[20] By the end of the 1820s, this aspiring gentry had made the Hunter Valley the second most populous region in NSW. The region had the highest proportion of free immigrant settlers as well as the greatest amount of alienated and cultivated land outside of Cumberland County, one fifth of the colony's cattle and almost a quarter of its sheep. Although they kept pigs, they were peripheral to the interests of these large landowners, and this remained the case, with just 16 500 pigs enumerated in the seven counties which made up the Hunter District in 1852, compared with 2.2 million sheep.[21]

Amongst these upper middle-class landowners were Cambridge-educated George Wyndham and his wife, Margaret, who arrived in Sydney in 1827 and bought an 842-hectare estate, renamed Dalwood, near Branxton. Wyndham experimented with many enterprises, including the winemaking for which he

116   *Nancy Cushing*

is best remembered, but his fortune was built on the backs of sheep and cattle, mainly grazed on much larger properties he acquired further north. Wyndham raised pigs at Dalwood, doing so responsibly, by building them styes and troughs and protecting his gardens from them with a fence.[22] If he followed best practice, the styes were set in a row, paved with stone and included a sleeping area lined with logs.[23] Although Wyndham carefully kept track of his growing flocks of sheep in his diaries, he did not make a record of pig numbers. Amongst Wyndham's peers were Robert and Helenus Scott who owned a property called Glendon near Singleton. When it went to auction in 1848, the list of animals for sale included specific numbers of sexes and ages of cattle but only the more general "about 20 to 30 pigs".[24] These pigs were kept in place on well-ordered properties, but other keepers of pigs were less careful. When harvesting maize in 1832, Wyndham found that wet weather, Aboriginal people and marauding pigs had knocked much of the crop down. Although he saw the other two former elements as out of his control, he resolved to wage war on the pigs.[25] For large landowners, pigs were a useful adjunct to their households that were of limited interest unless they caused trouble.

Pigs played a more important role for another group of valley residents: the former convicts, assisted immigrants and those born in the colony to parents from these groups who grew crops and kept a few animals on small parcels of land. Their occupation of the Hunter Valley had preceded that of the free settlers when, from 1814, a few trusted former convicts and public servants were permitted to establish small farms up the river from Newcastle. At Paterson's Plains and Wallis Plains (later Maitland), they grew maize, wheat, peaches and potatoes and raised pigs.[26]

Mixed agriculture on this modest scale continued as property owners established the great estates. Typical amongst the small settlers was convict Hugh Hughes, who, when he gained a ticket of leave excusing him from public labor in 1837, purchased land at Patrick's Plains (Singleton) to grow corn and tobacco and to raise pigs, fowls and a few cows.[27] Pigs were significant to these small farmers specifically because they could be eaten or sold either alive or cured as bacon, both locally and in Sydney market, and they did not require fodder or much in the way of husbandry.[28] These pigs might have a rudimentary stye, typically formed in the corner of a yard, with posts and rails made of rounded saplings for walls, a bark roof and a dirt floor, but they spent much of their time at liberty.[29] Pigs and settlers established a form of the traditional British practice of pannage, whereby peasants had the right to turn their pigs out to feed on mast (acorns and beechnuts) in private forests, and pigs were to some extent tolerated in public spaces.[30] However, although in the British context pigs had an attendant swineherd, in Australia, they roamed their neighbourhoods, whether in small towns or on agricultural lands, without any human oversight, having to be enticed back to their putative homes by occasional savoury meals.

Whether based on large or smallholdings or in towns, pigs were a well-established component of settler society in the Hunter Valley by the 1840s. They provided not only nourishment and income but also amusement. A pig race was

"*Cunning, intractable, destructive animals*"   117

the final event at an Old English sports competition in Maitland, the major urban centre of the valley, on Anniversary Day (26 January) in 1845. The pig itself was the grand prize.[31] Pigs outnumbered sheep at the Hunter River Agricultural Society's show that year, including Chinese pigs which the journalist reporting on the show described as beautiful.[32] People flocked to see the hanging carcasses of record-breaking "immense fat pigs".[33] Pigs were present and, when behaving well, were admired. Misbehaving pigs drew less positive attention.

Testing the boundaries

The free-ranging pigs of the smaller settlers did not discriminate between town and country, claimed and unclaimed lands, or between what was considered waste and what had value in settler society. Reflecting the general sense that pigs were independent actors, their transgressing of boundaries came to be viewed as a form of criminality, as Hartog found for New York City in a similar period, especially by town dwellers and the upper middle-class who least relied on pigs.[34] Perhaps reflecting the convict origins of the colony and of many owners of roaming pigs, the language used in Hunter Valley when complaining about pigs at large mirrored that used for human lawbreakers. They were not Descartes' automatons but enemies upon whom Wyndham declared war and "notoriously cunning animals" in the words of another victim, who accused pigs of duplicitously staying near home during the day but roving abroad at night, "fatten[ing] on plunder" amongst their neighbours' corn.[35]

Pigs were undoubtedly a disruptive force within the emerging colonial society. Although forbidden to roam the streets by the Towns Police Act, swarms of pigs disrupted traffic, undermined fences, destabilised buildings and opened gates to pillage gardens, chicken yards and kitchens.[36] They were housebreakers, in one case in Maitland in 1858, barging through a dwelling to feed on the front garden.[37] No respecters of persons, attacks by pigs on infants and older children were regularly reported, with appeals to parents not to trust these ferocious animals.[38] Pigs out of place could be lethal for themselves and others, as in 1856, when a train derailment near Hexham killed a man and the pig upon whom the accident was blamed, having been found nearly cut in two on the tracks.[39] Pigs' behaviour drove some people to extremes. In 1861, the police prosecuted Thomas Malthouse for maliciously stabbing and wounding a pig. He was found guilty but with a recommendation of mercy on the grounds of repeated provocation and served a reduced sentence of seven days in Maitland Gaol.[40]

The list of pigs' offences in the Hunter Valley in the mid-nineteenth century has many similarities to that compiled by Dolly Jørgensen from the surviving court rolls of the British town of Ramsey in the medieval period, where pigs obstructed roads, ate goslings and knocked over a baby's cradle.[41] Pigs, it seemed, were consistent in their actions, while humans struggled to either control or adapt to them. The attribution of malign intent and careless disregard for others on the part of pigs, and particularly the acceptance of Malthouse's defence of

118   *Nancy Cushing*

provocation, suggest that the courts regarded pigs as almost human in their exercise of agency and the extent to which they should be held liable for their actions.

Legislation was passed in NSW to try to control pigs. Within five years of the arrival of the first pigs in Australia, government orders had begun directing the use of nose rings and yokes to keep them out of gardens, along with the mandating of damages, forfeiture or death for pigs found running loose in towns.[42] A public pound for livestock was set up in Sydney in 1811, and increasingly complex impounding acts were passed from 1825. These acts established pounds around the colony to hold straying cattle, horses, sheep, goats and pigs until owners paid fees and penalties set by the local court of petty sessions.[43] Penalties doubled and then tripled for repeat offenders. If no one claimed an animal within an appointed period, it was sold at auction to cover costs, and any surplus went to local charitable organisations. In the published rates of penalties, pigs tended to be at the top.

As was the case for escaped convicts and runaway servants, detailed descriptions of impounded animals were published in the *Government Gazette* and in local newspapers to enable an owner to reclaim his or her animal. Convicts were described by name, age, height, the colour of their hair, eyes and complexion and distinguishing marks, such as scars and tattoos, and a reward offered for their return to the government.[44] For pigs, these verbal mugshots identified the sex (including sow, boar and barrow, meaning a castrated male), age (especially hog, an adult pig, and slips, pigs two to three months old) and colour (black or white, white streak on near side of neck and down face, white feet, foxy and black spotted). Some had their own distinguishing marks that provided evidence of their misadventures: hair very much rubbed off, lump on back, missing an ear and no tail.[45] They were not branded like cattle and horses, but owners earmarked them in a variety of ways, including a slit, a round hole, clipped on one or both ears or ears were noted as uncut. The advertisements record no breed, and it appears that the improved varieties of pigs, such as the Yorkshire, Hampshire, Berkshire and Poland China then being bred in Britain and the United States, did not arrive in Australia until the 1870s.[46] There was little point in paying hefty sums for well-bred pigs when they could not be isolated from the general run of free-roaming ones. As in the case of absconding convicts, money changed hands on the return of an impounded pig, in the form of a fine rather than a reward. There were close connections between responses to the misbehaviour of people and the misbehaviour of these animals.

An anonymous Hunter Valley settler of the 1830s observed that quarrels over livestock were not uncommon, but while those involving an ox or a horse were quickly settled, in those over pigs, people took on the character of the pig, keeping up the quarrel through generations and annoying one another in the "same insidious and indirect way in which Mr Pork approaches a cornfield and tho driven from their position a hundred times still return to the same point of attack to renew their vexatious proceedings". This attribution of "swinish" qualities to the owners of pigs was also noted by Catherine McNeur in her study of the hog wars conducted in New York City in the early nineteenth century, where Irish immigrants and African Americans vocally and sometimes violently defended their right to keep pigs in the "urban commons" of the city streets.[47] In NSW, authorities sided with the middle class, and although they could not cure pigs of their waywardness, over time they built up the penalties against pigs in public by charging high damages for their trespassing and permitting animal intruders on enclosed land to be shot.[48]

In the Hunter Valley, pigs did retain access to the informal commons of unalienated Crown land and the extensive unfenced portions of privately held land. They became the animal parallel of Australia's notorious bushrangers as they readily crossed the critical boundary between criminal and outlaw, between domestic and wild animal, occupying what Adrian Franklin called the domestic wild category.[49] Like free-living formerly domesticated cattle and later horses, goats and camels, fully independent pigs were regarded like their nominally owned relatives as both a pest and a resource. When three men struggled ashore on Long Island near Port Stephens from the wrecked cutter *Dove* in 1857, they survived on the raw meat of pigs which were the offspring of progenitors deposited there by a fisherman some 15 years earlier for just such a purpose.[50] The slippage between wild and domestic could create confusion, as in 1844, when an expensive, newly acquired boar was shot and killed by a neighbour at Fullerton Cove near Newcastle, who believed it to be a wild pig. The shooter was shocked to find that he faced possible imprisonment instead of praise for removing an unwanted pest.[51] To address such ambiguity, one settler of the 1830s was of the view that pigs should be "excommunicated and put out of the pale of the law", as in the West Indies, where, he maintained, locals could shoot pigs when found to be trespassing. In 1850, another writer recommended the classification of roaming pigs as wild beasts, which would mean that they could be destroyed at will when found on one's land, a regulation which was in place by the mid-1860s.[52]

Wider impacts

From the settler-colonists' point of view, pig numbers were not questioned in the Hunter Valley in the mid-nineteenth century. They were bothersome to many, and infuriating to some, but generally tolerated for the benefits gained from them. Taking a more comprehensive view, however, the activities least complained of were those through which pigs potentially had the greatest impact. Pigs played a distinctive environmental role by extending the effects of the colonial occupation beyond the paddocks grazed by sheep and cattle into the wooded areas and gullies which had become refuges for native plants and animals and for Indigenous Australians.

Although sheep ripped up and trod down native grasses, pigs sought out different food sources in different environments. Unable to cool themselves by sweating, by preference pigs spent their time in more damp and shaded areas, seeking protection from the sun. The tracts of non-arable, uncleared land that existed on and between Hunter Valley properties was excellent pig habitat. Dismissed as scrub by those seeking land for crops and grazing, the vegetation ranged from tea tree bush to open forests and thick vine brush. The latter was described as almost impenetrable jungle in the 1830s, with tall figs and cedar trees, and smaller myrtle, tree ferns and climbers creating a shady upper storey over a floor of decaying leaf litter.[53] Pigs' disruption of soils and surface vegetation as they rooted for tubers and bulbs encouraged the growth of exotic plant species and denied favoured foods to native animals both above ground and below, where species like bettongs dug for fungi.[54] Pigs ate bird chicks, eggs, reptiles, frogs, grubs and earthworms. Essig argued for the United States that pigs were perfect animals for colonisation because of their rapid breeding and the abundant meat they produced. In the Australian context, pigs' capacity to fend for themselves, and the effect of their omnivorous eating on unwanted native competitors, provided additional, if unintended, advantages for the settler-colonists.[55] The pig invaded areas that would have been left undisturbed as unsuitable for grazing or cropping.

This invasion impacted the Indigenous people of the Hunter Valley, the Awabakal and Worimi at the river mouth, the Wonnarua upstream and the Gringai in the Paterson River area. Pigs' preferences for the same foods as humans favour, an asset when there are surpluses to be stored and waste to be disposed of, can also lead to conflict. Crosby observed that the displacement and destruction of local fauna by pigs (and cattle) to the detriment of the diet of Indigenous people was an element of the Columbian Exchange. Essig gave the example of Calapooya people of the Willamette Valley in Oregon, who faced starvation in the 1850s after settlers' pigs began foraging in the wetlands where their staple, the roots of a marsh lily, grew.[56] Such conflict also occurred where pigs rather than people were the primary colonising force as in north-eastern Japan, where the failure of the soybean crop in 1749 led to a crisis when it was found that pigs had eaten the plants previously relied upon in times of scarcity, creating what was given the name the "wild boar famine".[57]

In the Hunter Valley, after mounting resistance to the invasion of their country in the 1820s and 1830s, the persisting population of some 300 Aboriginal people had been pushed to the margins – the wetlands, forests and broken country less favoured by the pastoralists and agriculturalists. Larger game like emu, wallaby and kangaroo was in decline as pastoralists protected the grass for sheep and cattle, land clearance had reduced habitat for possums and other tree dwellers, lagoons were being drained and bigger birds, including black swans, ducks and pigeons, were hunted by settlers. The loss of these essential sources of protein made smaller mammals, fish, grubs, goannas and cobbera (cah-bro) ever more important in the diet of Indigenous people.[58] Plant foods were also under threat as settler-colonists cleared land, leaving inhabitants more dependent on roots "which they procure in the bush".[59]

Although the changes undertaken by and for grazing animals and crops were acknowledged when local magistrates and clergy were asked about the state of Aboriginal people in the Hunter Valley in the mid-1840s, there was no local recognition that Aboriginal people were being placed in direct competition for food with pigs. This knowledge was in circulation in settler society, as William Thomas, assistant protector of Aborigines in the Port Phillip District of NSW

"Cunning, intractable, destructive animals" 121

(now Victoria), reported that although sheep did not destroy the root vegetables that were a staple of the diet of Indigenous people there, pigs did.[60] When Aboriginal people attempted to make up the deficits by hunting this new animal in their country, newcomers punished them for it. A Dungog magistrate reported in 1845 that he had witnessed an Aboriginal man spear his "fine barrow pig" and then delivered unspecified extra legal punishment of the man for this offence.[61] In 1847, one sympathetic observer linked pigs with Aboriginal people. He reported that the numbers of Indigenous people were so depleted in the Jerry's Plains area that they no longer formed camps but just crouched in twos and threes in wood heaps and the styes that pigs abandoned so readily and with such wide-ranging consequences.[62]

Conclusion

Pigs have largely been omitted from historical writings on and understandings of Australian agriculture, not only because of their lower numbers and economic contribution when compared with sheep and cattle but also because of their status. They were associated with the less powerful members of society who took advantage of pigs' capacity to exercise agency, to the advantage of the putative owner and often at the expense of those with fixed assets to protect. Therefore, much of the recorded opinion from the colonial period does not celebrate the pig but instead reflects the elite view that uncontrolled pigs, whether notionally domestic or wild, were troublesome and treacherous, even criminal, animals which had turned against humans and caused all manner of damage and costs in preventing their depredations.

Despite harsh criticisms of the pig, I found no written opinion that said there were too many. Relatively small numbers of pigs distributed around the countryside, providing breakfast bacon and serving as a tradeable commodity, were welcome and even celebrated when they grew very fat or provided light entertainment with their antics. This opinion draws attention to the subjective nature of assessments of whether animals are present in the right numbers. Taking a wider perspective, this chapter shows that the presence of pigs was contributing to a cataclysmic shift out of balance for remnant areas of the natural environment and the Indigenous peoples of the region. Colonial society did not recognise pigs for this service of co-colonisation and indeed in recent decades they have been further demonised for their ongoing environmental impacts. From the perspective of Indigenous Australians in the Hunter Valley in the mid-nineteenth century, pigs were indeed "cunning, intractable, destructive animals" of which any number could be considered excessive.

Notes

1 Brett Mizelle, *Pig* (London: Reaktion Books, 2011), 7.
2 Mark Essig, *Lesser Beasts: A Snout-to-Tail History of the Humble Pig* (New York: Basic Books, 2015).

122 Nancy Cushing

3 Ted Henzell, *Australian Agriculture: Its History and Challenges* (Melbourne: CSIRO, 2007); Richard Waterhouse, *The Vision Splendid: A Social and Cultural History of Rural Australia* (Perth: Curtin University Books, 2005); Adrian Franklin, *Animal Nation: The True Story of Animals and Australia* (Sydney: UNSW Press, 2006); Eric Rolls, *They All Ran Wild: The Animals and Plants That Plague Australia*, revised edition (London: Angus and Robertson, 1984).

4 For an account of this process, see Nancy Cushing, 'Animal Mobilities and the Founding of New South Wales', in Christof Mauch, Ruth Morgan and Emily O'Gorman (eds.) *Visions of Australia: Environments in History* (Munich: RCC Perspectives, Transformations in Environment and Society, 2017).

5 In June 1801, there were 6269 sheep, 4766 pigs, 1259 goats and 362 cattle at the Sydney settlement, with at least an equal number of pigs on Norfolk Island (Ian Parsonson, *Australian Ark, a History of Domesticated Animals in Australia* (Melbourne: CSIRO, 1998), 7. The *Returns of the Colony of New South Wales* record peaks of 13 059 324 sheep in 1851 (including the Port Phillip District, which became the colony of Victoria in that year) and 78 559 pigs in 1852 (NSW, *Returns of the Colony for 1850*, 'Return of Livestock in the Colony of NSW, on the 1st of January 1851', 945 and *Returns of the Colony for 1855*, 'Return of the Livestock in the Colony from the Year 1846 to 1855, Inclusive', 912).

6 The "big man's frontier" concept goes back at least as far as Brian Fitzpatrick, 'The Big Man's Frontier and Australian Farming', *Agricultural History*, 21.1 (1947): 8–12; Marvin Harris, *Good to Eat: Riddles of Food and Culture* (New York: Simon and Schuster, c1985), 74.

7 NSW, *Returns of the Colony*, 1845. Return of the Produce, Stock, etc., 490–1.

8 The conduct of agriculture along the Hawkesbury is discussed by Grace Karskens, *The Colony, A History of Early Sydney* (Sydney: Allen and Unwin, 2009) and 'Floods and Flood-mindedness in Early Colonial Australia', *Environmental History*, 21.2 (2016): 315–42.

9 Eileen Crist, quoted by Sarah E. McFarland and Ryan Hediger, 'Approaching the Agency of Other Animals: An Introduction', in S. E. McFarland and R. Hediger (eds.), *Animals and Agency: An Interdisciplinary Exploration* (Boston: Brill, 2009), 2–3.

10 Susan Nance, *Entertaining Elephants: Animal Agency and the Business of the American Circus* (Baltimore: Johns Hopkins University Press, 2013), 9.

11 Lisa Ford, 'The Pig and the Peace: Transposing Order in Early Sydney', in Shaunnagh Dorsett and Ian Hunter (eds.), *Law and Politics in British Colonial Thought: Transpositions of Empire* (Basingstoke: Palgrave Macmillan, 2010). The case turned on whether the military had the right to keep the peace in their own terms in a colonial convict town like Sydney and with an ambiguous verdict, which allowed ongoing negotiations about what sort of peace was to be upheld in the colony.

12 *Pig Bites Baby: Stories from Australia's First Newspaper*, Vol. 1, 1803–10, ed. Michael Connor (Sydney: Duffy and Snelgrove, 2003), 258–64.

13 Nance, *Entertaining Elephants*, 4, 9.

14 Mizelle, *Pig*, 94, 15.

15 Harris, *Good to Eat*, 67.

16 Dolly Jørgensen, 'Running Amuck? Urban Swine Management in Late Medieval England', *Agricultural History*, 87.4 (2013): 429–51; Hendrik Hartog, 'Pigs and Positivism', *Wisconsin Law Review*, 899 (1985): 1–26; Catherine McNeur, 'The "Swinish Multitude": Controversies over Hogs in Antebellum New York City', *Journal of Urban History*, 37 (2011): 639–60.

17 The Australian government's Department of Environment and Energy lists the "feral" pig as a serious pest because of its predation, habitat degradation, competition with other animals and disease transmission. It adopted a new plan for their threat abatement in 2017 which proposes a program of exclusion fencing, trapping, aerial shooting and poisoning, www.environment.gov.au/biodiversity/invasive-species/

"Cunning, intractable, destructive animals" 123

feral-animals-australia/feral-pigs (accessed 30 January 2018). Pig shooting is also a popular leisure activity, supported by such political groups as the Shooters, Fishers and Farmers Party formed in 1992, www.shootersfishersandfarmers.org.au/nsw_firearms (accessed 30 January 2018). The issue of labelling animals as feral is discussed in Anna Wilson, David Wilson and Libby Robin, 'The Ought-Ecology of Ferals: An Emerging Dialogue in Invasion Biology and Animal Studies', *Australian Zoologist*, 39.1 (2017): 85–102. They found that the pig was the animal most often described as feral after the cat.

18 Letter to Editor from Reform, *Maitland Mercury*, 10 August 1850, 4.

19 J. F. Campbell, 'The Genesis of Rural Settlement in the Hunter', *Royal Australian Historical Society Journal*, 12.2 (1926): 73–112; W. Allan Wood, *Dawn in the Valley: The Story of Settlement in the Hunter River Valley to 1833* (Sydney: Wentworth Books, 1972); T. M. Perry, *Australia's First Frontier: The Spread of Settlement in New South Wales 1788–1829* (Melbourne: Melbourne University Press, 1963).

20 Perry, *Australia's First Frontier*, 74.

21 Perry, *Australia's First Frontier*, 130–2, 135, 189.

22 George Wyndham, *The Diary of George Wyndham of Dalwood, 1830–1840: A Pioneer's Record*, ed. Alward Wyndham and Frances McInherny (Armidale: Dalwood Restoration Association, 1987), 4 and 13 October 1830; 12–19 March 1831.

23 James Atkinson, *An Account of the State of Agriculture and Grazing in New South Wales* [1826], facsimile edition (Sydney: Sydney University Press, 1975), 101.

24 'In the Insolvent Estate of Robert and Helenus Scott of Glendon,' *Sydney Morning Herald*, 27 July 1848, 4.

25 Wyndham, *The Diary of George Wyndham*, 15 May 1832.

26 Mark Dunn, 'A Valley in a Valley: Colonial Struggles over Land and Resources in the Hunter Valley, NSW 1820–1850' (PhD dissertation, University of NSW, 2015), 157–8.

27 Letter dated 25 March 1837, printed in *Devizes and Wiltshire Gazette*, 12 October 1837, cited by David Cragg in *I Am a Government Man to Mr Scott of Glendon: Hugh Hughes: From Convict to Free Man* (Sydney: David Cragg, 2015), 160.

28 See, for example, 'Exports from the District during the Week Ending 29 March 1850 Received in Sydney from Hunter River District,' when 91 pigs were received, *Maitland Mercury and Hunter River General Advertiser*, 3 April 1850, 2; and 'Exports from District during the Week to Sydney' for 3 December 1858 which included 52 pigs and 6.5 tons of bacon (*Maitland Mercury and Hunter River General Advertiser*, 3 December 1858, 2.

29 H. W. Potts, *Pigs and Their Management* (Sydney: NSW Department of Agriculture, 1910), 111.

30 Sam White, 'From Globalised Pig Breeds to Capitalist Pigs: A Study in Animal Cultures and Evolutionary History', *Environmental History*, 16 (January 2011): 96, 98–9.

31 'Anniversary Day in Maitland', *Maitland Mercury*, 1 February, 1845, 4.

32 'Hunter River Agricultural Society', *Maitland Mercury and Hunter River General Advertiser*, 19 April 1845, 4. For an account of the role of Chinese pig breeds in the development of modern varieties, see Sam White, 'From Globalised Pig Breeds to Capitalist Pigs: A Study in Animal Cultures and Evolutionary History', *Environmental History*, 16 (January 2011): 94–120.

33 'A Large Pig', *Maitland Mercury and Hunter River General Advertiser*, 14 July 1852; 'Immense Fat Pig', *Empire* (Sydney), 10 July 1858, 7.

34 Hendrik Hartog, 'Pigs and Positivism', *Wisconsin Law Review*, 899 (1985), 2.

35 Letter to Editor from Reform, *Maitland Mercury*, 10 August 1850, 4.

36 The act was applied in Singleton in August 1850 and credited with clearing the streets of swarms of pigs and goats ('Singleton', *Maitland Mercury*, 14 August 1850, 2); Letter to the Editor from Jeroboam, *Maitland Mercury*, 10 February 1844, 3; Letter to Editor from ABC, Morpeth, *Maitland Mercury*, 3 November 1855, 3.

124   *Nancy Cushing*

37 'Maitland Police Court,' *Northern Times* (Newcastle), 9 June 1858, 2. The defendant said it was the fault of the homeowner, who had no right to leave his back door open, but the magistrate disagreed.

38 'Savage Pig', *Maitland Mercury and Hunter River General Advertiser*, 14 February 1860, 3; 'Colonial Extracts, St Mary's, South Creek', *Newcastle Chronicle*, 12 June 1861, 3; 'Another Case of Animal Ferocity', *Newcastle Chronicle*, 24 July 1861, 3; 'Caution to Mothers', *Newcastle Chronicle*, 23 March 1861, 4.

39 'Late Railway Accident,' *Empire* (Sydney), 22 October 1856, 3.

40 'Stabbing a Pig', *Newcastle Chronicle*, 10 August 1861, 2.

41 Jørgensen, 'Running Amok?', 443–5.

42 Ford, 'The Pig and the Peace', 174; General Orders, *Sydney Gazette*, 6 April 1806 in Connor, *Pig Bites Baby*, 264.

43 'Government Public Notice, 24 August 1811, *Historical Records of NSW*, VII, 582–3. 'New Impounding Act', *Maitland Mercury and Hunter River General Advertiser*, 23 January 1856, 8–9 printed the full text of 'An Act to Regulate the Impounding of Cattle' (assented to 18 December 1855).

44 See, for example, notices placed by the Principal Superintendent of Convicts' Office in the *NSW Government Gazette*, 15 January 1840, 58.

45 'Impoundings', *Maitland Mercury and Hunter River General Advertiser*, 14 December 1844, 3; 12 August 1846, 2; 7 January 1852, 2; 17 December 1853, 2; 10 April 1854, 2.

46 Essig, *Lesser Beasts*, 159–60; E. B. Woodehouse's advertising flyer, 'New Circular Giving Pedigrees, Prices and Fullest Information of Undermentioned Famous Breeds of Pigs viz the Improved Berkshire, the Pure-bred Berkshire, the Magie or Poland China and Improved Essex' (Sydney: AW Beard Printer, 1880), indicated that his stock of these breeds had all been imported since the late 1870s.

47 McNeur, 'The "Swinish Multitude"', 641–2.

48 An Act to Regulate the Impounding of Live Stock, assented to 20 June 1865, *Government Gazette*, no. 125, 20 June 1865, 1305–12.

49 Franklin, *Animal Nation*, 144.

50 'Miraculous Escape', *Shipping Gazette and Sydney General Trade List*, 9 November 1857, 245.

51 'Shooting a Pig', *Maitland Mercury and Hunter River General Advertiser*, 25 May 1844, 2.

52 Author unknown, Hunter Valley Settler Manuscript, circa 1833, University of Newcastle Cultural Collections, A5094c(xv); Letter to Editor from Reform, *Maitland Mercury and Hunter River General Advertiser*, 10 August 1850, 4.

53 Wood, *Dawn in the Valley*, 2.

54 Jim Hone, *Applied Population and Community Ecology: the Case of Feral Pigs in Australia* (Chichester: Wiley Blackwell, 2012), 55–6.

55 Essig, *Lesser Beasts*, 151.

56 Essig, *Lesser Beasts*, 145.

57 Brett L. Walker, 'Animals and the Intimacy of History', *History and Theory*, 52 (2013), 61–2.

58 Joseph Docker, J. P., Scone and David Dunlop, J. P., Wollombi in NSW. Legislative Council. *Report from the Select Committee on the Condition of the Aborigines, with . . . Replies to a Circular Letter* (Sydney: WW Davies, 1845), 27 and 30, https://coalriver. files.wordpress.com/2018/01/1845-condition-of-aborigines-transcript-final.pdf. Evidence of William Ross, Church of Scotland, Paterson, 5 April 1846; Rev. George Middleton, Morpeth, 10 April 1846; Rev. Robert Thorley, Hexham, 15 April 1846; and Rev. C. P. N. Wilton, Newcastle, 1 May 1846, NSW Legislative Council. *Aborigines: Replies to a Circular Letter Addressed to the Clergy of All Denominations by Order of the Select Committee on the Condition of the Aborigines* (Sydney: Government Printer, 1846), 555, 559–60, 561–2, 576. Cobbera are a marine wood borer commonly called shipworms which live in wood submerged in brackish water.

59 Joseph Docker, J. P., Scone, *Report from the Select Committee on the Condition of the Aborigines*, 28 said stock feeding had driven out kangaroo, and William Ross, Church

of Scotland, Paterson, 5 April 1846, reported that there were few kangaroos in his district, as they had retreated from the "haunts of men" (*Aborigines. Replies to a Circular Letter Addressed to the Clergy of All Denominations*, 555); E. M. McKinlay and C. L. Brown, Magistrates in the District of Dungog, 1845 in NSW. Legislative Council, *Report from the Select Committee on the Condition of the Aborigines*, 27.

60 William Thomas, *Aborigines. Replies to a Circular Letter Addressed to the Clergy of All Denominations*, 55. Sheep were also capable of pulling out tubers – see Chalmer, this volume.

61 C. L. Brown, *Report from the Select Committee on the Condition of the Aborigines*, 27.

62 'Jerry's Plains,' *Maitland Mercury and Hunter River General Advertiser*, 7 August 1847, 2.

10 Wine worlds are animal worlds too

Native Australian animal vine feeders and interspecies relations in the ecologies that host vineyards

Julie McIntyre

The common Eurasian grape *Vitis vinifera* is among many invasive plant species introduced to Australia by British colonists from 1788 with the intention of creating plantation-style commercial agriculture.[1] Since then, *V. vinifera* vineyards in Australia have been interspecies battlegrounds between those humans who cultivate grapes – for eating fresh or drying or to make into wine – and the insects, birds and mammals that feed on the vines and ripe fruit. As opportunistic feeders, the animals that are construed as vineyard pests, whether themselves native or introduced, are unconcerned by the invasive status of *V. vinifera*. Indeed, some native species are closely entangled with grapevines, especially the caterpillar of the vine moth (*Agarista glycine*) and the tiny grape bird, the silvereye (*Zosterops lateralis*). To achieve a balance that allows for the profitable production of wine, grape-growing humans have historically deployed many methods, including poison and guns, to control the numbers of these animals that they characterise as pests. Grape and wine producers then gloss over this animal-human conflict in the consumer-facing narratives of their products, allowing drinkers to assume wine is produced without harming animals.

Until now, Australian historians have taken an economic rather than a critical environmental or ecological view of animals in vineyard environments. David Dunstan, as the authority on the arrival of the aphid-like grape phylloxera in colonial Victoria, has treated the politics and impact of the vine-pull solution to eradicate this insect but does not discuss the nature of its presence or that of other animals in vineyards.[2] I have published widely on Australian wine growing across several themes but previously viewed insects, mammals and mildews in vineyards only as problems to be solved for the economic and social sustainability of the wine industry.[3] This approach is also common among historians addressing vine cultivation and winemaking in other wine countries due to the exclusion of ecological approaches in source materials on wine communities and wine as a commodity, in favour of economic and social methodologies.[4]

In her environmental history of grape growing in the nineteenth-century United States, Erica Hannickel presents a strong critique of grape growing and

Wine worlds are animal worlds too   127

wine manufacture in the twentieth century as industrial processes involving chemicals and waste. Although she discerns that 'wine growing easily outpaces romanticized images of other agricultural goods', she does not extend her analysis or commentary to consider animals in the ecologies that host vineyards, as either agents or as sentient beings.[5] It is significant, too, that one of Australia's most important voices on interspecies relations, Eric Rolls, is an agent of the 'vineyard mythos' identified by Hannickel.[6] Rolls frames grapes and wine within a classical first foods mythology rather than as an invasive plant crop in the Australian context. In *A Celebration of Food and Wine: Of grain, of grape, of Gethsemane* (1997), Rolls is briefly attentive to other non-human nature in winegrowing and manufacture: yeasts, disease mildews, the timbers used in wine barrels and animal pests, including native caterpillars and vinegar flies; the invasive vine insect phylloxera; native birds, such as eastern and crimson rosellas, silvereyes, crested pigeons and ravens; and invasive starlings.[7] Rolls touches on organic viticultural practices that encourage natural predators to control caterpillars and mentions the difficulty of excluding some birds from vines with netting. Yet the overriding story Rolls tells is one of reverence for grapes and wine, with little of the concern for native species expressed in his work elsewhere.[8]

Anthropocentric paradigms of economic and social sustainability have naturalised the notion that native Australian animals can be trespassers in the space occupied by commercial crops of introduced plants. As Emily O'Gorman notes in identifying the paradoxes of 'biocultural belonging' in the Anthropocene, 'a native duck can cross into a rice field and become an invasive pest', although the rice is the invader and the duck the native.[9] Wine grape vineyards can similarly be defined as invasive plant cultivation within wider ecologies which include animals identified as pests. This chapter will highlight the agency of native animals that feed on vines and grapes and emphasise that wine is an animals-present product. As such, it contributes to the environmental humanities project of disrupting naturalised anthropocentric thinking through the rewriting of 'inaccurate narratives about human relationships to ecosystems and nonhuman species'.[10]

Beginning with a discussion of contemporary wine discourse as animal-free, I then identify the genesis of the lexical normalisation of certain native animals as vineyard pests in the 1840s, prior to the arrival of the invasive animals which later became vineyard pests. Following on from this, I suggest that it was in the 1970s that a consumer-facing silence became common to disguise the reality of the control of native and invasive animal feeders in vineyards, even as a new generation of winegrowers faced the same animal 'pest' species as had the early settlers. Historical sources for the early nineteenth and late twentieth centuries, although temporally discrete, offer a glimpse of continuities and changes in animal behaviour and human intentions in wine grape vineyards.

Terroir as an animal-free narrative of wine

Since the second wave of wine globalisation in the 1990s, grape wine is produced in many parts of the world and consumed in most nations.[11] This has led to fierce

128   *Julie McIntyre*

competition among producers seeking to differentiate their wines in the global market and has given rise to producer-driven narratives that privilege the idea of certain vineyards as the source of the highest-quality wines. This contemporary producer-driven narrative of wine and vineyard nature is epitomised in the concept of terroir, a French word synonymous with locale and a powerful discursive tool in global wine marketing. As Hannickel argues, the concept of terroir employed in some specialist producer-driven narratives of wine has the effect of veiling actual vineyard practices, such as the use of synthetic chemical fertilisers, pesticides and herbicides.[12] Through the notion of terroir, some producers claim that the vineyard environment of grapes for premium wines is a guarantee of the characteristics and quality of the wine and therefore a determinant of its price.[13] By contrast, marketing narratives for less expensive bottled or bulk wines – or indeed for eating grapes – do not focus on unique individual vineyard qualities.

Wine grape marketing of vineyard imagery not only trades on the beauty of vineyards but also on the idea of terroir and the apparent immutability of the non-human environment of vineyard locations it suggests. This imagery excludes both human vineyard laborers[14] and the animals that feed on the vines. When animals are featured in marketing materials, it is because, like the kangaroo on some Australian wine labels, it has positioning value for the wine producer. The discursive power of terroir as a conceptual vacuum allows producers to elide the existence or agency of pest animals in vineyards. The construction of vineyards as animal-free is what Nicolaas Mink has referred to as a weakness in producer-centred narratives;[15] a silence about human relationships with non-human nature that, once revealed, enables a more complete view of wine production as occurring within an economic value chain dependent on ecosystems.

Making native animals into invasive pests

The development of specialist colonial knowledge on animal pests in Australian vineyards can be traced from the 1820s. The young agriculturalist James Busby emigrated to New South Wales with his family in 1824 when his father took up an engineering position in Sydney. The British government encouraged wine growing in its temperate colonies, and based on several months' residence in a French wine region, Busby intended to promote this industry in New South Wales in return for government employment and land grants. To this end, drawing upon French wine-growing manuals, Busby self-published *A Treatise on the Culture of the Vine and the Art of Making Wine* (1825) a year after his arrival in Sydney. In the *Treatise*, Busby remarked briefly on caterpillars and borer grubs (translated from French as 'cut buds' and 'vine worms') and explained that in France these insects were controlled by the same means recommended by ancient Greek agriculturalist Cato the Elder: surrounding the vines with 'pitch, sulphur and [olive?] oil'.[16] This advice captured the tremendous continuity or *longue durée* of cultivation practices in Europe which had accumulated an air of authority through tradition. According to Busby, winter ploughing also succeeded in removing European grubs from the soil near European vines. In the Cape Colony vineyards of Constantia, which Busby visited on the voyage to Sydney, he observed that growers repelled vine grubs by suspending vine leaves dipped in brandy below each grape bunch. His advice was directed at countering pests which might arrive with imported vines. If Busby anticipated that native Australian animals would be attracted to feed on vines and grapes, he did not reveal this to his readers.

The *Treatise* was not as successful as Busby hoped, and within a few years, he tried again to boost his reputation in colonial wine growing with a new book designed to appeal to the more numerous small-hold settlers, emancipists and those born in the colony to parents of limited means. *A Manual of Plain Directions for Planting and Cultivating a Vineyard and for Making Wine in New South Wales* (1830) drew on local knowledge from another 1820s immigrant, nurseryman Thomas Shepherd, who had become a regular columnist on horticulture in the colonial press. The *Manual* presents vine growing and wine making as effortless and as socially and economically transformative. Busby refers in it to native caterpillars as pests, which may well have been on Shepherd's advice, as Busby himself yet had little vine-growing experience. According to the *Manual*, insects that fed on vines might be dealt with cost-effectively by occasionally sending children to 'look out for, and destroy, the large green caterpillar' that attacked young vine leaves.[17]

Also in 1830, Frederick Hely, superintendent of convicts and a wine grower, inked in the flyleaf of his copy of Busby's *Manual* that a redheaded caterpillar appeared around the same time as blossoms on his vines north of Sydney. He noted that a 'small grub' attacked sweetwater grapes shortly after fruit set in the Australian Agricultural Company's vineyard at Port Stephens.[18] These accumulating knowledge processes reached a crucial point a decade later when, in the 1840s, William Macarthur wrote a series of columns in *The Australian* newspaper under the pen name Maro. These articles were collated and published as the well-received book *Letters on the Culture of the Vine, Fermentation, and the Management of Wine in the Cellar* (1844). Macarthur's experience arose from observing vineyards in France and Switzerland, and European colonies, such as Madeira and the Cape, combined with more than two decades of vine-growing experiments at his family's properties, and he gave the first detailed attention to Australian vineyard pests.

Macarthur identified the insects attracted to feed on vines as moth larvae hosted by acacia, casuarina and other soft woods. These larvae, Macarthur said, would Trojan-horse into vineyards in the wood of trellising stakes. The black and yellow caterpillar of the *Agarista glycine* moth (the vine moth) was an especial pest. Besides insects, 'Opossums, squirrels, and native cats . . . occasionally make an inroad into a vineyard, and devour the fruit', wrote Macarthur, 'but they are easily traced to their haunts'. At Camden Park near Sydney, Macarthur encouraged Aboriginal people to capture these mammal pests. The Aboriginal people presumably killed and ate the animals, according to long-established tradition, and perhaps made the skins into cloaks. Although these Aboriginal people were welcome at Camden Park, other would-be grape thieves (Macarthur does not stipulate settler or Aboriginal) were hunted away. Macarthur advised that 'no

130   *Julie McIntyre*

one possessing a vineyard will omit the protection of a formidable hedge fence, as well as a watchman with a gun, assisted by faithful dogs, when the grapes are ripe'.[19]

The principal animal threat, however, lay skyward. The silvereye, Macarthur tells us, 'would seem almost to forbid the cultivation of the vine; for they destroy twenty times as much as they consume'. These tiny green and grey birds, marked with a distinctive white eye ring, 'select the finest and ripest berries upon a bunch, and having pierced them with their bills, suck out a little of the richest juice, and then attack another bunch'. Compared with the silvereyes, some larger birds (presumably the rosellas, ravens and magpies that lived in the Sydney Basin) 'are not nearly so formidable, as they are easily seen and shot or scared away'. But the silvereyes

> steal unperceived amongst the vines, and in a short time, do an incredible amount of damage. The only methods I have found effective in restraining, and, I may almost add, in altogether preventing their ravages, are, to pursue and shoot them, if possible, at all seasons of the year, and to seek out their nests and destroy them. By keeping up this system at all times, particularly when there is no fruit to tempt them, it is remarkable what an impression may at length be made upon these little marauders. Although for a time their numbers may not appear to diminish, still, if the gun be constantly used, they become so thinned, and the remnant so scared, that in the fruit season they may be frequently seen passing over a *well-kept* garden or vineyard without venturing to alight within its precincts.[20]

To control silvereyes, Macarthur furnished Aboriginal children with firearms and paid them a 'pittance' for each bird carcass they shot and produced as evidence.

The notion that fear of noise or death led silvereyes to avoid Macarthur's vineyards is an intriguing glimpse into their learned behaviour. Macarthur also noted that native mammals were alert to danger and 'will not approach watchful dogs, and may, by this means, be kept away'. Although Macarthur saw the animals as pests, he also recognised their agency. He perceived the animals weighing up their desire for food against the potential for harm.

The behaviour of insects is not so readily accessed as birds and mammals, although some observations survive. In 1842, Ludwig Leichhardt found the vine moth's adaptation to feeding on *V. vinifera* to be 'the most striking example' of native animals turning to introduced sources of nourishment compared with, say, native ants eating cow dung. The caterpillar of the vine moth continued to feed on native plants as previously, especially one 'with the knots and tendrils of the grape vine with beautiful dark-green, oval leaves', but preferred 'the introduced grape-vine'.[21] Henry Carmichael reported to the Hunter River Vineyard Association in 1849 that a 'green knob-headed' species of caterpillar had transferred its attention from vine leaves to vine blossoms, which posed a far greater threat to Carmichael's fruit crop.[22] Caterpillars appeared annually in larger or smaller numbers, depending on other environmental factors, such as rainfall. Some other native insects ranged more widely, and their feeding habits were less predictable. In 1851, for example, grasshoppers destroyed twenty acres of vines in the Upper Hunter Valley.[23]

Invasive diseases and pests that attacked V. vinifera in other countries were not identified in Australia until the 1860s. Powdery mildew (Oidium tuckerii) appeared in Queensland in 1867 and subsequently spread to the other eastern colonies, and in 1877, grape phylloxera was detected in Victoria. These invasive species both originated in the United States and arrived in Australia via Britain and Europe. Powdery mildew devastated wine production in Europe and elsewhere until scientists identified sulphur spray as the remedy. Phylloxera also caused tremendous damage to grapevines and, as a result, to wine volumes and traditions of wine trade globally before the solution of grafting V. vinifera onto phylloxera-resistant rootstock from America, such as Vitis labrusca, which became widespread in the 1880s. This grafting process is still used today to control phylloxera.[24]

From the 1870s, invasive hares and rabbits caused ecological havoc in vineyards. Victorian vine growers were among those farmers seeking permission to cull hares in opposition to the settler sportsmen and acclimatisers who supported the spread of lagomorphs for hunting. The debates that raged over the fate of hares in the colonial press also referred to continuing problems in vineyards from native parrots and invasive sparrows.[25]

After the 1870s, the nature of pesthood in Australian vineyards as configured within wine science and industry indiscriminately encompassed native and invasive animals, insects and mildews. With the inauguration in 1890 of the *Agricultural Gazette of New South Wales*, formal communication with grape growers and winemakers about pests and other matters in the colony transferred away from the newspaper press to this exclusive, specialised publication. When an expert viticulturalist was appointed, the modern separation of the development and circulation of scientific knowledge on vines and wine from public eyes was complete.

Although animals continued to feed in vineyards, their presence disappeared from broader view as their treatment as destructive pests became further naturalised. In the 1920s, another American fungous disease was detected in Australia. Downy mildew affecting grapes (*Plasmopara viticola*) proved more destructive than powdery mildew but could also be controlled with sulphur spray.[26] In the 1930 federal parliamentary inquiry into the Australian wine industry, vineyards were conceived of only as economic places, with pest removal factored as an expenditure, not in relation to the lives of the animals. At the national scale, discussion of animals in vineyards, whether native or invasive, was outweighed by concerns to promote industry growth through attention to economic inputs and to licensing and export.[27] The fate of animals was subsumed into the notion of the environment as an externality which could be omitted from economic calculations. The animals were still there, however, and the historical lacing together of silvereyes, grapes and humans is captured beautifully in Mary Card's 1930s Grape Vine and Silvereye Tea Cloth and Table Mat (see Figure 10.1). Biocultural

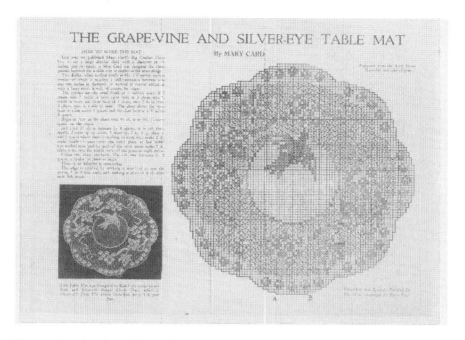

Figure 10.1 This design for a table mat, and one for a larger and more complex tea cloth, captured the popular association of silvereyes with vineyards in the 1930s.

Source: Grapevine and Silver Eye Table Mat, 1937. *Collection of Mary Card's crochet patterns and giant crochet charts*, held by State Library of NSW, Q746.43/8.

belonging is evident in Card's design which symbolises the many generations of silvereyes (as well as vine moths and other animals) which had by this time been heartily nourished by the wood, leaves, shoots and fruit of *V. Vinifera*, although the industry chose not to acknowledge such connections. The recommendations of the Report on the Wine Industry had little effect, and the industry remained in stasis until the 1960s.[28] Australia's increasing urbanisation and modernity further disconnected public consciousness from wine and narratives of wine generally, and the possibility of a popular conception of vineyards as complex ecological spaces sank further from view.

Morkit and dieldrin in the 1970s wine industry

Post-war prosperity and a rising middle class with new social freedoms and transport mobilities led to a reinvigoration of the Australian wine industry from the 1960s. The many cultural changes of the period included the first national campaigns encouraging women to drink wine and the expansion of

Wine worlds are animal worlds too   133

opportunities to drink wine in company with the relaxation of restrictions on the service of alcohol and the establishment of new city restaurants. By the end of the 1970s, although beer remained the dominant alcohol of choice, many white, urban Australians viewed themselves as belonging to a wine-drinking country.[29]

Thanks to new mobilities offered by motor cars, wine tourism and festivals in wine regions became a popular form of entertainment. From 1965 to 1973, as Hunter Valley vineyard plantings extended beyond Pokolbin near Cessnock to Muswellbrook in the Upper Hunter, the Cessnock Vintage Festival metamorphosed into the Hunter Vintage Festival. What is of interest for animal studies scholars is that brochures for these festivals capture a narrative on vine growing and wine in which native animals as vineyard pests suddenly appear and then disappear within the space of a few years. Consumers were briefly provided with a candid insight into the conflict between animals and humans in vineyards and then firmly excluded from this more realistic view of the destruction of animals for winegrowing.

The tourist guide for the 1969 Greater Cessnock Vintage Festival features a range of maps and articles instructing visitors about wine history and wine appreciation. Among these pages is a short section titled 'Some Bird Pests in the Vineyard', by Athel D'Ombrain, a well-known Hunter Valley naturalist.[30] D'Ombrain argued that although Australian birds are a great source of aesthetic pleasure, farmers have no alternative but to protect their livelihood through 'controlled killing'. The (invasive) starling, he says, is the 'greatest menace' in sultana vineyards in the New South Wales Riverina, although, in their favour, these birds eat vine insects out of fruiting season. According to D'Ombrain, silvereyes helped growers control aphids, thrips and caterpillars. But once the grapes ripened, this tiny tenacious bird committed the greater crime than starlings by puncturing individual berries, allowing juice to flow and causing bunch rot. The solution for vine growers? 'Science has come up with a spray known as "Morkit", an imported spray which causes an upset to the bird's digestion' (a euphemism for killing them), although he noted that some growers expressed reservations about this method. D'Ombrain explained that rosellas were not as much of a problem as ravens which smash off whole grape bunches, and there were fewer of these large birds at the winemaking centre Pokolbin because cattle slaughtering facilities had been relocated to another town. Other problematic birds for winegrowers were honey-eating friar birds and the common black-backed magpie. D'Ombrain concluded by advising that such pesticides as dieldrin were very effective to control vine moth caterpillars but harmed bird species, 'good and bad', and shooting (to kill and scare), along with explosive devices, such as carbide cannons, 'are the most direct and positive ways of combating' birds.

Following D'Ombrain's frank description of interspecies warfare in the ecologies that host vineyards, the tourist guide for the following event, the Hunter Vintage Festival of 1973, did not refer to vineyard pests or their eradication. From the 1970s, the Australian wine industry's public relations staff ensured

134   Julie McIntyre

that the reputation of wine remained untarnished by association with unsociable outcomes of drinking, including drunkenness.[31] Surely, with a long-developed sense of consumer-facing storytelling about wine, the Hunter Valley wine community quickly discerned that stories of animal deaths by poisons and gunfire would also fail to win them customers, especially among women, who the industry was working hard to reassure about the respectability of wine, and members of the new post-war incarnation of Australia's environmental movement, who were certainly lovers of wine.[32] Prominent environmental campaigners have acknowledged the 'personal impact' of Rachel Carson's *Silent Spring* (1963), which drew attention to the devastation of American bird life, from chemical solutions to insect pests.[33] Some connection is also likely between wine industry awareness of rising consciousness of the toxic effect on ecosystems of chemical use in agriculture and the concealing of the use of pesticides and other pest-control methods in wine discourse.

Although interspecies conflict was concealed from wine consumers, it increased as more vineyards were planted. Birds were a problem for people forging new relationships with non-human nature through grape growing for wine. In new wine-growing regions in Western Australia, there were intense responses by silvereyes, and growers' experiences echoed those of Macarthur in the 1840s. Oral history interviewee Tom Cullity planted his Margaret River vines in 1967, and they first fruited in 1970, but 'the first vintage – oh, God, the vines were all rotten. The grapes were rotten . . . I thought it was birds – silver-eyes. A lot of it was but I think a lot of it was bunch rot as well. . . . My heart sank, I know that. But we made some wine out of it'.[34] Fellow Margaret River winegrower Tony Devitt perceived that the vines were a lifeline for birds. 'Amazing silvereyes', he recalls, 'They really got to know about the grapes.' They 'tended to breed in the coastal scrub'. He continues, 'Numbers increased. Summer came, it got pretty hot and most of the birds died out. Went back to something normal, and then bred up. Back and forward, back and forward. They went to the forest for their food during the flowering of the red gums and things like that'. But when the flowering of the gums was delayed, 'grapevines came along and filled in a bit of a gap – a hard gap – for them'.[35]

When the River Red gum blossoms failed, silvereyes flocked to Betty Quick's vines in Denmark, Western Australia. One year, Quick and her family drove continually up and down vine rows in her car to prevent birds alighting on ripening grape bunches. The motion of the car coated the grape bunches in dust, but there were grapes to harvest, and the wine won awards.[36] Other interviewees recall children of vineyard families firing guns to deter or kill the birds (echoing the practices in Macarthur's vineyard), and some growers used new methods, such as the musical scares involving the loud playing of recorded music as a bird repellent.[37]

As with this range of bird deterrents, from the 1970s to the 1990s, the use of chemicals against vine moths and other insect pests in vineyards lessened. At first, as Drew Hutton and Libby Connors point out of the wider use of agrichemicals, anti-pesticide campaigns had little effect against the powerful the pesticide industry, but this changed with the banning of certain toxins in agriculture.[38] Growers welcomed bans on chemicals that were highly toxic to humans, animals outside of vineyards and vineyard soils, although other chemicals are still used in many vineyards to control insect 'pests'. As for the birds, the small western silvereye destroyed wine grape crops, 'three years out of five' into the 1990s, when netting became an affordable means of protecting grape crops against them.[39] Wine producers demonstrate greater awareness of sharing vineyards with non-human nature other than the grapevines, and today the reality of this troubled biocultural interconnection is shared by some wine producers with consumers.

Virtuous *Vitis*?

This chapter's survey of evidence on the configuration and control of native animals as pests in Australian wine grape vineyards reveals a continuity of native animal opportunism, from Macarthur's experience in the 1840s in New South Wales to those of Cullity, Devitt and Pearse in Western Australia more than a century later. My argument has been intended to achieve two outcomes. First, it serves as a step towards recasting the conceptual specialness of wine grape vineyards as they are now understood by wine consumers by demonstrating that they do not exist in an animal-free monocultural terroir. Vine growers have, of course, always known that their vineyards are part of a wider ecosystem, the animal inhabitants of which had impacts on their crops. Although ecologists employed by the state prioritise and, where necessary, protect native animals, other state experts and officeholders focused on other forms of science and economics agree with winegrowers that native animals are pests.

Second, this chapter has aimed to untangle the identities of native animals from a blanket pesthood where all the animals that feed on grapevines, whether native or invasive, are unwelcome in the ecologies that host vineyards. Despite the actions taken against them, of the native animals best known as vine and grape feeders, neither vine moths nor silvereyes have become endangered species. Their symbiosis with *V. vinifera*, although fatal for many individual animals, has produced a state of equilibrium which has not reduced the species per se and in certain seasons spurred their breeding practices.

Finally, towards a clearer sense of 'biocultural belonging', a few remarks are due on *V. vinifera* as invasive in Australia. As Rolls implies with his passionate reflection on vines and wine, this plant is not a pest in wider Australian ecologies. It rarely escapes the bounds of human control in its new environments. *Vitis* plants are slow growing compared with grasses and not aggressively self-seeding. *V. vinifera* does not behave in the 'way of the weed', such as purslane, knotgrass and snakeweed, which, as Alfred Crosby observes, highlighted 'the vulnerability of the Australian flora to Old World invasion'.[40] Although larger invasive fruiting plants, such as blackberry and lantana, are problematic in Australia, grapevines are not.[41] *V. vinifera* has co-invaders that are greatly destructive of grapevines, but powdery mildew and phylloxera do not appear to adversely affect any other plants and animals. Nevertheless, the relative virtues – and indeed the great pleasures

136 Julie McIntyre

to be had from consuming wine or visiting wine grape regions – should not cloud perceptions of the processes of wine production that implicate animals as well as people and plants. An ecological understanding of wine disrupts the power balance of the Anthropocene that allows humans to consciously erase the existence of animals as co-inhabitants of the ecological spaces cultivated by humans. Re-entangling animals into consumer awareness of economic processes in the commodity production of wine encourages greater attention to environmental as well as economic and social sustainability in viticulture and perhaps in agriculture more broadly.

Notes

1 Grateful thanks are due to editors Nancy Cushing and Jodi Frawley for their guidance and patience, to Liz Downes for intelligence on hares in Victorian vineyards and to David Harris for sharing memories of silvereyes in Melbourne. On the introduction of grape species, see Julie McIntyre, *First Vintage: Wine in Colonial New South Wales* (Sydney: University of NSW Press, 2012).

2 David Dunstan, *Better Than Pommard!: A History of Wine in Victoria* (Melbourne: Australian Scholarly Publishing, 1994).

3 See, for example, McIntyre, *First Vintage*.

4 See Fernand Braudel, *The Identity of France, Volume One: History and Environment*, translated by Sian Reynolds (New York: Harper & Row, 1990); Fernand Braudel, *The Identity of France, Volume Two: People and Production*, translated by Sian Reynolds (New York: Harper Perennial, 1986); see also Gwyn Campbell and Nathalie Guibert (eds.), *Wine, Society, and Globalization: Multidisciplinary Perspectives on the Wine Industry* (New York: Palgrave Macmillan, 2007).

5 Erica Hannickel, *Empire of Vines: Wine Culture in America* (Philadelphia: University of Pennsylvania Press, 2013), 1, 3.

6 Hannickel, *Empire of Vines*, 3.

7 Eric Rolls, *A Celebration of Food and Wine: Of Grain, of Grapes, of Gethsemane* (St Lucia: University of Queensland Press, 1997), esp. 44–173.

8 Eric Rolls, *They All Ran Wild: The Animals and Plants That Plague Australia* (Sydney: Angus & Robertson, 1984), the first Australian account of introduced plants and animals as agents of ecological change. Rolls argues that methods of dealing with these change agents were problematic. See also Eric Rolls, *A Million Wild Acres: 200 Years of Man and an Australian Forest* (Sydney: Hale & Iremonger, 2011).

9 Emily O'Gorman, 'Belonging: Living Lexicon for the Environmental Humanities,' *Environmental Humanities*, 5 (2014): 283–6.

10 Joni Adamson, 'Introduction', in Joni Adamson and Michael Davis (ed.), *Humanities for the Environment: Integration Knowledge, Forging New Constellations of Practice* (Abingdon UK: Routledge, 2017), 15.

11 Julie McIntyre and John Germov, 'The Changing Global Taste for Wine: An Historical Sociological Perspective', in *A Sociology of Food and Nutrition: The Social Appetite* (Melbourne: Oxford University Press, 2017), 202–18.

12 Hannickel, *Empire of Vines*, 1–8, 228.

13 There is an extensive research literature on the politics of terroir and the possibility of its scientific basis. Soils may be managed to achieve 'expression of place' for premium products versus generic wines undistinguished by their origins. Soil management strategies to determine wine specificity include encouragement of soil organisms, application of fertilisers and the quantity of water available to grapevines. Robert E. White, *Understanding Vineyard Soils* (Oxford: Oxford University Press, 2015), 225. See also

Julie McIntyre, 'Resisting Ages-old Fixity as a Factor in Wine Quality: Colonial Wine Tours and Australia's Early Wine Industry', *Locale: The Australasian-Pacific Journal of Regional Food Studies*, 1.1 (2011): 42–64.

14 Marion Demossier, *Burgundy: A Global Anthropology of Place and Taste*, (Oxford: Berghahn, 2018).

15 Nicolaas Mink, 'It Begins in the Belly', *Environmental History*, 14 (April 2009): 315; see also Alfred Crosby, *Ecological Imperialism: The Biological Expansion of Europe 900–1900* (Cambridge: Cambridge University Press, 2004).

16 James Busby, *A Treatise on the Culture of the Vine and the Art of Making Wine: Compiled from the Works of Chaptal, and Other French Writers; and from the Notes of the Compiler, During a Residence in Some of the Wine Provinces of France*, facsimili edition (Sydney: David Ell Press, 1825/1979), 114–15.

17 James Busby, *A Manual of Plain Directions for Planting and Cultivating a Vineyard and for Making Wine in New South Wales* (Sydney: Printed by R. Mansfield, for the executors of R. Howe, 1830), 49–50.

18 Inscription in the flyleaf of Frederick Hely's copy of Busby, *Manual*, n.p. The State Library of New South Wales holds eight copies of the *Manual*. Hely's copy is Dixon Library (DL) 634.8/B copy 1.

19 Maro (William Macarthur), *Letters on the Culture of the Vine, Fermentation, and the Management of Wine in the Cellar* (Sydney: Statham and Forster, 1844), 34.

20 (Macarthur), *Letters on the Culture of the Vine*, 34. Macarthur's emphasis.

21 Assembled from diary entries, Ludwig Leichhardt, *The Leichhardt Diaries: Early Travels in Australia During 1842–1844*, eds. Thomas Darragh and Roderick Fensham (South Brisbane: Queensland Museum, 2013), 33–40.

22 *Maitland Mercury*, 5 May 1849.

23 *Maitland Mercury*, 8 March 1851.

24 This section draws on McIntyre, *First Vintage*, 117–51. *V. vinifera* is the common grape for wine and for eating fresh and dried. There are also North American *Vitis* species in Australia, such as *V. labrusca*, but these are not used for wine and are omitted from this discussion for the sake of clarity.

25 See, for example, 'Hare Protection', Letter to the Editor, *Geelong Advertiser*, 31 August 1871 and 'The Geelong Vinegrowers' Association,' *The Age*, 14 June 1872.

26 Julie McIntyre and John Germov, *Hunter Wine: A History* (Sydney: NewSouth, 2018), Chapter 7, forthcoming.

27 John Gunn and R. M. Gollan, *Report on the Wine Industry of Australia*, presented to Federal Parliament, 17 July 1931 (Canberra: Commonwealth of Australia, 1931).

28 The emergence of Australian wine culture from the 1960s to 1980s is explored in Julie McIntyre and John Germov, '"Who Wants to Be a Millionaire?" I Do: Postwar Australian Wine, Gendered Culture and Class', *Journal of Australian Studies*, 42.1, 2018: 65–84.

29 The emergence of Australian wine culture from the 1960s to 1980s is explored in Julie McIntyre and John Germov, 'Who Wants to Be a Millionaire?'.

30 The Greater Cessnock Vintage Festival 1969, SLNSW call no. Q634.8105/1, 36–7.

31 McIntyre and Germov, 'Who Wants to Be a Millionaire?'.

32 For example, Arnold Ewald, who is known to the author and mentioned in Drew Hutton and Libby Connors, *A History of the Australian Environmental Movement* (Melbourne: Cambridge University Press, 1999), 213; also see Rolls, *Celebration*, 104–5.

33 Hutton and Connors, *A History*, 96; Rachel Carson, *Silent Spring* (London: Hamish Hamilton, 1969), 84–105.

34 Interview with Dr Tom Cullity, 25 July 2000 by Rob Linn, OH 692/30, Treading Out the Vintage, National Wine Centre, Wolf Blass Foundation Oral History Project, recordings and transcripts held at State Library of South Australia (SLSA).

35 Interview with Tony Devitt in Perth on 26 July 2000, interviewer Rob Linn, OH 692/34, SLSA.

138 *Julie McIntyre*

36 Interview with Betty Quick/Betty Pearse, at Denmark Western Australia, 5 October 2001, interview by Rob Linn OH 692/137, SLSA.
37 Interview with Micky Clifford and Leila Glen Clifford, 23 July 2002, interviewed by Rob Linn, OH 692/23, SLSA.
38 Hutton and Connors, *A History*, 212–15.
39 Interview with David Hohnen in Adelaide on 5th December 2002, interviewer unstated, OH 692/68, SLSA.
40 Crosby, *Ecological Imperialism*, 162.
41 Rolls, *They All Ran Wild*, 269.

11 Defending nature
Animals and militarised landscapes in Australia

Ben Wilkie

Introduction

Warfare is one of the most intense and far-reaching of human activities in its ecological and geographical impacts over time and space. The legacies of war for the environment and animals are publicly well understood and, indeed, are well documented in more specific cases. White phosphorous used in grenades has been linked to the deaths of thousands of waterfowls in Alaska; cadmium, lead, mercury, and uranium from bombing ranges in Puerto Rico have entered the food chain of the island; flame retardants at air force bases in the United States have proven toxic to fish; herbicides, such as the infamous Agent Orange, defoliated vast swathes of Southeast Asian forest cover during military operations in the 1960s, and to this day, high levels of dioxins are still found in the food chain, particularly in ducks and fish.[1] As Charles E. Closmann summarised it, 'Military conflict is often a cause and consequence of environmental decline . . . military operations (and occupations) can have devastating effects on natural resources, making the study of the relationship between war and the environment vitally important'.[2]

To help us to understand some of the impacts of conflict, ecologists Gary Machlis and Thor Hanson put forward a taxonomy of warfare that includes preparations for war, war itself, and post-war activities. All stages of warfare produce ecological impacts of various intensities and scales. Among post-war activities are long-term alterations to land use and settlement patterns, continued contamination and health risks, groundwater pollution, and socioeconomic disruption leading to loss of resource management programmes.[3] It would seem that, given the nature of war and the military, the question of impacts on animals and their habitats appears settled: war is destructive of animal life. Emerging from the relationship between war and the environment, however, is something of a paradox: some war-related activities may benefit animal habitats, especially if we move beyond the battlefield. Military training areas in particular cover at least 50 million hectares of land globally, an area approximating the size of France. Due to the frequently opaque and uneven nature of information regarding military assets, this is likely a significant underestimate.[4] Among conservationists and ecologists, it is increasingly understood that these training sites and defence bases often have significant conservation values, and – with the correct policy settings – can play a critical complementary role in international biodiversity conservation.[5] This chapter uses the Puckapunyal Military Training Area in central Victoria, Australia, case study as a springboard for exploring the history of environmental policy in the Australian armed forces and the broader implications for animal populations in militarised landscapes. It reveals the evolution of military environmental discourses and practices that have developed along highly contingent, path-dependent lines, and highlights the complicated, multifarious nature of military training sites and the relationships between their human and non-human occupants. The question of animals in militarised landscapes is far from settled and significantly more complex than a relationship of domination at the hands of destructive forces.

Geographer Rachel Woodward has dismissed the assertion of military lands assisting with conservation as a discursive strategy emanating from the defence establishment to legitimise militarised environments and military control of land, describing the attempts to connect biological diversity with defence estates as 'a sort of military creationism'.[6] This extends on the central critique of the political consequences of military-owned lands, which is that 'militarism and military activities in nonconflict situations exert [discursive and material] control over space in ways and through means which frequently render this control invisible'.[7] Both positions can be accepted, however, with a recognition that military environmentalist discourses have a political function – to assert control over military lands – while also acknowledging that the ecological diversity of defence estates remains a material reality. As Chris Pearson argues, 'the relationships between war, militarization and the environment are more nuanced and complex than the pro-/anti-military dichotomy suggests', although, of course, we must always subject politically charged military discourses around the environment to critical analysis.[8]

Indeed, the picture emerging from ecological studies of military training areas is that cycles of disturbance from shelling or heavy armour, for example, combine with a lack of intensive land use (agriculture, forestry, and mining) and public exclusion to create heterogeneous conditions which provide rich opportunities for biological diversity.[9] Patrick Wright has written of 'crater as habitat' in reference to landscapes, shaped by military activity, which favour some species that otherwise struggle in 'civilian landscapes'.[10] In fact, the withdrawal of military activities, and thus disruption of such ecological dynamics, from some sites has been accompanied by concerns over the future of threatened species that previously found sanctuary at these active military sites.[11] As Pearson notes, 'the relationship between war, militarization, and landscape is more complex than one characterised by military domination and destruction of the environment'.[12]

Furthermore, the subject of conservation at military training areas has implications beyond military geographies. The increasing awareness of the ecological and conservation value of military training sites worldwide and, in recent decades, a shift of policy discourse towards the language of sustainability and environmental responsibility, highlights the subjective, contested nature of land and wildlife conservation measures more generally.

Protected areas, such as national parks, have been established to protect ecosystems and species, but their ability to do so optimally is contingent on the historical conservation, as well as political and economic, contexts in which they were established. The oldest reserves protect areas that are aesthetically pleasing, geologically and topographically unique, or, frequently, areas that were then unsuited to agricultural, pastoral, or extractive industries and development. It is only more recently that protected areas have been established to safeguard biological diversity and ecological processes and to encourage ecosystem and species restoration. This historical gap in protected area types is filled to an extent, however, by a range of typically human-affected landscapes, including military training sites, which often overlap otherwise historically underprotected ecosystems and species but which encompass significantly different ecological disturbance regimes than, for instance, agriculture.[13]

As this chapter observes, however, the protection of ecological diversity at these sites is often, but not always, subject to and limited by the requirements of maintaining defence capabilities. Woodward rightly notes that a metaphor of balance between environmental protectionism and the needs of military training is central to military environmental discourse. As in the United Kingdom and North America, the boundaries of conservationism on Australian military training areas have been set by normative understandings of national defence requirements.[14] Furthermore, although the maintenance of landscapes has obvious benefits for the utility of training sites – to avoid soil erosion, for instance – the presence of various animal populations pose more complicated sets of issues that intersect with competing political interests and with evolving cultural attitudes towards both defence activities and environmental protection.

The restoration and revegetation of Puckapunyal, 1971–85[15]

In 1975, a technical memorandum from the Commonwealth Scientific and Industrial Research Organisation (CSIRO) observed that 'As well as deferring to a growing public awareness of ecological values and concern for the environment it is advantageous for the Defence Forces to conserve areas under their control and to maintain them in a condition suitable for the purposes for which they were acquired'.[16] The language of deferment to public environmental concern highlights the shaping of a new military environmentalist discourse in Australia that, much like similar strategies in the United Kingdom and North America, emphasised military environmental stewardship. Indeed, the CSIRO researchers continued:

> The Army may derive satisfaction in giving a lead in the conservation of land used by Governments – ecological studies and revegetation works began on Army Training Areas before the Australian Government established a Department of Environment and Conservation.[17]

142   *Ben Wilkie*

As an outcome of discussions between the Australian Army and the CSIRO in 1969, the latter organisation agreed to begin ecological studies of military training areas, with a focus on land management and environmental conservation. The initial sites designated for CSIRO studies throughout 1970 included army training areas at Puckapunyal in Victoria in addition to four Queensland bases at High Range, Shoalwater Bay, Canungra, and Tully. By the middle of the 1970s, the research programme had been extended, and studies were completed at training sites across Australia: Enoggera and Mount Stuart in Queensland; Bindoon, Lancelin, and Swanbourne in Western Australia; Murray Bridge, Cultana, and Lincoln Park in South Australia; Holsworthy in New South Wales; Queenscliff and Portsea in Victoria; and Buckland in Tasmania.[18]

This research was to provide information on the sites that would 'permit their continued use for military training purposes and as far as is consistent with their use for such purposes permit their management for the conservation of vegetation, soil, wildlife, and related matters'. Furthermore, the CSIRO was to 'advise the Army on remedial measures necessary to halt degeneration on new training areas and to regenerate and re-establish vegetation on areas which have been degraded by military operations'.[19] Conservation was permissible but within limits: environmental programmes and policies were to be subject to and limited by the requirements of maintaining defence capabilities.

Perhaps the most significant of such projects at the time – 'one of the largest single landscape revegetation operations yet attempted in Australia and perhaps anywhere', suggested the CSIRO – took place at the Puckapunyal Military Training Area in central Victoria, which had been used for military purposes since the First World War.[20] Today, Puckapunyal is home to 44,000 hectares of box-ironbark ecosystem, of which over three quarters has been cleared elsewhere in the state. There are 12 endangered or vulnerable vegetation communities, 481 indigenous and 225 introduced plant species, and 170 species of lichens, mosses, and fungi. It is a rich site of biodiversity and holds high conservation value, now forming an extensive wildlife corridor with neighbouring state parks. It is registered as a Land for Wildlife property, has been placed on the Register of the National Estate, and is listed as a Commonwealth Heritage Site on the grounds of its biological significance.[21] The area forms integral habitat for a range of animals. Puckapunyal today supports 185 native bird species, 17 indigenous and 15 introduced mammals, 12 kinds of bat, 18 species of reptile, and 12 species of amphibian, 7 native and 4 introduced kinds of fish, and over 140 species of invertebrates.[22]

At the same time, Puckapunyal is one of the Department of Defence's most intensively used training areas, and it is a significant element in the maintenance of Australia's defence capabilities (see Figure 11.1). Between 60,000 and 70,000 training days, involving 12,000 vehicles and 1,000 live-firing exercises, are undertaken at Puckapunyal every year, and up to 3,500 people are present at the site on any given day.[23] Its restoration and conservation since the 1970s has been driven by both environmental protectionism and militarism, and it represents a

Figure 11.1 The Puckapunyal military training area, circa 1940, showing the initial degradation of the environment.

Source: *Argus* Newspaper Colllection of Photographs, State Library of Victoria.

144 *Ben Wilkie*

useful case study of how militaries – and other organisations – have attempted to establish a balance of these two interests.

In the aftermath of European colonisation in the mid-nineteenth century, the land around Puckapunyal – traditionally belonging to the Taungurung people – was utilised for intensive sheep and cattle grazing, later followed by gold mining and logging for timber and firewood in the area's box and ironbark forests. Land degradation and accelerated soil erosion was severe in most of the area by the early twentieth century – the soils at Puckapunyal were and are particularly susceptible to erosion after disturbance – and caused siltation of the nearby creek systems that formed tributaries of the Goulburn River.[24] Military training commenced at Puckapunyal during the First World War, and the Department of Defence formally purchased the site from pastoral landowners during 1939. It was one of the largest infantry training sites in Australia, becoming home to the 1st Infantry Brigade, the 3rd National Service Training Brigade, the Royal Australian Army Service Corps Centre, and even school cadets. During the Second World War, the US 41st Infantry Division trained there, and from 1949, Puckapunyal was home to the 1st Armoured Regiment.[25]

Historical land use impacts and heavy military usage, with little attention paid to land management or maintenance, eventually left the area barren and denuded. One newspaper described it in 1953 as the 'most desolate and barren military camp in Victoria'.[26] Some early attempts to improve the area were made, although it is unclear whether this was for environmental remediation or for purely aesthetic reasons; certainly, animals were not a core concern at this point. In the early 1950s, the Australian Army in consultation with the Commonwealth Arboculturalist and the Department of Works and Housing 'embarked upon a programme of reafforestation at Puckapunyal in an attempt to remedy the damage caused to the camp by the endless tramping of hundreds of thousands of soldiers'. *The Age* reported:

> Seventy trees have already been planted on the camp by ex-servicemen who trained at Puckapunyal. . . . All associations of former wartime units which trained at Puckapunyal will be asked to help in the reafforestation plan. Every national service trainee who enters the camp to do his 98 days' service is now obliged to plant a tree.[27]

The enlistment of defence personnel would presage later attempts at restoration. By the 1960s, however, half of the range area was impassable in winter because of waterlogging and severe erosion. For the tanks of the armoured division, these areas were unsafe and unusable. By 1969, the army was faced with two alternatives: '(1) to rehabilitate the area, or (2) to abandon it with consequent loss of facilities and the certainty of having to face similar problems elsewhere in the future'.[28] The former option was taken, but it presented numerous challenges: the soils were of low fertility, made worse by widespread erosion; and the climate was not amenable to standard practices in revegetation works. Furthermore, as one report acknowledged ten years after the commencement of the project, 'Cost

Defending nature   145

and time considerations rule out the use of normal farm techniques of ploughing and harrowing to prepare seedbeds. Unexploded bombs and shells (UXOs) posed serious hazards to ploughing and deep ripping'.[29]

Despite these unique challenges, the Puckapunyal Restoration and Conservation Project began work in 1971. Officially operating under the auspices of defence, the research and scientific support for the project was provided by the CSIRO, while the Victorian Soil Conservation Authority managed operations and provided its expertise in soil erosion and land restoration. By 1985, the extensive program of earthworks, soil and water erosion control, and revegetation had been completed on 20,000 hectares of land. Some 5,000 hectares of barren and denuded landscape was repaired, and 16,000 hectares of improved pasture had been established. At the completion of the project, land management and scientific officers were appointed to continually monitor and research the Puckapunyal site. A rest and restore program was implemented, creating 'no-go' areas where the land was overused, where new vegetation was establishing itself or was otherwise sensitive to environmental changes, or where research was being conducted.[30] Up to this point, the focus had been on restoring a landscape, not on a habitat for animals. The question of animal populations inevitably arose, however, as the ecology of Puckapunyal was re-established, and they would be shaped in large part by emerging public and political concern about biological diversity in Australia.

Conservation and controversy: animals at Puckapunyal since the 1980s

The evolution of land management and wildlife conservation at Puckapunyal since the large-scale restoration projects of the 1970s and 1980s has occurred in the context of a similarly evolving state and national policy framework. The recognition of the need for a national approach to conservation and biodiversity brought about the Commonwealth Endangered Species Advisory Committee in 1988, a national Endangered Species Program in 1989, and the creation of an Endangered Species Unit as part of the federal environment agency in the same year. Building on the United States' Endangered Species Act of 1974 and the Victorian Flora and Fauna Guarantee Act of 1988, a federal Endangered Species Protection Act was passed in 1992; Australia ratified the Convention on Biological Diversity in 1993.[31]

The prominence of environmental awareness and concern in the Australian community from the 1980s onwards therefore found expression in various state and Commonwealth policies and laws, and it was in this milieu of change that the Australian defence forces started to consider their environmental impact in a more systematic and serious way. It was in the wake of the Endangered Species Protection Act that Australia's Department of Defence began to consider further country-wide environmental management and protection programmes.

In March 1995, the facilities division of the Department of Defence and the chief executive officer of the Australian Nature Conservation Agency signed a

146 Ben Wilkie

new Memorandum of Understanding. It broadly described how Australia's armed forces would go about meeting their obligations under the new Endangered Species Protection Act with regard to the 'lands and waters under control of the Department of Defence'. The department agreed to 'commence a review in 1994/95 of existing biological information for Defence land, to prepare a preliminary inventory of the presence and abundance of listed species and to identify priorities for further inventory work as well as recovery action'. It agreed to prepare and implement recovery plans for listed species on the lands it owned, develop threat abatement strategies, and incorporate this work into existing environmental management plans for its military sites. In return, the Nature Conservation Agency would 'provide educational materials on endangered species issues and the ESP Act . . . for distribution to Local Commanders and Environmental Advisory Committees'.[32] Importantly, the text of the memorandum does not equivocate on the priority of adhering to the Endangered Species Protection Act, distinguishing it from earlier agreements – such as that between the army and the CSIRO in 1969.

For animals at Puckapunyal, the practical impacts of these policy shifts have been evident in the results of monitoring programmes. Bush stone-curlew, tuan, common dunnart, powerful owl, barking owl, and lace monitor, among many others, are regularly recorded today.[33] In the 1990s, however, all these species were otherwise considered threatened in Victoria.[34] The tuan, for example, was thought rare in Victoria in the early to mid-1990s; assessments at Puckapunyal since 1995, however, have recorded a 65% increase in juveniles. Reports of the common dunnart increased from 13 sites at Puckapunyal in 1995–96 to 67 sites in the mid-2000s. Similarly, the bush stone-curlew, although believed to inhabit parts of Puckapunyal in the 1950s, was rare by the time of environmental assessments in 1995; numbers increased from 3 breeding pairs and 9 individual birds, at that time, to 14 pairs and 31 birds in the mid-2000s. Two pairs of powerful owls were known to live at the base in the 1970s, and by 2006, 11 breeding pairs and 3 single birds were recorded.[35]

Although conservation programmes emphasised utility for defence requirements, the restoration project of the 1970s and 1980s had, in reality, reimagined Puckapunyal as both a military training area *and* a natural landscape for vegetation and habitat for animals. This is evident in the re-emergence of native fauna at the site but also in the treatment of 'pest' species. Since the late 1980s, the site has been managed under various range standing orders, land management plans, and environmental management plans and systems that focus on the management of land, water, fire, and pollution. A key component of these plans since the mid-1990s has also been the management of rabbits, red foxes, and feral cats through baiting, shooting, trapping, and habitat control. The first baiting treatments in 1994 reduced the red fox population, for example, from 84 to 34 individuals (at selected monitoring sites); between 1995 and 2006, 121 cats have been shot or trapped, and in the 2000s, only 4 to 10 cats have been observed on the range – some of these are roaming domestic pets.[36] In any case, the management of these animals has likely been a significant factor in the flourishing of native faunal species.

Defending nature 147

The management of animals at Puckapunyal, however, has also been subject to controversy, thus further reflecting the intersection of defence environmental policy with changing attitudes to land management and conservation in the public sphere. Since the 1980s, a significant issue at Puckapunyal had been an increasing population of eastern grey kangaroos. A major drought in 2002–03 pushed kangaroo populations south from the northern areas of Victoria; population monitoring undertaken since 1983 put the number of kangaroos at Puckapunyal by the drought years at 80,000; the site, it was claimed, was unable to support a population this size. A plan to hire contractors to kill 15,000 kangaroos was met with protest from animal activists – one group referred to the cull as the Puckapunyal Military Massacre – although the RSPCA provided inspectors to ensure the cull was conducted humanely.[37] A second cull in 2003 was met with more objection, this time from the RSPCA itself.[38] More culls in 2013 and 2016 sparked further protest from animal rights groups.[39]

Broadly, however, the restoration project appears to have been a net benefit to native animal populations, providing habitat and sanctuary for various species that are endemic to the grassy woodlands that have otherwise not been well protected under traditional conservation models. The overall effect of the Endangered Species Protection Act on defence environmental policy was to provide impetus for creating a broader framework for wildlife and land conservation at military sites across Australia. Furthermore, it opened up possibilities for the Department of Defence to respond to increasing public and community interest in environmental and conservation issues. As it was during the emergence of early environmental policy in the military forces, Puckapunyal provided a testing ground for defence approaches to animal conservation that continue to develop to this day.[40]

Animals and militarised landscapes in an international perspective

The Puckapunyal case, and the broad discussion around the management of animals on defence estate in Australia, draws attention to some far wider, global considerations. As we have seen, the place of animals at Puckapunyal has been determined in part by the emergence of military environmental policy and practice and in part by the evolution of environmentalist discourse in the Australian community. This reflects the development of policies for outlining and establishing the environmental responsibilities of militaries internationally, which can also be attributed to the broader growth of environmentalism in the 1960s. This is true, at least, for the United Kingdom, where a Defence Lands Committee, chaired by Lord Nugent, was established in 1973 in response to growing public and political concerns about the environmental impacts of non-conflict military activities. An important and immediate outcome was the establishment of conservation officers at major military training areas in the United Kingdom. The Nugent inquiry set the tone for future military environmental policymaking: environmental and military needs could be balanced, although with priority given to the latter, with the correct managerial practices and policy settings. One

148   *Ben Wilkie*

critique of the framework established, however, is that little regard was given to remediating already-existing environmental damage at military training sites.[41] At the centre of military environmentalist discourses in the United Kingdom during the 1970s was the humble fairy shrimp, which found sanctuary at the Salisbury Plain tank training grounds, where it inhabits the ditches and ruts created by tank activity; the Salisbury Plain fairy shrimp became, in the wake of the Nugent inquiry, a 'weapon in the battle for hearts and minds of those who opposed military land ownership'.[42]

A key point, in any case, is that conservation at training areas has been limited by military requirements and that defence departments have tended to set the terms of environmental protection. In 1987, for example, the United Kingdom Ministry of Defence affirmed, 'In managing land which it owns or uses within the national parks, the MoD declares that it will endeavour to promote the objectives of the park authorities wherever these are compatible with the needs of national defence'.[43] In Australia, the origins of the relationship between environmental protectionism and militarism have been similar, with the distinct exception that defence environmental policy did not ignore the importance of remedying existing damage but rather emerged from remediation and restoration projects themselves.

Similar concerns have arisen in the United States, which has increased its defence training estate by around 1,200 hectares per year in recent times. Indeed, lands under the mandate of the United States National Parks Service only slightly exceed Department of Defence holdings in terms of their representation of ecological diversity.[44] As elsewhere, military landscapes in the United States have provided unexpected benefits for some species. Preble's meadow jumping mouse, for example, was endemic to streamside meadows in Colorado and south-east Wyoming, but its numbers have declined as 90% of its habitat has been occupied by agriculture, commerce, and residential developments since the 1960s. The Front Range base in Colorado has provided sanctuary for this threatened animal.[45] Elsewhere in Colorado, at the Rocky Mountain Arsenal and Rocky Flats military areas, militarisation led to 're-wilding' after the cessation of intensive cattle grazing. From the 1970s, prairie grasses began to re-establish themselves and created habitats for native herbivores, such a mule deer, and their predators. Outside the protection of this militarised area, the same animal populations have otherwise dwindled.[46]

The extent of conservation practice at such sites is bounded, as we have seen, by the needs and priorities of defence capability. How the defence forces approach issues of habitat and wildlife conservation has, however, moved in concert with broader public concerns about ecological and biological diversity. The question of animal populations has emerged as a significant feature of wider considerations of how an equilibrium might be established by the sometimes competing, sometimes complementary demands of militarism and environmentalism. In the twenty-first century, this question has become increasingly complicated as the social, political, and technological contexts of warfare have evolved. Of particular concern to conservationist and environmentalists will be the privatisation of military activity. Although this chapter focused on the ability of governments to determine military environmental policy and outcomes for animal populations, the growth of private military and security firms has raised a host of issues around transparency and accountability for misconduct that will, no doubt, intersect with concerns touched upon here.[47]

The place of animals and their habitants in militarised landscapes should remain a significant issue as preparations for war use up to 50 million hectares of land across the Earth and make up 6% of global raw material consumption. Wars and military activities account for perhaps 10% of annual global carbon emissions. Over 80% of major armed conflicts between 1950 and 2000 occurred within recognised global biodiversity hotspots, areas that harbour over 40% of terrestrial vertebrate species and at least half of all plant species but which cover less than 2.5% of the Earth's land surface.[48] It is essential, therefore, to continue to seek an understanding of the complex relationships between animals and the militarised landscapes they inhabit, in times of war and peace, and on both battlefields and homefronts.

Notes

1 R. Woodward, *Military Geographies* (Malden: Blackwell, 2004), 77–80.
2 C. E. Closmann, 'Landscapes of Peace, Environments of War', in Closmann (ed.), *War and the Environment: Military Destruction in the Modern Age* (College Station: Texas A&M University Press, 2009), 1.
3 G. E. Machlis and T. Hanson, 'Warfare Ecology', *BioScience*, 58 (2008): 729.
4 R. Zentelis and D. Lindenmeyer, 'Bombing for Biodiversity – Enhancing Conservation Values of Military Training Areas', *Conservation Letters*, 8 (2015): 299–305; J. L. Aycrigg et al., 'Bombing for Biodiversity in the United States: Response to Zentelis & Lindenmeyer 2015', *Conservation Letters*, 8 (2015): 306–7.
5 Zentelis and Lindenmeyer, 'Bombing for Biodiversity', 299–305; J. L. Aycrigg et al., 'Response', 306–7.
6 Woodward, *Military Geographies*, 92.
7 Woodward, *Military Geographies*, 3.
8 Chris Pearson, 'Researching Militarized Landscapes: A Literature Review on War and the Militarization of the Environment', *Landscape Research*, 37 (2012), 117.
9 R. A. Hirst et al., 'Assessing Habitat Disturbance Using a Historical Perspective: The Case of the Salisbury Plain Military Training Area', *Journal of Environmental Management*, 60 (2000): 181–93; R. A. Hirst et al., 'Ecological Impacts of Military Vehicles on Chalk Grassland', *Aspects of Applied Biology*, 58 (2000): 293–8; S. D. Warren et al., 'Biodiversity and the Heterogeneous Disturbance Regime on Military Training Lands', *Restoration Ecology*, 15 (2007): 606–12; D. G. Milchanus et al., 'Plant Community Structure in Relation to Long-Term Disturbance by Mechanized Military Manoeuvres in a Semiarid Region', *Environmental Management*, 25 (2000): 525–39; J. W. Rivers et al., 'Long-term Community Dynamics of Small Landbirds with and Without Exposure to Extensive Disturbance from Military Training Activities', *Environmental Management*, 45 (2010): 203–16; S. D. and R. Buttner, 'Active Military Training Areas as Refugia for Disturbance-dependent Endangered Insects', *Journal of Insect Conservation*, 12 (2008): 671–6.
10 P. Coates, T. Cole, M. Dudley and C. Pearson, 'Defending Nation, Defending Nature? Militarized Landscapes and Military Environmentalism in Britain, France, and the United States', *Environmental History*, 16 (2011): 470.

150 *Ben Wilkie*

11 J. Reif et al., 'Abandoned Military Training Sites Are an Overlooked Refuge for Threatened Bird Species in a Central European Country', *Biodiversity Conservation*, 20 (2011): 3645–62; A. Jentsch et al., 'Assessing Conservation Action for Substitution of Missing Dynamics on Former Military Training Areas in Central Europe', *Restoration Ecology*, 17 (2009): 107–16.

12 C. Pearson, 'Researching Militarized Landscapes: A Literature Review on War and the Militarization of the Environment', *Landscape Research*, 37 (2012), 117.

13 O. Cizek et al., 'Conservation Potential of Abandoned Military Areas Matches That of Established Reserves: Plants and Butterflies in the Czech Republic', *PLoS One*, 8 (2013), http://doi.org/10.1371/journal.pone.0053124.

14 Woodward, *Military Geographies*, 95–6.

15 This chapter extends on material first presented in B. Wilkie, 'Australian Environments in War and Peace: Toward an Environmental History of Australia's Defence Estate' (Paper Presented at the Australian Historical Association Conference, Ballarat, Australia, 2016) and B. Wilkie, 'Bombs and Biodiversity: A Case Study of Military Environmentalism in Australia', *Arcadia: Explorations in Environmental History*, 15 (2016).

16 R. M. Moore et al., *Ecological Studies and Conservation Projects on Army Training Areas, 1974* (Canberra: CSIRO Division of Land Use Research, 1976) 33.

17 Moore et al., *Ecological Studies*, 33.

18 Moore et al., *Ecological Studies*, 2.

19 Moore et al., *Ecological Studies*, 2.

20 Moore et al., *Ecological Studies*, 3–10.

21 Bob Anderson et al., 'Habitat Management for Tanks and Tuans: Evolving Approaches at Puckapunyal Military Area', *Ecological Management & Restoration*, 8 (2007): 11–13.

22 Anderson et al., 'Habitat Management', 12.

23 Anderson et al., 'Habitat Management', 14.

24 J. F. McDonagh, J. Walker and A. Mitchell, 'Rehabilitation and Management of an Army Training Area', *Landscape Planning*, 6 (1979): 376.

25 'Puckapunyal', in Peter Dennis et al. (eds.), *The Oxford Companion to Australian Military History* (Melbourne: Oxford University Press, 2008), 435.

26 *The Age*, 7 January 1953, 9.

27 *The Age*, 7 January 1953, 9.

28 J. F. McDonagh, J. Walker, and A. Mitchell, 'Rehabilitation and Management', 376.

29 J. F. McDonagh et al., 'Rehabilitation and Management of an Army Training Area', 379.

30 Anderson et al., 'Habitat Management', 14–15.

31 John Woinarksi and Alaric Fisher, 'The Australian Endangered Species Protection Act 1992', *Conservation Biology*, 13 (1999): 959–60.

32 R. Carey and P. Bridgewater, *Memorandum of Understanding between the Department of Defence and the Australian Nature Conservation Agency on the Application of the Endangered Species Protection Act 1992 to Lands and Waters Under the Control of Department of Defence* (Canberra, 1995).

33 Anderson et al., 'Habitat Management', 21.

34 A. Bennett, *Wildlife Extinction in the Box-ironbark Forests* (Melbourne: Department of Natural Resources and Environment 1999).

35 Anderson et al., 'Habitat Management', 21–2.

36 Anderson et al., 'Habitat Management', 20.

37 Anderson et al., 'Habitat Management', 17; *Sydney Morning Herald*, 21 May 2002; 'Puckapunyal Military Massacre', Australian Society for Kangaroos, www.australiansocietyforkangaroos.com/puckapunyal_massacre.html (accessed 14 August 2017).

38 'Kangaroos Starving at Puckapunyal Army Base', *ABC Radio: The World Today*, www.abc.net.au/worldtoday/content/2003/s889035.htm (accessed 14 August 2017).

Defending nature 151

39 'Puckapunyal Kangaroo Cull "Our Dirty Little Secret": Activists,' *The Age*, www.theage.com.au/victoria/puckapunyal-kangaroo-cull-our-dirty-little-secret-activists-20131221-2zs5c.html (accessed 14 August 2017); '25,000 Roos for Culling in Victoria', *The Weekly Times*, www.weeklytimesnow.com.au/news/politics/25000-roos-for-culling-in-victoria/news-story/033bf63998fc54d9e4115ad08aa4acaa (accessed 14 August 2017).

40 B. Wilkie, 'Defence White Paper Shows Australian Forces Must Safeguard Nature Too,' *The Conversation*, https://theconversation.com/defence-white-paper-shows-australian-forces-must-safeguard-nature-too-55386 (accessed 24 October 2017).

41 Woodward, *Military Geographies*, 85–9.

42 Coates et al., 'Defending Nation, Defending Nature?', 470.

43 Woodward, *Military Geographies*, 86.

44 Zentelis and Lindenmeyer, 'Bombing for Biodiversity', 299–305; J. L. Aycrigg et al., 'Response', 306–7.

45 Coates et al., 'Defending Nation, Defending Nature?', 471–2.

46 Coates et al., 'Defending Nation, Defending Nature?', 473–4.

47 On the legal issues arising between governments and private firms in military and conflict scenarios, see, for example, B. Sheehy, J. Maogoto and Virginia Newell, *Legal Control of the Private Military Corporation* (London: Palgrave Macmillan, 2008).

48 T. Hanson et al., 'Warfare in Biodiversity Hotspots', *Conservation Biology*, 23 (2009): 578–87.

Part IV

Scarcity

Homecoming (Alpine Strata)

1. Mountain and River

The snow's come early,
King Lear's beard swelling quietly
Before unfurling,
Nebulous
Along the horizon.

Upon the shore
Last year's run-off
Soothes a brumby's dying
Belly,

Sickled branches mourn
The earth.

I've been taught the basics:
Gravity, orbits, lunar tides,
But to no avail –

The grass shivers off its morning frost,
Indifferent to my knowing.

2. Lake and Forest

Clover and wild mints seed,
Stones retire beneath reptile moss,
The lake succumbs
To its double vision –

Clear waters, clouded sky.

154 *Scarcity*

Perhaps the world was sprung
From this alpine wilderness? –
A spasm of pine needles,
And cities, deserts, herds
Were born,

Like the lone tree
That quakes its passion,
A tambourine struck by wind,
Its leaves the birth of music.

3. Field and Home

I cross the field on foot,
Where bones and birds
Thicken in their muddy caul,
Hooves shoal between
Stone and bracken.

To live here
Above a million years
Of humus, debris
And animal waste
Is to fathom

The hunt for evolution,
The sacrificial end.

Whereupon the horizon
Ossifies to village,
My childhood home:

Flint, skull and viscera,
Exotic realm.

                    – Emma Carmody

12 A slow catastrophe?
Fishing for sport and commerce in colonial Victoria

David Harris

Introduction

The bays and inlets along the Victorian coast formed between 10,000 and 1,000 BP following the end of the last ice age. Archaeological evidence suggests the more recent exploitation of marine life by Indigenous people in south-eastern Australia began as the movement of wind, sand and water brought changes to the shoreline. Although current research locates the creation of present-day Port Phillip Bay about 1,000 BP, there is evidence of other changes – in Gippsland, for example, amongst the Gunaikurnai nation from about 2,500 BP, when land-based economic activity shifted to include more fish and shellfish.[1] By comparison, the older inland riverine environments, such as along the Murray River, had a much longer history of fishery exploitation stretching back over 40,000 years.

By the 1850s, the coastal and riverine fisheries that had sustained Aboriginal populations for several thousand years had become part of the commercial and recreational lives of the colonising invaders, including recently arrived gold rush immigrants. Perhaps it was the unfamiliarity of the bounty they had taken, but amongst the new arrivals, a curious ambivalence evolved towards the fishery. Gentleman anglers initially despaired at the quality of native fish in colonial Victoria and the difficulty of casting a line from the steep banks of local rivers into water littered with large tree branches and other natural debris. A comparatively small number of marine commercial fishers earned livelihoods working the inshore fishing grounds that bordered Bass Strait, and many blamed fluctuating catches on competition from predators, such as sharks, sting rays and cormorants, that limited the consistent achievement of expected bounties. Melburnians marvelled at the seasonal appearance in Port Phillip Bay of seemingly familiar species, such as Australian pilchards (*Sardinops neopilchardus*), and were equally despairing when the pilchards failed to appear for several years in a row.

Although, as will be discussed next, human-induced boom-and-bust cycles characterised the early colonial marine fishery, the period after the 1860s was less a boom and bust than it was an unfolding 'slow catastrophe'.[2] Between the 1860s and 1900, the tragedy of the colonial fishery unfolded at a cumulative pace that was imperceptible to some, yet there were many for whom the earlier excesses remained a warning of what was possible. Arising from the meeting of

156   *David Harris*

colonial politics, culture, economics and scientific thought and the local environment, the slow catastrophe was not a story of inevitable decline. Colonists made choices shaped by a diverse array of understandings about the fishery that found expression in the competition to exploit a shared natural resource for sport or commerce.

This chapter explores the commercial and recreational exploitation of the marine and riverine fisheries in Victoria during a period of rapid economic, social and political change that characterised the last half of the nineteenth century. I argue that the meeting of commercial and recreational fishing interests in nineteenth-century Victoria highlighted tensions in colonial society over how the colony's fishery should be harvested and how it should be managed. Key participants in the debates were the fish acclimatisation societies and angling clubs, colonial politicians, local tourism interests and a loose alliance of commercial fishers. Complicating the debate was the absence of any scientific fieldwork into the fishery or any accurate indication of how many fish were being taken by anglers or commercial fishers.

The fishery debate

In Victoria by the late nineteenth century, the colonial fishery debate was shaped by its position at the intersection where colonial political, social and economic interests met international thinking about the growth of industrialised fisheries and recreational angling. International perspectives from the growth of the British fishing industry drove expectations about the assumed commercial potential of the colonial fishery, and from North America came the proposal for how fish hatcheries could supplement native fish stocks.[3] At the same time, differing local perceptions of the fishery provided the basis for either resisting these expectations or for driving support for the further expansion of recreational fishing and the associated hatcheries or for the growth in commercial fishing and the fish trade. It was in this context that the decline of the fishery slowly evolved, imagined by some but unimaginable to others.

Historians writing on colonial fisheries in Australia have generally taken three overlapping approaches. The colonial exploitation of the fishery has been variously interpreted as a narrative of shifting bureaucratic regulation,[4] as a contested political battle over access to fish as a resource[5] or, more recently, as a scientific response to a damaged environment that drew on international ideas about fishery management.[6] Woven through these interpretations has been a discussion about fish acclimatisation, angling and commercial fishing. Acclimatisation was a scientific fad that attracted members from the scientific community, government and academia. It has also been identified as a cultural and scientific expression of a European response to nature by the generations that established settler colonies in Australia, New Zealand and North America. Peter Minard, drawing on earlier research by Drew Hutton and Libby Connors, has suggested the fish acclimatisers and their associated fish hatcheries were the precursors of a modern conservation movement.[7] More recently, Anna Clark – echoing the anthropologist Adrian

Franklin's image of communitarian angling in nineteenth-century Tasmania – has identified a key characteristic of recreational angling that was democratic and diverse in nature.[8] In Victoria, where the ties between angling and fish acclimatisation were close, recreational angling was neither specifically democratic nor diverse. The sport grew in Victoria during the late nineteenth century amongst the urban middle class in tandem with the spread of railways, the linked growth in tourism and the emergence of the suburban boom in Melbourne during the 1880s. Yet at the same time as nineteenth-century angling was an expression of privilege, the holidaying anglers at some holiday destinations also provided income for commercial fishers over the summer. Some fishing families let out the front rooms of their houses to holidaymakers, and commercial fishers used their boats to ferry visitors to good fishing locations on the water.

Victoria's colonial fishing history, like that of other Australian colonies, was shaped as much by geography, climate and the colony's social and political history as by influences from across the empire. Writing on the acclimatisation of salmon in Victoria, Peter Minard partly addresses the failings of previous historical interpretations when he argues: 'salmonid acclimatisation was simultaneously embedded in the particularities of colonial Victorian politics and science while being linked to broader transnational acclimatisation, aquaculture and conservation networks'.[9] Although Minard's concern is with acclimatisation, his comments are relevant to the broader fishery debate that was shaped by local circumstances as much as by ideas from beyond Australia. Colonial governments sent representatives to the International Fisheries Exhibitions to gain insights into the organisation of commercial fishing, and historians have generally overlooked how, as part of different imperial networks, there was also international interest in colonial fisheries coming from Britain, Europe and North America. A transnational perspective was embedded in colonial discussions about recreational and commercial fisheries, as there was a parallel growth in these activities across the Anglophone world. Local circumstances in Victoria, such as the region's recent colonisation, the character of colonial politics and the small size of the fishery, merged with transnational ideas about fisheries to produce a fishery debate that was distinctly Victorian.

Sport and commerce

Recreational angling, as a sport, came to the colony with gentlemen colonists armed with their copies of Izaak Walton's book on angling etiquette, *The Compleat Angler*.[10] As early as 1850, more than a decade before the creation of the Victorian Acclimatisation Society and the attempts to introduce trout, salmon and other exotic fish into colonial waterways, the Waltonian Club lobbied the colonial government about the use of nets by commercial fishers at the mouth of the Saltwater River flowing into Port Phillip Bay. A critic of the Waltonian Club's objection called it 'a piece of class prosecution' and wrongly characterised it as an attempt to introduce the 'infernal system of the English Game Laws'.[11] This was a minor skirmish, but the hostility evident in the complaint, and also the misunderstanding about the types of nets used by commercial fishers, would be repeated over the following decades. For the anglers, the sporting aspect of their hobby involved confining themselves to using a hook and line, and for commercial fishers, the only way to make a living was to use the traditional seine fishing net that was designed with different-sized mesh according to the target species.

The use of fishing nets by commercial fishers attracted criticism, as inexperienced fishers often used them inappropriately, and there was also little understanding about their use outside fishing communities. Commercial fishers imported herring nets from Britain that were then cut into widths to suit fishing in the colony.[12] Mesh varied according to the target species, and restriction on mesh size varied across the period, but there were government regulations on the weight of fish caught and how the catch was removed from the net, and there were also regulations about where nets could be used. Depending on the target species, commercial fishers also used lines and hooks but not long lines.[13]

With some notable exceptions, much of the recent writing about the history of Victoria's colonial fishery has concentrated on angling or acclimatisation.[14] The perception in Victoria of recreational angling as a privileged pastime or the way its critics considered angling – and the associated practice of fish acclimatisation – as a threat to particular riverine fish species have been overlooked. The following section is a brief overview of the meeting between commercial fishing, fish acclimatisation and recreational angling in colonial Victoria.

Two photographs taken during the 1880s reflect one of the key differences between the fish acclimatisers and commercial fishers in colonial Victoria, a difference that was often highlighted when conflict arose between commercial fishing interests and their opponents. On a still morning at Metung on the Gippsland Lakes – possibly in 1886 – the photographer Nicholas Caire captured a nostalgic view of commercial fishing that he knew would appeal to visiting holidaymakers (see Figure 12.1). The image was at odds with the reality of commercial fishing on the Gippsland Lakes, where, at the time, more than 100 baskets a day, each weighing about 25 kilograms, were loaded onto passing pleasure steamers for delivery to the railhead at the nearby town of Sale. The two fishers loading their catch into baskets also represented an era of the artisanal fisher that, as this photograph was being taken, was already fading, overwhelmed by the commercial demands of a market that had a greater interest in exploitation than moderation. By contrast, a photograph – probably taken in the late 1880s – presents a scene at the Ballarat Fish Hatchery (see Figure 12.2). The image formed part of an informative display at the Melbourne Aquarium that celebrated the industry of the colony's fisheries and the science of fish hatcheries. In the photograph, a line of gentlemen act out the maintenance tasks at the hatchery, a job presumably done by the person squatting in the corner of the shot. It was gentlemen like this group who organised campaigns against commercial net fishing during the colonial era.

Figure 12.1 Packing fish for Melbourne, circa 1886. Photographer, N. J. Caire.
Source: State Library Victoria. SLV H27501.

Figure 12.2 Ballarat Fish Hatchery, circa 1890.
Source: State Library Victoria. SLV H84.202/12.

160   *David Harris*

The photographs highlight one aspect of the colonial fishery debate involving the question of who had power over whom in the use of a common resource.

Early on, as Geoffrey Bolton has suggested, the shadow of the English Game Laws lay across the relationship that the first generation of colonists had with the native wildlife, but in colonial Victoria, class continued to exert a significant influence in the fishery debates into the 1890s.[15] It was sustained in part by the emergence of fish acclimatisation societies and the political lobbying they undertook of colonial politicians. Although the fish acclimatisers were initially part of the Acclimatisation Society of Victoria (ASV) established in Melbourne in 1861, they did not share the views of social improvement that were part of the broader acclimatisation movement and instead confined their activities to lobbying for stricter controls on the use of commercial fishing nets and with improving the fish stocks for sporting anglers in waterways across the colony.[16] They brought to the colonial fishery a view of nature and a set of rules about fishing that commercial fishers invariably contravened the moment they used a fishing net. In the acclimatisers' imagined nature, trout and salmon were superior to the available native fish, although, over time, such native species as the Gippsland perch, Murray cod and grayling attracted significant murmurs of approval.[17]

To an extent, class was embedded in the nineteenth-century fishery regulations and other associated government policies in the colony. Acclimatised fish received protection upon release in colonial waters, and acclimatisation societies received government funding for hatcheries as well as free rail transport to deliver hatchlings from the hatcheries to the site of release.[18] At different times, depending on government policies and sufficiency of staff, members of the societies and angling clubs also had the power as honorary fishery inspectors to enforce fishery regulations. In country towns, this led to instances where a commercial fisher who broke the law regarding the use of nets could find that the arresting officer and prosecuting barrister were both members of the local acclimatisation society, as was the magistrate hearing the case.[19] In one instance at the town of Sale, close to the Gippsland Lakes, the local acclimatisation society was characterised following such a case as previously outlined as being unsympathetic to the interests of 'poor men'. The secretary, a local surveyor, responded that the acclimatisation society was instrumental in 'preventing poor men destroying the means by which other and perhaps poorer men gained a living'.[20] Looking beyond the patronising tone of the elevated perspective, it illustrated an element that had been embedded in the fishery debate from the beginning: the acclimatisation societies and angling clubs were considered by their supporters to take a greater interest in the protection of fish and upholding the law than commercial fishers.[21]

Although the rhetoric of the angling clubs and fish acclimatisation societies portrayed commercial fishers as reckless and destructive in the way they fished, the reality was more complex, and it varied during the period under discussion as knowledge about the fishery was acquired by non-Indigenous fishers. Commercial fishers were a diverse group both in terms of ethnicity and in the skills they possessed. According to the 1871 Victorian census, there were 552 men identified as 'fishermen', and a decade later, there were 557 with three women included in the number, but it was not clear whether these statistics included Chinese and Indigenous fishers or those who fished only on a casual basis.[22] Until the 1870s, Yorta Yorta fishers supplied Melbourne fish companies with Murray Cod, while Gunaikurnai and other Indigenous fishers at the two missions on the Gippsland Lakes sold and bartered fish to tourists.[23] There were Scots from fishing villages on the east coast of Scotland, from Cellardyke and elsewhere, who had fished for herring in the North Sea, and there were Chinese fishers from Canton province who had fished the Pearl River Delta.[24]

Contemporary commentators and government bureaucrats drew a distinction between the commercial fishing families who approached the trade as a long-term prospect and those who were interested only in immediate returns. The Scots dominated the politics of commercial fishing and were the most active in searching for ways to reform the trade. In particular they pursued a greater share of the profits obtained by the fishing companies who controlled the sale of fish at the Melbourne Fish Market.[25] Another aspect of the fish trade was the involvement of Chinese fishers who traded in traditionally cured fish for sale to Chinese consumers in the Australian colonies and for export to Hong Kong and Singapore. They also appeared to be involved in a smaller export trade of shark fins and abalone. Alister Bowen's ground-breaking research on Chinese fishers at Port Albert has revealed the importance of Chinese fishers in the early years of commercial fishing from the 1860s.[26]

The colonial government did not gather statistics on commercial fishing until 1889, and even then, no records were kept of the catch, and they did not identify the ethnicity or nationality of the fishers.[27] Accordingly, evidence about who fished and how many fish they caught remains impressionistic, although the frequent government inquiries into Victorian fisheries reveal something of the difficulties that commercial fishers faced. For example, in 1892, when a commercial fisher named Robert Patterson gave evidence to a government inquiry, drawing on his 50 years of fishing in the colony, he lamented how he did not realise catching snapper and Australian salmon in Port Phillip Bay between October and December was the time when they were spawning.[28] Later, in 1919, another inquiry reported that 'so little is known of the habits of any of our fishes that no one can say authoritatively what effect the operations of the fishermen are having upon the shoals'.[29] In the absence of statistics and scientific knowledge, discussions about the health of the fishery often reflected prevailing political circumstances, cultural expectations about what the fishery should be or the anxiety about an unfolding catastrophe.

Scarcity or plenty

Between the 1850s and 1880s, colonial perceptions about the marine and riverine fisheries oscillated between the expectation of a bounteous nature and the fear that the absence of a particular species was a sign of careless commercial fishing practices or some other cause. And although Hutton and Connors, mentioned earlier, have identified the acclimatisers as the proponents of 'efficient and wise use' of natural resources, the fish acclimatisers were no different from other

162   *David Harris*

groups in colonial society who were equally concerned about creating a sustainable fishery.[30]

For some colonists, fears of scarcity were based on memories of earlier episodes of uncontrolled exploitation. Events from the early part of the nineteenth century when the Bass Strait fur seals were hunted almost to the point extinction[31] or the way prawns and oysters were plundered during the gold rush[32] remained in the minds of many colonists as warning of the dangers arising from a boom-and-bust cycle. At the beginning of the 1860s, a widely published report by James Putwain, Victoria's first inspector of fisheries, identified the destructive exploitation of the fishery in Port Phillip Bay and Westernport Bay. Putwain considered whiting, garfish, mullet and bream numbers to have declined, and he also lamented the destruction of the mud oyster (*Ostrea angasi*) beds in Westernport Bay that had occurred during the gold rush when they were harvested indiscriminately for a quick sale on the streets of Melbourne and in the oyster bars.[33]

The fears of uncontrolled exploitation remained in the minds of government officials, such as Charles Mandeville, the chief fishery commissioner, who reported on the difficulty of farming oysters in Westernport Bay in 1885. Recalling what had happened during the gold rush, he dismissed the local folklore from 'the oldest and most experienced fishermen' that the once productive oyster beds had disappeared due to disease.[34] Although disease, such as the *bonamia* parasite, was a credible explanation, the commissioner rejected the suggestion, arguing instead that 'the real fact is that [the oysters] were destroyed from the want of supervision and from the greed of the men who fished for them'.[35] With palpable fury, he then launched into a description as though he were watching the events unfold again:

> When a bed was found it was dredged up and down never missing a foot of the ground, say from north to south till they got across the bed, then at right angles say from west to east then again diagonally till there was nothing left. When one man found a bed and dredged it he threw the mullock he had in his boat outside the bed, but he was usually followed by others, he then threw it on top of the oysters to discourage or allay the newcomers, . . . in fact the whole of the oysters were cleaned out.[36]

Mandeville's correspondence regularly simmered with this type of outrage as he thundered at the greed and carelessness he identified in the fish trade: female crayfish offered for sale at the Melbourne Fish Market after having the eggs stripped from them; tons of fish dumped each week at the market, particularly during summer; fish offered for sale after having millions of spawn stripped and buried; underweight fish offered for sale; nets not emptied in the water as required by regulations, with the consequence that small fish caught in the nets were left to die on the beach. Yet he also had no time for anglers who, with 'plenty of time to spare', would fish out the lakes where they cast a line or would immediately blame the scarcity of fish in rivers on the practice of illegal netting.

A slow catastrophe? 163

Mandeville's solution to the wastage was to encourage commercial fishers with a long-term interest in the fishery who would sustain the old family traditions of artisanal fishing.

By the final decades of the nineteenth century, the fishery debate had expanded beyond the impact of careless commercial net fishing. Attention shifted to the impact of angling on native fish and to the effects that the acclimatisers were having on fish in the colony's rivers. A survey on the native grayling (*Prototroctes maraena*) suggested that numbers had declined due to the impact of angling combined with the introduction of Murray cod, trout, perch and other imported species, and during a debate in the colonial parliament, one politician argued that salmon were as voracious as sharks, eating all other fish in the river.[37] Meanwhile, in New South Wales, a government inquiry raised concerns about the destructive impact that Murray cod were having on the rivers into which they had been introduced by the acclimatisers.[38]

In the absence of any scientific fieldwork into the Victorian fishery, discussion relied on scientific theories drawn from elsewhere, politics and occasionally the perspectives of experienced commercial fishers. For example, driving the hopeful expectations of the bounteous harvest was a strand of popular scientific thinking about the unlimited wealth of the ocean, a perspective affirmed by seasonal events in Port Phillip or along the coast where pilchards appeared in apparently limitless number.[39] Regularly in colonial debates, the argument was presented that an acre of the ocean had a more productive yield than an acre of land, a view presented during an inquiry into British fisheries in 1868.[40] Extending the image further, some colonials believed that a land-based harvest occurred once a year, but the ocean could provide an unlimited harvest at any time. Yet commercial fishers who had sailed in Bass Strait, such as William Carstairs, a Scot whose family had fished for herring in the North Sea, thought otherwise. He, like others in the colony, argued that due to the lack of rivers flowing into Bass Strait, nutrient levels were low and that this limited fish and invertebrate activity. In one government inquiry, he attempted to explain how the low numbers of fish in central Bass Strait would not support a trawling industry, although fish could be caught following floods when they gathered, attracted by the nutrients in the outflow from the rivers.[41] Subsequent scientific research in the twentieth century confirmed that Bass Strait was nutrient poor partly due to the influence of the East Australian Current and to other low-nutrient water masses that flowed through the Strait.[42]

It is likely that even with substantial scientific research, politics would have continued to shape the debate about the condition of the fishery particularly as, by the end of the century, a fishing industry had become entwined with notions of national development. Accordingly, the local political momentum that produced federation and gave the states control over their fisheries also combined with the international growth of industrialised fisheries to promote commercial fishing as a potential lucrative economic activity into the twentieth century. In this atmosphere of national progress, debate about decline of the fishery became muted, although it never disappeared. And with the growth of tourism as a potential

164 *David Harris*

boost to the new state economy, the task of breeding exotic fish for anglers passed to government-run hatcheries.

Fishery management

A tenet of British colonialism was that nature could be improved through the meeting of British culture, science and technology under the management of an efficient government bureaucracy. Exotic fish introduced into native waterways by the Acclimatisation Society were protected under legislation, while local fauna, such as cormorants or sharks or stingrays that were seen as competing with the colonisers' commercial interests, were identified as pests, and bounties were offered for their destruction.

Fisheries management involved the holding of several parliamentary inquiries between the 1860s to the 1890s, and there were fisheries acts introduced in 1859, 1864, 1873 and 1890.[43] As much as they were statements of political alignments and power, the different fishery acts were works of imagination that attempted to balance the competing political and economic interests in the colony. They contained regulations reflecting how politicians, commercial fishers and fish acclimatisers imagined nature should be and who should have access to it. As knowledge of the fishery increased, regulations were adjusted, but the absence of any long-term information about native fish species amongst the colonisers meant politicians, at worst, drew up regulations arbitrarily or, at best, followed customary fishing practices that often varied between commercial fishers.

Politicians did not seem to understand, for example, the relationship between the legal size limits of fish caught, the assumed breeding cycle of fish and the size of the mesh used in fishing nets. During the parliamentary debate on the 1873 fishing inquiry's recommendations on the legal weights for the sale of flounder, pike, garfish, sole, whiting and flathead, politicians arbitrarily reduced all the weights suggested by the inquiry.[44] The weights had been determined on the advice of experienced fishers during the inquiry and were suggested in the context of other advice about the size of mesh in the nets. Lesley Moody, the inspector of fisheries, later advised the politicians to increase the minimum weight, but a petition from a group of fishers countered this by arguing a more extreme point of view.[45] Based on a different logic, derived from fishing in Britain, the petition claimed that 'flatheads are fish which need no protection, as the large ones eat the small; and, like the herring at home, the more that are caught the more are left'.[46] From a modern perspective, this was an ineffective way of managing a fishery, but it was a logical consequence of how the legislators conceived the relationship between state regulation and the environment.[47]

Conclusion

The character of Victoria's colonial fishery was shaped, in part, by the conflict between commercial fishing interests and the fish acclimatisation societies. Given the diversity of challenges that the colonial marine and riverine fisheries faced from commercial fishing, angling, acclimatisation, agriculture, industry and mining, it is difficult to quantify the impact of colonisation on the colony's fish and invertebrate species.

The degree to which the fishery was in decline during this period is also unclear. It was being more heavily exploited than previously, and there was the fear of its decline across sections of the colonial population. There was also an apparent indifference to questions of supply, as some fishers regularly ignored regulations on the size of fishing nets, on location or seasonal restrictions, on the size of fish or whether it was the breeding season. Victorian waterways during the period under discussion were also transformed in the first place by the gold rush when land was cleared for farming and water quality was compromised by pollution and various drainage, irrigation and river clearing or controlling schemes. Later, the railway expansion of the 1870s put additional pressure on marine and riverine fisheries, as previously inaccessible areas of the colony were opened to intensive commercial and sport fishing.

The character of the colony's fishery was shaped by different understandings of the environment that found expression in political decisions and in the legislation that was introduced. Although there was never a consensus about how the colony's fishery would be best harvested for commerce or recreation, there seemed a significant level of engagement amongst colonists with the idea that the fishery was a limited resource and required management.

Notes

1 K. Thompson, *A History of the Aboriginal People of East Gippsland: A Report for the Land Conservation Council, Victoria* (Melbourne: Land Conservation Council, 1985), 83.

2 In this chapter, I use the term 'slow catastrophe' to discuss the colonial fishery, in part as an alternative to the concept of boom and bust that characterised other aspects of Australia's environmental history. See discussion in Libby Robin et al. (eds.), *Boom and Bust: Bird Stories for a Dry Country* (Melbourne: CSIRO Publishing, 2009), 3–5; the idea of the slow catastrophe is taken from Rob Nixon's work on 'slow violence', but the focus of my discussion is with the European exploitation of, and impact on, the marine and freshwater fisheries during the colonial period. See Rob Nixon, *Slow Violence and the Environmentalism of the Poor* (Cambridge: Harvard University Press, 2011), 1–46; Rebecca Jones also used the term in a different sense than it is used here in her analysis of farming families and their experiences of droughts in *Slow Catastrophes: Living with Drought in Australia* (Melbourne: Monash University Publishing, 2017).

3 T. D. Smith, *Scaling Fisheries: the Science of Measuring the Effects of Fishing, 1855–1955* (Cambridge: Cambridge University Press, 1994), 51–5, 63; J. M. Knauss, 'The Growth of British Fisheries During the Industrial Revolution', *Ocean Development and International Law*, 36.1 (2005): 1–112.

4 See, for example, G. C. Bolton, *Spoils and Spoilers: Australians Make Their Environment 1788–1980* (Sydney: George Allen & Unwin, 1981), 15, 98; Joseph Christensen, 'Recreational Fishing and Fisheries Management: A HMAP Asia Project Paper' (Perth: Asia Research Centre, Murdoch University, 2009).

5 David Harris, 'It's Just Fly Fishing against Net Fishing' in Erik Eklund and Julie Fenley (eds.), *Earth and Industry: Stories from Gippsland* (Melbourne: Monash University, 2015), 135–6.

6 Peter Minard, 'Salmonid Acclimatisation in Colonial Victoria: Improvement, Restoration and Recreation 1858–1909', *Environment and History*, 21 (2015): 179–82.

166 David Harris

7 Peter Minard, 'Assembling Acclimatisation: Frederick McCoy, European Ideas, Australian Circumstances', *Historic Records of Australian Science*, 24 (2013): 1–2.
8 Anna Clark, *The Catch: The Story of Fishing in Australia* (Canberra: National Library of Australia, 2017), 79–91; Adrian Franklin, 'Performing Acclimatisation: the Agency of Trout Fishing in Postcolonial Australia', *Ethnos*, 76.1 (2011): 19–40.
9 Minard, 'Salmonid Acclimatisation'.
10 Izaak Walton, *The Compleat Angler or the Contemplative Man's Recreation* (London: A. and C. Black, Ltd., 1928).
11 *Argus*, 30 July 1850, 4.
12 Public Record Office, Victoria (PROV), VPRS 16182/P0001 'Outward Letter Book, Inspector of Fisheries and Game', Unit 1, 1885–1894, Captain James Anderson to J. H. Bates 3 December 1888.
13 PROV, 'Outward Letter Book', Anderson to Bates.
14 See the following theses for a scholarly discussion on colonial commercial fishing in different parts of Victoria: Brad Duncan, 'The Maritime Archaeology and Maritime Cultural Landscapes of Queenscliffe: a Nineteenth Century Australian Coastal Community' (PhD dissertation, James Cook University, 2006). Alister Bowen, *Archaeology of the Chinese Fishing Industry in Colonial Victoria* (Sydney: Sydney University Press, 2012); Coral Dow, 'Tatungalung Country: An Environmental History of the Gippsland Lakes' (PhD dissertation, Monash University, 2004).
15 G. C. Bolton, *Spoils and Spoilers*, 15.
16 David Harris, 'Imagined Natures: The Gippsland Lakes, Australia: 1860s – 1900' (PhD dissertation, La Trobe University, 2014), 150–7.
17 *Argus*, 22 December 1887, 5 and 12 August 1872, 4; J. E. Tenison-Woods, *Fish and Fisheries of New South Wales* (Sydney: Government Printer, 1882), 109.
18 Lindsay G. Thompson (ed.), *History of the Fisheries of New South Wales with a Sketch of the Laws by Which They Have Been Regulated* (Sydney: Charles Potter, Government Printer, 1893), 103; Samuel Wilson, *The Californian Salmon, with an Account of Its Introduction into Victoria* (Melbourne: Sands and McDougall Printers, 1878), 115.
19 Harris, 'Imagined Natures', 249–150, 156.
20 *Gippsland Times*, 7 October 1881, 3 and 12 October 1881, 3.
21 *Victorian Parliamentary Debates (VPD)*, 1873, vol. XVI, 639, 1202.
22 *Census of Victoria, 1881*, 273, http://hccda.ada.edu.au/pages/VIC-1881-census_02-13_273 (accessed 13 December 2016).; *Census of Victoria, 1871*, 117, http://hccda.ada.edu.au/pages/VIC-1871-census-18_117 (accessed 13 December 2016).
23 D. J. Leslie, 'Moira Lake – A Case Study of the Deterioration of a River Murray Natural Resource', (MSc dissertation, University of Melbourne, 1995), 36–8; M. Bennett, 'The Economics of Fishing: Sustainable Living in Colonial New South Wales', *Aboriginal History*, 31 (2007): 86–7, 91–6, 99.
24 Peter Stokes to David Harris email 30 November 2011; Bowen, *Archaeology*, 61–7.
25 *Gippsland Times*, 21 May 1879, 3–4.
26 Bowen, *Archaeology*, 61–85.
27 PROV, 'Outward Letter Book', 379–93.
28 VPP (Victorian Parliamentary Papers) 1892–93, vol. 1 'Final Report from the Select Committee Upon the Fishing Industry of Victoria, Together with the Proceedings of the Committee', Robert Patterson 24 June 1892, questions 2290–2230.
29 VPP 1919 vol. 2 'Report of the Royal Commission on Victorian Fisheries and Fisheries Industries', 6.
30 Drew Hutton and Libby Connors, *A History of the Australian Environment Movement* (New York: Cambridge, 1999), 45.
31 Alister Gilmour, 'Fishing in Bass Strait', in Stephen Murray-Smith (ed.), *Bass Strait, Australia's Last Frontier*, rev. ed. (Sydney: ABC Enterprises for the Australian Broadcasting Corporation, 1987), 69; Marcus Blake Brownrigg and Stephen Murray-Smith,

Mission to the Islands: The Missionary Voyages in Bass Strait of Canon Marcus Brownrigg, 1872–1885 (Launceston: Foot and Playsted, 1987), xvi.

32 Horace Wheelwright, *Bush Wanderings of a Naturalist* (Melbourne: Oxford University Press), 248.

33 *Argus*, 3 September 1862, 4.

34 PROV, 'Outward Letter Book', Mandeville to Commissioner of Trade and Customs, 21 August 1885, 85/60, 75.

35 S. Corbeil et al., 'Bonamiasis in Australian *Ostrea angasi*', *Australia and New Zealand Standard Diagnostic Procedure*, January 2009: 2, www.scahls.org.au/Procedures/Pages/Aquatic-ANZSDPs.aspx (accessed 8 March 2013); PROV 'Outward Letter Book', 21 August 1885.

36 PROV, 'Outward Letter Book'.

37 VPP 1888, vol. 1 'Fisheries Report return to an order of the House dated 27th June 1888 for the fisheries reports prepared and submitted by Mr. Saville Kent', 15; Fish Preservation Committee, *Report of the Fish Preservation Committee to the Victorian Fish Protection and Angler's Club* (Melbourne: Kain and Thompson, 1893), 9; VPD 1886 vol. LIII, 2387–2388.

38 Tenison-Woods, *Fish*, 156.

39 *Argus* 28 August 1865, 5.

40 *Argus*, 15 February 1873, 1 and 21 March 1873, 6.

41 VPP 1892–93, vol. 1 'Final Report', William Carstairs 23 July 1892, question 3863.

42 P. S. Roy et al., 'Structure and Function of South-east Australian Estuaries,' *Estuarine, Coastal and Shelf Science*, 53.3 (2001): 354.

43 Act for the Protection of Fisheries of Victoria 1859; Act for the Regulation of the Oyster Fisheries in Victoria 1859; Act for the Preservation of Fish in the Lakes and Rivers of the Colony of Victoria 1859; Fisheries and Game Statute 1864; Fisheries Act 1873; The Fisheries Act Amendment Act 1878; Fisheries Act 1890, www.austlii.edu.au/ (accessed 20 August 2012).

44 VPD 1873 vol. XVII, 1539.

45 VPD 1875–6 vol. XXIII, 2587.

46 VPD 1875–6 vol. XXIII, 2587.

47 Harris, 'Imagined Natures', 145–50.

13 The palatability of pests
Redfin in the Murray-Darling Basin

Jodi Frawley

The stories we tell

In the story of redfin, the dominant narrative circulating in Australia is a scientific rendering of belonging. Redfin are not natives but invaders. In the Murray-Darling Basin, a system made up of thirty-seven rivers that encompass one eighth of the Australian continent, binaries continue to structure fisheries research, natural resource management and riverine conservation that have implications for the lives of redfin.[1] While geographers, historians and philosophers have all challenged these binaries, seeking to make a more complex reading of environments and their creatures, fisheries scientists continually reinforce them in everyday practices. Symptomatic of this approach is Mark Lintermans' *Fishes of the Murray Darling Basin: An Introductory Guide*, which is used by natural resource managers and lay people across the basin to identify redfin as an alien fish. In this body of work, Lintermans carefully constructs two groups of fish, natives and aliens, and these categories flow through into the day-to-day management of the rivers. On the other hand, the memories of local people who lived on the rivers, and their everyday fishing practices, challenge this scientific perspective and are generally not included in the management approaches to these rivers.[2]

To add to the growing body of scholarship about people, animals and their rivers, I consider how local fishing communities remember redfin as a fish that was easy to catch and good to eat. Although science-based river managers celebrated the loss of redfin in the 1980s from the epizootic hematopoietic necrosis virus (EHNV), fishers experienced this scarcity differently. The death rate resulted in low numbers of redfin, which conservationists applauded but fishers saw as a loss because they associated these fish with memories of everyday life. As such, the story of redfin opens a space for the consideration of life lived in a hybrid settler colonial environment: one made up of natives and a broad range of human and non-human newcomers.

This chapter emerges from *Talking Fish*, an oral history project conducted in the Murray-Darling Basin in 2010–11. A multidisciplinary team of aquatic ecologists, natural resource managers, a radio producer and two environmental historians conducted fieldwork in twelve sites across the Murray-Darling Basin. The project drew oral history participants from local fishing communities of recreational,

The palatability of pests 169

Aboriginal and professional fishers, who shared life narratives shaped by their fishing along these river systems. To them, the native/exotic divide registered as a contemporary, not historical, concern. Instead, fishers recalled enjoying redfin as one of a suite of native and introduced fish that were plentiful over the twentieth century. Once redfin populations diminished and became scarcer, in contradistinction to the prevailing wisdom of conservation biology, fishers framed this change as a loss. These oral histories, with their recording of fishers' laments for the redfin, capture histories of fish populations that are not based on the rigid divides of science.

Scientific storytelling

In the contours of the scientific narrative, redfin emerges as a problematic invasive species because of the way they interact with the environment and compete for space and food with native fish. As fish biologist Mark Lintermans explains: 'The perch is a voracious predator, with large and small individuals in the Basin consuming small native species such as carp gudgeons and the young of Murray cod, golden perch and Murray trout.'[3] Curiously, Lintermans does not articulate whether the predation habits of redfin include other invasive fish, like carp or gambusia. For Lintermans, here reflecting a dominant scientific perspective, the redfin's predation creates an imbalance in the Murray-Darling Basin river systems. The focus for fisheries scientists is on the carnivorous activity of the fish only in relation to native fish without consideration of the eating habits of the humans who lived along the river.

In the 1980s, a new threat emerged for the fish of the Murray-Darling Basin, as EHNV spread through fish populations. Such natives as Macquarie perch, sliver perch and mountain galaxias were particularly susceptible. But it was the redfin that took the brunt of the disease, dying in the hundreds of thousands. In 1985, scientific trials proved that redfin was the host of the disease; even though no one is sure how this came about 120 years after the translocation of redfin populations. Scientists celebrated this demise and the scarcity it created as a win for the native fish.

The importance of consumption of fish is underplayed or deliberately downplayed in much of the commentary about fisher 'behaviour'.[4] The only national survey of recreational fishers undertaken to date asked fishers to scale their motivations for fishing, separating out different elements that contribute to a sense of enjoyment when fishing.[5] Lyle and Henry had participants rate the fishing experience and then presented these 'fisher motivations' as a hierarchical list, with eating fish placed last in a group of eight categories, largely dismissed as irrelevant.[6] Changing systems of food production have undermined the importance of knowing how to fish to feed a family or community. However, when asked, all Murray-Darling Basin fishers interviewed provided a favourite style of cooking fish, suggesting that eating fish continues as a key motivator in contemporary fishing cultures.

170   *Jodi Frawley*

As these fish recipes suggest, the fishers interviewed for *Talking Fish* whose childhood memories of fun and food connect them to redfin, and the rivers they fished, did not see the redfin's precipitous decline in the same light as the scientists did. It is lament that best describes how they felt. Tracey Bye, who loved fishing with her father around Katarapko Creek in South Australia, remembered:

> It wasn't unusual to catch [catfish]. And redfin. We used to catch a lot of redfin. But you just don't anymore. We haven't seen a redfin for quite some time. But the catfish to me was always the yuck one. It's just because they're ugly, that's all. And then the redfin, they were beautiful to look at. Absolutely beautiful fish. But I haven't seen them for a while.[7]

Bye was not alone in her lament; this sentiment came through in a number of interviews where fishers discussed redfin. To explore this quandary between the scientific and everyday narratives, I turn to the history of redfin and how she was entangled in the daily lives of fishing communities from the time of her migration in the nineteenth century right through to the 1980s.

Origin stories

Perca fluviatilis is a European fish. She makes herself at home in many corners of Europe: from south-eastern England, west to Siberia as well as south to Italy and across to the Black and Caspian Seas. In these places, she is called the European perch.[8] She is a very beautiful fish; deep bodied, olive green and striped with thick dark bands. But it is her fins that help us humans to recognise her. Sometimes they are bright orange and other times glowing red. Fish biologists think her fins change colour as a flight-or-fight mechanism. We see her red fins, and in Australia, this is what we call her. Redfin.

In the nineteenth century, both people and fish from Europe were on the move to Australia. Such is the violence of migration by human hands, that four times – in 1857, 1858, 1859 and 1360 – redfin died en route to Tasmania. But in 1861, eleven redfin shared a cabin with solicitor and acclimatisation enthusiast Morton Allport as they travelled to Hobart. From ship to shore, Allport translocated the fish into purpose-built ponds in his brother Joseph's gardens. The Allports called her the English perch, paying homage to their heritage, more than that of the fish, who always ranged more widely on the European continent than might be assumed from this kind of naming.[9]

The Allports added another batch of fish the following year, and by 1866, they had grown this fledgling group to 30,000 by their account. The fish stock was now ready to move to the mainland, being first transported to Victoria in the Allport enterprise in the 1860s.[10] Harriet Ritvo writes of the motivations of people like the Allports: 'frivolous (or worse) as they may seem from a contemporary vantage point, the instigators of all these acclimatization attempts understood themselves to be acting in the public interest, and not just for their idiosyncratic satisfaction.'[11] The Allports may have been operating under the peculiar altruism 'in

The palatability of pests   171

the public interest', which understood that any introductions advanced Australia from its original strangeness to a place better suited to the British lifestyle, but they were also savvy businessmen. They sold these fish for others to release into impounded dams and ponds that did not connect to the river systems but also into the lakes, rivers, creeks and streams across Victoria. Through this process, redfin became mainland dwellers. The river systems into which she went provided connectivity to places foreign to these fish.

Such origin stories have an inherent attractiveness, providing precision and singularity that oversimplifies. The Allports were not the only ones responsible for the introduction of *Perca fluviatis*, English perch, redfin. Other fish travelled with other human companions. Maybe they came from England; perhaps they didn't. Who is to say that perch didn't come from a tributary of the Moskow River in Russia or one of the inlets of the busy immigration port at Hamburg in Germany? For example, from 1849, ships like the *Goddefroy*, *Wappaus*, *Dockenhuden* and *Emmy* disembarked more than 347 immigrants from Prussia, Silesia and Saxony.[12] All these places are also freshwater homes for redfin. And why should we think only of the Allports in this story of introduction? Like many Australian stories, the English documents overwrite these other more-than-human tales.

These stories contribute to the power Britain gained to assert that it was remaking Australia in its image rather than acknowledge the multiplicity of people and the non-linear arrival of species new to the continent. Here ecological imperialism and science's cultural imperialism converge: it becomes essential to establish the precise dates of the arrival of species to categorise them as invaders. Despite the dominance of the Allport narrative, colonial records show redfin in Ballarat, in Victorian Acclimatisation society lists[13] and that Mr. E. H. K. Crawford of Pinnacle Station between Forbes and Grenfell in New South Wales released fish into his station dams, which subsequently migrated into tributaries of the Lachlan River during flooding.[14] Safe to say, these records do not show releases by the local farmer on the Murrumbidgee River, who liked to fish, or the cook from the local pub in a town like Seymour, who wanted to dish up a fresh feed of fish to her patrons. Instead of having a unique origin story, the numbers of redfin swelled as a result of multiple entry points and the complex food needs of new and old locals.

These new rivers welcomed redfin, who needed little help to establish herself. Into the waters of Kangaroo Creek, Wendouree, and the Young district she went. She liked it in Australia. Or to be more accurate, she liked some bits of the Australian rivers. She is a freshwater fish and prefers slow-moving or still water. In Australian rivers, this means the mid-range sections. In the headwaters, in our so-called mountains, the water runs too fast. And down in the estuaries, the fluctuations from brackish to salty and back to fresh again did not suit her so well. In the mid-range, Australian rivers of the Murray-Darling system were a labyrinth of billabongs, floodplains, wetlands and appealing little creeks and tributaries. All were of the perfect velocity for a redfin finding her way.

She also liked the water to be warm but not too warm. Higher water temperature was one of the reasons that she was not so fond of the Darling River. The plains of western Queensland and New South Wales raise the water temperature

172   *Jodi Frawley*

just a little bit too much. She had found a niche in the mid-range of the Victorian, South Australian and southern reaches of the Murray-Darling system, and there she continued to breed in self-sustaining populations from the late nineteenth century. Unlike the trout and salmon, whose fingerlings acclimatisers and anglers still regularly release into the rivers, redfin did not continue to require human intervention to survive. Redfin laid eggs in gelatinous strings of hundreds of thousands. It is this volume that offered a modicum of protection in the streams of Europe. Plentiful newborns equal viable populations of adults, despite predation by larger fish. In Australia, none of the native fish found these eggs palatable. Instead of enabling equilibrium, the volume of eggs that protected her from the attrition of consumption assisted her to multiply beyond imagining. She, on the other hand, found the locals pretty tasty; the eggs, spat and fingerlings of the Murray and trout cod, the eel-tailed catfish and the large-bodied yellow belly were delicacies to be picked off in the twentieth-century rivers of Australia. She grew fat and plentiful.

Ecologies of leisure

By the 1960s, the Murray-Darling Basin was a different place than that first encountered by redfin in the 1860s. One hundred years had turned these rivers into an organic machine.[15] Settler colonialism changed the river into a system of dams and weirs, irrigation channels and series of off-channel dams and tanks that reduced flow. To assist with the passage for their boats, settlers cleared riverbeds of snags and debris, and the banks were stripped of vegetation to create watering points for cattle, sheep, horses, donkeys and camels. The vastness of the system, over one million square kilometres, was incomprehensible to the individual farmer, pastoralist or fisher who saw only their small component of it. The rivers became sewers for both humans and animals and drains for agricultural runoff, which increasingly meant chemical loads as the use of herbicides and pesticides became more common.[16] Anecdotally – because there is no science yet that successfully tested this proposition – this was a time when the redfin populations did very well indeed. It was a time, too, when the native fish populations dropped.[17] The native fish of the Murray-Darling Basin didn't much like the changes, and pushed along by the professional and non-professional fishing, the balance of fish species in the river shifted in favour of introduced fish. By the 1990s, fisheries scientists estimate that native fish populations are 10% of a pre-1788 baseline.[18]

The 1960s was also a time when the socioecology of the riverbank changed. Recreational fishers began to move around the basin in ways that they had not before. Two effects enhanced settler mobility. Firstly, full employment within a stable labor market delivered regular holidays and the ubiquitous 'weekend'. The 1950s saw the rise of two full days out of seven where Australians could pursue recreation. Secondly, this was also a time when cars, trailable boats and caravans, along with better roads, camping facilities and boat ramps, enhanced the access to rivers. Jim Davidson and Peter Spearritt point out that by 1965, locals established over 2,000 caravan parks and camping grounds across the continent.[19] Australian

The palatability of pests   173

historian of travel and tourism Richard White traced these changes along the coast, declaring that it was the camping grounds close to estuaries and beaches that became the magnet for city dwellers during summer holidays.[20] Many of the towns along the Murray-Darling rivers, which were close enough to large populations of people to attract weekend holidaymakers, installed these facilities. White has called the period between 1945 and 1975 the heyday of the family holiday, with the car as the critical technology in these changes.

These changes in the river catchments saw the bait and tackle shop established alongside the camping and caravan parks as a new amenity and business enterprise driven by these new patterns of leisure and recreation. Leisure, technology, small businesses and mobility all converged and placed more humans on the water's edge or midstream in lightweight, cheap aluminium boats. For fishing as leisure to grow as a very Australian pastime, fishers also needed to catch fish. Redfin obliged.

Redfin has folded into the memories of fishing these rivers on family holidays. Learning to fish etches those moments with mum or dad, aunt or grandparent, into a structure of feeling about fish and these rivers.[21] Imagine if you are learning to find bait. If you are looking for bardi grubs, which all the fish of the river love to eat, then you need to find the right kind of tree, where the caterpillar lives just underground within the root structure that lay close to the surface. Threading them onto the hook is an engrossing experience, as is taking the weight of the rod, as your teacher helps you to manoeuvre the line behind your head and then swiftly whip it towards the river so that the line, sinker, hook and bait sail over your head and plunk into the water. Anna Clark captures this sense of body, timing and memory when she opens her book on the history of fishing in Australia with 'When they shut their eyes and pause for a minute, fishers have a place to go in their mind. A special place, a fishing place. Mine is called Paradise, but you won't find it on any map'.[22]

The *Talking Fish* oral history project collected stories in which fishers told of their love of fishing in ways that echo the shape of Clark's memories. Donny Richter, who grew up in Melbourne, remembered learning to fish with his siblings:

> My first memories of fishing was with Dad: We used to go camp up to Yarra – not Yarrawonga – up to Echuca – and, back in them days we used to catch fish, like, redfin. We were only kids like seven, eight, nine, ten maybe.[23]

It is a critically important but often ignored premise that fishing requires fishers to catch fish. Without catch, there *is* no fishing experience. When redfin were plentiful, fishing was fun for children and adults alike. Many fishers of the Murray-Darling Basin told of that first fish rising out of the water, dancing across its surfaces, resisting the pull of the line with the species' characteristic strength. Redfin and river attach to emotion and memory, drawing recreational fishers into those new ecologies of leisure of the 1950s and 1960s. These Murray-Darling fishers identified redfin as their first catch, while others talk about how, if redfin were on the run, then they could catch their fill without any problem.

174 *Jodi Frawley*

Dividing fish

Paul Sinclair, in his masterful book, *The Murray: a river and its people*, rightfully acknowledges the vital place of fishing in the lives and memories of the people of the Murray River catchment.[24] In this book, he focuses on the loss of native species, the destruction of native habitat and the alteration of the natural river. The lens he uses to bring this story into sharp relief is one that privileges indigenous fish and an ecosystemic balance found somewhere in the past. He argues that in this place, in these rivers, the only fish that rightfully belong were those that existed prior to non-Aboriginal settlement. Following this thread, Sinclair states that by the mid-twentieth century, the scarcity of Murray cod in the river was an indicator of diminished biological biodiversity and widespread degradation.[25] But what should we make of the people who were new to the river in the 1960s? What of those who happily fished for redfin and who did not see a diminished river but one which provided all they needed for recreation and consumption?

Fish biologist Daniel Pauly coined the term 'shifting baselines' in 1995 to capture an idea about the different perceptions that people build about ecosystems when they do not have the reference points of the past.[26] When they don't understand the changes, then they take what they see and experience as natural, although through a scientific lens that same place may be viewed as degraded in a longer view. The fisheries managers of the Murray-Darling Basin called this creeping normalcy.[27] By the time that visitors and locals who undertook recreational fishing associated with new leisure patterns, the people who were fishing were seeing a different river than the one that had accepted the introductions of redfin from the 1860s. To the fishers, there was no association of the river with loss or unnaturalness, but instead, they imbued it with wonder, beauty and plentiful fishing.

In ruminating about the cultural importance of fishing, Sinclair reveals a stark difference between the way that he looks at this story and the approach of those fishers involved in the *Talking Fish* project. Like many people trained to listen to science, to think about conservation and to make assessments of places to contribute to policy debates, when Sinclair looks at fish, he sees a binary: native or exotic. This scientific thinking, in turn, classifies them as belonging or not belonging. Sinclair describes the desirable fish of the Murray River, in terms of fishing, by making this list: 'Murray cod, golden perch, silver perch, freshwater catfish and bony bream'.[28] He does not include any non-native fish, therefore mirroring the science that supports his approach attributing responsibility to the negative impacts of settler colonialism.

When recreational fishers make the same list of desirable fish, they also demonstrate a means of categorising these animals. In this case, fishers base these constructions on what they have caught. Kay Gibb, who fished from the Goulburn River, told us that 'Redfin, yellow belly, perch, cod' were the common fish caught and valued by her and her family.[29] Ken Gilmore, who grew up on a large pastoral property that bordered the same river, made a similar list when asked what he had fished for as a child: 'Cod. Yeah. You'd get cod and trout, all sorts. Redfin too.'[30]

The palatability of pests   175

Jim Hanley from Seymour, who had journeyed all over the Victorian reaches of the Murray-Darling rivers, said of learning to fish with his family, 'my dad used to fish it for Murray cod, Macquarie perch, redfin'.[31]

These linguistic strings show a different perspective on the question of value and how that contributes to the way we see the animal populations of the river. Sinclair emphasises the native by setting aside the introduced fish. In doing so, he isolates the native fish and accords all emotional attachment to them and their loss from the system. The fishers do no such thing. Instead, they collapse the imaginary boundary of native and exotic and arrange fish by a schema that relies on the catch-ability and edibility of redfin and other table fish that were popular with recreational fishers over the twentieth century.

Consuming redfin, making memories

For fishers, redfin entangles herself in these family and holiday memories because she was easy to catch and good to eat. In the early twentieth century, in myriad ways, Australians were intimately connected to food production far more than they are today. In the urban centres, as Andrea Gaynor details in her book, *Harvest of the Suburbs*, suburban backyards supported vegetable patches, chicken coops and fruit trees. A dairy could be local enough for suburbanites to collect milk and cream from the farmer or to have it delivered by horse and cart.[32] Whether city or country, food production for the kitchen was the norm because providing for the table was a part of everyday life. Class emerges as one marker of the difference between practices that value table fish versus those that value trophy fish. Of the 110 interviews collected for *Talking Fish*, only two participants self-identified as sports fishers. Such phrasing is widely considered to represent fishers engaged in a middle- and upper-class pursuit, who did not eat the fish they caught.[33] As Adrian Franklin shows, trout and salmon, which continue to be restocked throughout the basin, always aligned certain fishers with the pursuit of angling as a sport and therefore with patrician sensibilities. Redfin, on the other hand, is a workers' fish associated with consumption. The participants who provided the following evidence were all from working-class backgrounds.

The Lean family lived in Yarrawonga on the Victorian side of the Murray River through the twentieth century. Three generations ran the local barbershop, and in the 1960s, they dedicated half of their retail area to fishing tackle and bait. As a boy, Dennis and his brothers and sisters lived right on Lake Mulwala, a reservoir created after a weir was placed across the Murray in 1939, with a menagerie of dogs, chooks, birds and cats. A jetty in the backyard gave them access to the lake, but there they also kept a wire cage filled with redfin. In a time when refrigeration was not yet ubiquitous, this was one way to keep the fish fresh. By filling and refilling the pen, the siblings could supply dinner for their mother's table. For Dennis, remembering redfin also captured the pleasures of childhood games that were intertwined with the very real need to feed the family.[34]

In regional areas in particular, hunting and fishing formed part of this continuum of self-provisioning. In some parts of the Murray-Darling Basin, fishing mixed up leisure and food in interesting ways. Howard Hendrick lived and fished in the Riverland area in South Australia. Howard's family came to the Riverland as 'blockers', part of a group of settlers that helped to establish the fruit or orchard industry. The South Australian government provided them with a small block next to the Murray River for orchard production. There his parents built a home and raised six children. In the dry, nutrient-poor soils of their blocks, this was hard work, and the children worked in the orchard beside both parents outside of school hours. Howard described an austere life, but the nearby river provided a refuge of sorts. The cool waters with large overhanging trees became a place for swimming and larking about with siblings on the weekend. The family also used time at the river to catch fish for the table. It didn't matter to Howard or his siblings whether the fish was native. It mattered that there was something to share for dinner.[35]

Indigenous fishers maintained connections with the rivers of the Murray-Darling Basin throughout the colonial period. Although indigenous cultural kinship systems held a place for native fish, this did not mean Aboriginal people spurned introduced fish. Wally Cooper, a Moitheriban man who grew up on Yellima Station on the main stem of the Murray River, recalled:

> One of the good things was redfin, but it was an introduced species. I viewed that as . . . I liked the dry taste of the redfin, it was a good fish.[36]

Cooper worked extensively with the natural resource managers from the Murray-Darling Basin Authority as they delivered the Native Fish Strategy between 2003–13.[37] It is clear that he has been encouraged to believe that as redfin was an introduced species, it also was a problem. However, the hesitation that Cooper shows in this extract of his interview acts as an example of the way that his memory of the fish when it was plentiful contradicts the science. In his memory, the fish is a 'good thing' with a dry taste that he liked. He also understands that an articulation of the concept of 'the introduced' brings with it a way of constructing the environment that drives conservation.

In a different part of the basin, Barry Porter fished the horseshoe bends of Katarapko Creek. Porter said:

> Our family always used to like the redfin best of all. [Fish were cooked on an] old metal frypan or a wire mesh over the fire, . . . either grilled, fried, battered, you name it. It was a completely different texture and flavour to the callop.[38]

Porter's experience aligns with the new leisure ecologies of the mid-twentieth century. His family spent weekends exploring the rivers around the camping sites they set up all around the Riverland area. In small boats and from the side of the bank, Barry and his family fished for all kinds of river fish. These fish became part of the provisioning that was crucial to the pleasure of Barry's family trips.

Where recreational fishers were mobile through the twin developments of structured holiday time and increased availability of cars, camping was the

The palatability of pests 177

preferred mode of holidaying on the banks of the Murray River. Although providing supplies and services for these holidaymakers saw local town economies flourish, keeping food fresh during the weeks away from home presented a practical challenge to campers. Like Howard Hendrick's family, fishing held a dual role for Porter in this kind of recreation. As Porter shows, the redfin caught went straight from the river to the campfire.

Listening to the words of the fishers from across the Murray-Darling Basin reveals the way that for fishers it is not the scientific narrative that explains what connects them to redfin. Tracey Bye's voice caught with sadness as she talked of this fish, as did Barry Porter's when he explained that 'we used to catch a lot more redfin than we do now. They seemed to have dropped right off'.[39] Although the interviews do not offer explanations for participants' awareness of the disease, this sadness was at odds with the scientific storytelling. Rather than the binary, they show the way that introduced disease can manifest as a positive effect in one paradigm and as having a negative impact in another.

Conclusion

As Libby Robin shows in her chapter about cane toads, the local response to an introduced species is multifaceted and fraught. Understandings of communities living with introduced species are often at odds with scientific assessments and government interventions. In this case, redfin disrupted any clean division between native and introduced because of the way they are entangled with the memories of fishing in the Murray-Darling Basin. Fishers lament their loss. And yet this hasn't brought calls for continued introductions as it has in the case of trout and salmon. Fishers accepted the loss of redfin as part of the changing patterns of understanding about the river. Nevertheless, fishers' emotional response demonstrates different ways of experiencing fish from a fisher perspective.

The relationship between redfin, local fishing communities and science-based natural resource management is complex. This chapter shows some of the changing contours of these relationships over the twentieth century. The catch-ability and edibility of fish leads fishers to remember groups of fish differently and creates a way of including native and non-native together. The changes to consumption patterns and expectations for leisure influence behaviour on the rivers. In these histories, various elements combine and re-combine to shape the way fishing communities appreciated redfin at different times in the history of the Murray-Darling Basin.

Notes

1 I would like to thank Margaret Cook, Adam Gall, Scott Nichols, Heather Goodall, Fern Hames and all the wonderful people at the now closed Native Fish Strategy. The Murray-Darling Basin Authority (MD1489) and the Australian Research Council (DE130100634) supported this research. Mark Lintermans, *Fishes of the Murray Darling Basin: An Introductory Guide* (Canberra: Murray Darling Basin Authority, 2007).
2 Jodi Frawley, 'Dancing to the Billabong's Tune: Oral History in the Environmental Histories of the Murray-Darling Basin Rivers', in Katie Holmes and Heather Goodall (eds.), *Telling Environmental Histories* (London: Palgrave, 2017), 51–79.

3 Murray Darling Basin Authority, 'Alien Fish, Redfin Perch', https://www.mdba.gov. au/sites/default/files/archived/mdbc-NFS-reports/2201_factsheet_alien_redfin_perch. pdf (accessed 14 November 2017).

4 Ian G. Cowx, Robert Arlinghaus and Steven J. Cooke. 'Harmonizing Recreational Fisheries and Conservation Objectives', *Journal of Fish Biology*, 76 (2010): 2194.

5 Gary W. Henry and Jeremy M. Lyle, *The National and Indigenous Fishing Survey* (Canberra: Fisheries Research and Development Corporation, 2003).

6 Henry, *The National Fishing Survey*, 95–6: The list is: relax and unwind; to be outdoors; for solitude; to be with family; to be with friends; fishing competitions; fish for sport; fish for food.

7 Tracey Bye, (Katarapko Creek) interview by Jodi Frawley, Loxton, South Australia, 29 October 2010.

8 FishBase, '*Perca fluviatilis* Linnaeus, 1758', www.fishbase.org/Country/CountryList.php? ID=358&GenusName=Perca&SpeciesName=fluviatilis (accessed 14 November 2017).

9 John Clements, *Salmon at the Antipodes: A History and Review of Trout, Salmon and Char and Introduced Coarse Fish in Australasia* (Skipton, Vic: John Clements with the assistance of Eels Pty Ltd, 1988).

10 Clements, *Salmon at the Antipodes*, 48.

11 Harriet Ritvo, 'Back Story: Migration, Assimilation, and Invasion in the Nineteenth Century', in Jodi Frawley and Iain McCalman (eds.), *Rethinking Invasion Ecologies from the Environmental Humanities* (London: Routledge, 2014), 26.

12 Perca fluviatilis Linnaeus, 1758, FishBase.

13 'English Perch', *The Evening News*, 13 August 1881, 5.

14 'Acclimatising Perch in Station Waters,' *The Sydney Mail and The NSW Advertiser*, 8 October 1887, 764.

15 Richard White, *The Organic Machine* (New York: Hill and Wang, 1995).

16 Paul Sinclair, *The Murray: A River and Its People* (Melbourne: Melbourne University Press, 2001).

17 Lintermans, *Fishes of the Murray Darling Basin*; Dean Ansell and Peter Jackson (eds.), *Emerging Issues in Alien Fish Management in the Murray-Darling Basin* (Canberra: Murray-Darling Basin Authority, 2007).

18 Murray Darling Basin Ministerial Council, *Native Fish Strategy 2003–2013*, (Canberra: Murray-Darling Basin Authority, 2004), 12.

19 Peter Spearritt and Jim Davidson, *Holiday Business: Tourism in Australia since 1870* (Carlton, Vic: The Miegunyah Press at Melbourne University Press, 2000), 178.

20 Richard White, *On Holidays: A History of Getting Away in Australia* (North Melbourne, Vic: Pluto Press, 2005).

21 Frawley, 'Dancing to the Billabong's Tune'; Jodi Frawley, 'Kissing Fish: Rex Hunt, Popular Culture, Sustainability and Fishing Practices', *Journal of Australian Studies*, 39.3 (2015): 307–25.

22 Anna Clark, *The Catch: The Story of Fishing in Australia* (Canberra: National Library of Australia, 2017), 3.

23 Donny Richter (Goulburn River), interview by Jodi Frawley, Murchison, Victoria, 27 October 2010.

24 Sinclair, *The Murray*.

25 Sinclair, *The Murray*, 136.

26 Daniel Pauly, 'Anecdotes and the Shifting Baseline Syndrome in Fisheries', *Trends in Ecology and Evolution*, 10 (1995).

27 Jodi Frawley, Heather Goodall, Scott Nichols and Elizabeth Baker, *Talking Fish: Making Connections with the Rivers of the Murray-Darling Basin* (Canberra, Murray-Darling Basin Authority, 2012).

28 Sinclair, *The Murray*, 141–2.

29 Kay Gibb (Goulburn River), interview by Jodi Frawley, Seymour, Victoria, 25 October 2010.

30 Ken Gilmore (Goulburn River), interview by Jodi Frawley, Thornton, Victoria, 27 October 2010.

31 Seymour Anglers (Don Collihole, Geoff Vernon, Jim Hanley, Keith Jones) (Goulburn River), interview by Jodi Frawley, Seymour, Victoria, 26 October 2010.

32 Andrea Gaynor, *Harvest of the Suburbs: An Environmental History of Growing Food in Australian Cities* (Crawley, WA: University of Western Australia Press, 2006).

33 Adrian Franklin, 'Neo-Darwinian Leisures, the Body and Nature: Hunting and Angling in Modernity', *Body and Society*, 7.3 (2001): 57–76; Adrian Franklin, 'Australian Hunting and Angling Sports and the Changing Nature of Human-Animal Relations in Australia', *Journal of Sociology*, 32.3 (1996): 39–56; Adrian Franklin, 'Performing Acclimatisation: The Agency of Trout Fishing in Postcolonial Australia', *Ethnos*, 76.1 (2011): 19–40.

34 Dennis Lean (Murray River), interview by Jodi Frawley, Yarrawonga, Victoria, 25 November 2010.

35 Howard Hendrick (Katarapko), interview by Jodi Frawley, Loxton, South Australia, 1 October 2010.

36 Wally Cooper (Murray River), interview by Jodi Frawley, Glenrowan, Victoria, 23 November 2010.

37 Murray Darling Basin Ministerial Council, *Native Fish Strategy*.

38 Barry Porter (Katarapko), interview by Jodi Frawley, Berri, South Australia, 28 September 2010. Callop is the golden perch, *Macquaria ambigua*.

39 Barry Porter (Katarapko), interview by Jodi Frawley, Berri, South Australia, 28 September 2010.

Part V

Extinction

'Tis the last fly of summer

'Tis the last fly of summer
Left buzzing alone;
All its black-legged companions
Are dried up or gone;
Not one of its kindred,
No blue-bottle nigh,
To sport 'mid the sugar
Or in the milk die.

I'll not doom thee, thou lone one,
A victim to be;
Since the rest are all vanished,
Come dine thou with me.
Thus kindly I scatter
Some crumbs of my bread,
Where thy mates on the table
Lie withered and dead.

But soon you will perish,
I'm sadly afraid,
For the glass is at sixty
Just now in the shade.
When wasps have all vanish'd,
And blue-bottles flown,
No fly can inhabit
This bleak world alone.
 – From *Punch*, republished in
 *Bell's Life in Sydney and
 Sporting Reviewer*,
 3 June 1848, p. 3.

14 After none
Memorialising animal species extinction through monuments

Dolly Jørgensen

Upon entering the Old New Land gallery of the National Museum of Australia in February 2016, I was confronted with a large box-like galvanised iron structure.[1] Its slightly angular walls leaned out at the top towards the visitor, giving the impression that it might perhaps tip over. On the end facing me was a wall with an epigraph in front of a vanilla-coloured web of sketched lines. 'Endling' it said in indistinct cursive text on the sunken panel, with the words 'disappearing' and 'vanish' at the bottom. On the semi-transparent layer on top, words in black text stood out more clearly: 'Endling/The last of a species'. Underneath that was a text about extinction in Australia:

> In the past 200 years, 18 mammal species and about 100 plant species have become extinct. The loss of the thylacine has become legend, but many smaller animals and plants have also vanished unnoticed. Australia's current rate of extinctions is the highest in the world.

A thylacine, also known colloquially as a Tasmanian tiger, appeared to gaze back at the viewer from a black-and-white photograph just beside the text. This thylacine and all others of its kind have long since vanished – there are none left. As I looked at this epigraph, it struck me that the walls of the box were filled with engravings of the common and scientific names of extinct Australian species. These are the 'unnoticed' of the inscription, and there is an abundance of them (see Figure 14.1).

Passing through the door of the box, I entered a tomb – a sepulchre or mausoleum – for the thylacine. The body remnants of the thylacine stood on display like the bones in an ossuary. When I was there, these included a prehistoric mummified head and a full skeleton, but they change over time for conservation purposes: when the exhibit opened in 2001, it featured a thylacine skin and a full body preserved in formalin. None of these thylacines on display were the last thylacine, the endling, which was discarded by the zoo in Hobart after it died, yet they take the place of this last, serving as a tactile stand-in for the end of the species.

This is no ordinary museum exhibit. It is a monument to extinction and an intentional one at that. The feeling of this exhibit as a 'memorial' to extinction was specifically chosen according to the senior curator, Mike Smith, who led the

184 Dolly Jørgensen

Figure 14.1 'Endling' at the National Museum of Australia, Canberra, February 2016.
Source: Photograph by author.

exhibit design process.[2] How can we understand this monument as a physical manifestation of human remembrance of a species reduced to none?

Monumentalisation is a key element in the remembrance of the dead, from grave headstones to war monuments. These serve as markers of history to remind viewers of the past as well as to envision potential futures. Yet the meaning of a monument is not fixed. A monument embodies a particular time and place but is then experienced and re-read at later times.

Monuments have been criticized for creating static images of past events that culturally reify simplified and often nationalistic histories.[3] A poignant example of the debate around monuments and memory arose in the context of a white supremacist march tied to a Civil War Confederate monument in Charlottesville, Virginia, in August 2017 that caused the death of one anti-march protester. An outpouring of public commentary by historians tried to contextualise the place of American Civil War monuments and question their contemporary uses.[4] The monument, in these critiques, replaces the work of cultural memory with its physical form, with the possible end result of the loss of memory instead of bolstering it. The viewer is reduced to passive spectator instead of active contemplative

After none 185

participant in commemoration of the event or person being memorialised. An alternate criticism is that public monuments are easily rendered invisible, as Robert Musil famously argued.[5] Monuments can become banal through both familiarity and overdramatic representation of events which are seen as irrelevant for the viewer. In spite of these criticisms, monuments continue to be erected for civic figures, the fallen dead of war, and heroes of all types.

Although monumentalisation is thought of as a practice by humans to remember the loss of other humans, these memory practices stretch to encompass the non-humans in forms from pet cemeteries to warhorse memorials.[6] Because humans are the commissioning agents of these works, studying memorials and the sentiments behind them gives us a glimpse into how those humans think about the relationship between humans (past, present, and future) and animals. Because monumentalisation generally involves honouring the subject, the animal commemorated is by definition considered as worthy of being remembered. At the same time, monuments fix the human-animal relationship in space and time, which may lock the remembering into particular forms that could prove relevant for future viewers, or not.

This chapter examines monuments to animal extinction in public settings, covering several different types of public art, including statuary, murals, and funerary forms. Some of the monuments honour a particular species that has become extinct, whereas others mark extinction as a general event. These are works set up after the species' population had been reduced to zero as a way of remembering the missing.

Work in environmental humanities has called for the cultivation of a new ethos in our human relationship with the more-than-human world, one that recognises and makes a place for all.[7] Extinction stories, in particular, might have the potential to raise awareness of the connections between humans and the non-human through mourning or care.[8] Although non-humans like crows show some fleeting signs of grief, only humans as a species set up monuments to remember the past with the intention of bridging generational gaps and forming long-lasting collective memory. Just as Maurice Halbwachs's foundational work on collective memory prompted a surge in historical studies of the function of memory and commemoration of human-centred events, in particular the Holocaust and other traumatic histories,[9] we need to theorise how we remember the histories of non-humans lost to violence and tragedy. Remembering extinct species through monumental works gives species death a materiality that lasts into future generations, ensuring the remembrance of absence.

The novelty of monumentalising extinction should not be underestimated. Species extinction was only recognised as a potential reality in the eighteenth century when losses of species like the Stellar sea cow became known.[10] As Elizabeth Kolbert points out in her Pulitzer Prize-winning book *The Sixth Extinction*, we are now living through the Earth's sixth mass faunal extinction event. The current rapid loss of species is fast gaining widespread attention, including the claim by scientists that it represents an act of 'biological annihilation'.[11] Although the mass extinction of species has happened five times before, this time

186 *Dolly Jørgensen*

around, the extinction is being recorded when it happens; it is being remembered in human narrative. As humans have become aware of the extinction or imminent end of non-human animal species over the last 200 years, there have been active attempts to understand, confront, or memorialise the loss of species which have zero individuals remaining.

Marking the passing of a pigeon

Wyalusing State Park in the far south-western tip of Wisconsin sits in an old landscape. The indigenous population constructed effigy mounds, often in the shape of animals, on the ridges from 1400 to 750 years ago. The Sentinel Ridge Trail in the park passes through a landscape of these mounds, marking the spot as a meeting point of life and death. Midway on the ridge, a dusty brown stone wall frames the edge of the steep bluff to the valley below where the Wisconsin River meets the mighty Mississippi. On a late March day in 2017 when I visited, the sky was grey and the trees were leafless, but the honking of some geese echoed in the distance. A rectangular bronze plaque stands out from the highest brick section (see Figure 14.2). A raised figure of a bird perching on a branch dominates the plaque. Coming nearer, the inscription comes into focus:

DEDICATED
TO THE LAST WISCONSIN
PASSENGER PIGEON
SHOT AT BABCOCK, SEPT 1899
THIS SPECIES BECAME EXTINCT
THROUGH THE AVARICE AND
THOUGHTLESSNESS OF MAN.

This monument to the passenger pigeon dedicated in 1947 by the Wisconsin Ornithological Society commemorates the passing of a species, lamenting the direct role of humans in the event. The last known passenger pigeon (*Ectopistes migratorius*) had not died in Wisconsin but in nearby Ohio in 1914, only a month after the beginning of World War I. That last pigeon, named Martha, died in captivity of illness rather than being killed in the wild. But many millions of her kind had been shot or netted since the mid-1800s as food to be consumed both locally on the US Midwestern frontier and in distant east coast cities crammed with immigrants. The species' quick decline from flocks which blackened the skies to none confounded many commentators. By the time this monument was set up, the passenger pigeon was fading into the distant past, making the monument all the more poignant.

The passenger pigeon monument in Wisconsin was the first public memorial to a species whose population had been reduced to none. In Aldo Leopold's speech published on the occasion of the monument's unveiling on May 11, 1947, he characterised the monument as a symbol of sorrow and grief not only for the now-extinct passenger pigeon but also because of the lingering doubt that the

Figure 14.2 Memorial to the passenger pigeon in Wyalusing State Park, Wyalusing, Wisconsin, March 2017.

Source: Photograph by author.

extinction had been unnecessary. A bird which had been ridiculously abundant – numbering in the billions – became extinct within half a century of the beginning of large-scale hunting.[12] Leopold was unsure that the monument could have any function other than as a public confession of guilt – a collective guilt that he and his ancestors had thought it 'more important to multiply people and comforts than to cherish the beauty of the land in which they live'.[13] Leopold recognised this grief as something new, noting that the sportsman who shot the last pigeon had not grieved, and the sailor who clubbed the last auk did not mourn.[14] The monument was explicitly for remembering this guilt because, although there were still living men who as youngsters had seen the birds, 'but a few decades hence only the oldest oaks will remember, and at long last only the hills will know'.[15] The inscription on the monument would remain, and tourists would read it, 'but their thoughts, like the bronze pigeon, will have no wings'.[16] He doubted, then, that people's attitudes would be easy to change. Hartley H. T. Jackson, who delivered the dedication address at the unveiling, was more positive about the monument's function for the future: 'Let us not look upon this beautiful work of art as a token to the dead and the past, but rather as a symbol to the living and the future

188 *Dolly Jørgensen*

that never again will we permit through our ignorance or our indolence a native species to vanish from our midst'.[17]

A monument, as a physical remnant, is more than plaques and words – it also sits in a landscape. For Leopold, the monument 'perched like a duckhawk on this cliff . . . will scan this wide valley', seeing many birds pass by, but alas, no passenger pigeons.[18] But to astute observers today, the monument to a dead bird placed along the effigy monuments of Native Americans is noteworthy. This was a landscape long used to honour and remember the dead. The pigeon monument is a fitting addition to the landscape of memory on the prominent clifftop.

In southern Pennsylvania, only a few months after the Wisconsin dedication, another monument to the passing of the passenger pigeon was set up. This time it was not a group of specialist bird lovers but a group of Boy Scouts who took the initiative. In October 1947, the Conewago District Boy Scouts sponsored an eight-foot-high stone shaft topped with a bronze passenger pigeon and bearing a granite plaque.[19] According to the plaque, the monument was placed in an area known as Pigeon Hills near Harrisburg, where the passenger pigeon had flocked 'from earliest pioneer days until the 1800's [sic]' and 'was once so plentiful its numbers darkened the skies'.[20] The monument was destroyed in 1981, and a replacement was relocated to a nearby state park and substantially redesigned so that it is now quite similar to the Wyalusing monument.

Unlike the Wyalusing monument, which clearly blamed human greed for the pigeon's demise, the Boy Scout monument called the species 'ill-fated', implying it was destined to fall. Although the scouts specifically dedicated the memorial 'in the interest of the preservation of wild life', the reading of this monument is quite different from the other. This monument evokes the sadness of inevitable loss of the pigeon to death rather than a feeling of guilt for overharvesting the bird. The difference is subtle, but it is there. Both the grief and the guilt approaches to the commemoration of the pigeon appear on roadside historical markers in states from Wisconsin to Mississippi.[21]

Passenger pigeon monuments take on an additional significance in Cincinnati where the last known specimen, a female called Martha, died on September 1, 1914, in the city's zoo.[22] For the 70th anniversary of her death and thus the extinction of the species, the zoo made the pavilion in which she had died into a memorial (see Figure 14.3). The Japanese-style pagoda was one of seven aviaries built in 1875 when the zoo first opened and is the only one remaining after a new gorilla exhibit was added, although the building was relocated when it became a museum/memorial.[23] The building featured three taxidermied passenger pigeons on display and wall exhibits detailing the hunting practices that led to the extinction.[24] In a sad twist of fate, the last known Carolina parakeet (*Conuropsis carolinensis*), who was called Incas, had also died in the same building in 1918. The original dedication plaque named both birds as the object of the memorial, even though it is placed under a bronze passenger pigeon statue.[25]

The passenger pigeon has always received more attention than other North American birds which became extinct in the same era, but these, too, have been monumentalised. The artist Todd McGrain created a series of large-scale bronze

Figure 14.3 Passenger pigeon memorial in the Cincinnati Zoo, Cincinnati, Ohio, June 2017.

Source: Photograph by author.

statues of five extinct North American bird species: great auk (*Pinguinus impennis*, extinct 1844), Labrador duck (*Camptorhynchus labradorius*, extinct 1878), passenger pigeon, Carolina parakeet, and heath hen (*Tympanuchus cupido cupido*, extinct 1832). Individual copies of the statues have been placed into the landscapes relevant to the extinction events for each bird, with species-specific installations in Newfoundland, New York, Florida, Massachusetts, and Ohio (see Figure 14.4). One set of the statues was displayed as a group in 2014–15 in the gardens of the Smithsonian Castle, except for the passenger pigeon which was placed next to the National Museum of Natural History where the body of Martha, the last live passenger pigeon, was put on display to commemorate the 100-year anniversary of her death. I saw this set of statues, their large, smooth black bodies seemingly caught in the act of preening or stretching or squawking in the garden. McGrain modelled 'these gestural forms to contain a taut equilibrium, a balanced pressure from outside and from inside – like a breath held in'.[26] The breath does look to be held in, but it cannot be released from these lifeless figures. They are like giant silhouettes, shadows of things that had been but were no more.

Figure 14.4 Passenger pigeon bronze from the Lost Birds project in place at the Audubon Center, Columbus, Ohio, June 2017.

Source: Photograph by author.

Unlike heroic soldiers, national founders, intellectual thinkers, or tenacious reformers who often have statues put up in their honour, the birds these statues commemorate did nothing special – except that every last one of their kind died because of humans. These monuments mark the tragedy of an extinction as a loss that should be remembered by generations long after those who saw these individual animals. The monuments attempt to make the birds real to us now through images of the species, whether as McGrain's three-dimensional models or the more picture-like plaques of the pigeon monuments. We have to be reminded of what these birds looked like because we cannot see them alive again. These monuments (especially outside of the temporary group setting in which I saw them) tell a directed story about specific species with specific histories. They mark the species' demise but do not necessarily ask the viewer to see the bigger picture of extinction.

Memorials to mass extinction

A partial move from commemorating species extinction to marking mass extinction is what we find in the 'Endling' display at the National Museum of Australia (NMA) described at the beginning of this chapter. In both appearance and function, it serves as an extinction memorial not only to the thylacine but also to the many named species that cover the walls. The original NMA exhibit that opened in 2001 housing 'Endling' was named 'Tangled Destinies'. It was conceived as a space to explore 'how people have responded to the Australian environment over tens of thousands of years and how the environment has responded to them'.[27] As the epigraph notes, the European colonisation of Australia has resulted in the extinction of hundreds of species. Many of these species are not iconic like the Tasmanian tiger – in fact, a good number of them listed on the walls did not even have a common name, indicating their obscurity to the general public. The problem is that these names, too, are obscured: the etching of the names into the metal is hard to read, and only the thylacine has a picture or artefacts to catch the eye. As an attempt to lift a species-level monument to an event-level one, the design is not particularly successful.

The same can be said about the Cincinnati Zoo monument. The multi-species nature of the Cincinnati Zoo extinction site led to a change of focus when the memorial was redone for the 100-year anniversary of the passenger pigeon extinction in 2014.[28] The exhibit inside the building was renamed 'Martha's Legacy: Lessons from the Passenger Pigeon for a Sustainable Future'. Although there was still one wall covering the history of passenger pigeon 'from billions to none' and one case with a pigeon net and stuffed pigeon, the two other long walls now displayed 'A Wake-up Call to Save Wildlife', featuring the American bison, wild turkey, and American alligator, and 'Saving Species: Conservation Champions of the Zoo', with stories of contemporary international wildlife conservation efforts involving the Cincinnati Zoo. There are no stories of other extinctions – even though one important one, the Carolina parakeet, happened in that very room. Although the pagoda is still labelled on the zoo map as 'Passenger Pigeon Memorial', it has become more of an exhibit to wildlife conservation actions in general than a monument to extinction.

A different aesthetic informs 'Monument to Extinction' at the Louisville Zoo (see Figure 14.5). This installation of reddish-brown, mustard yellow, and grey-blue titles by sculptor Bob Lockhart was dedicated in 1987 and now graces the limestone-covered side of the educational building. The work features 45 square ceramic titles with lost and nearly lost species, from the dodo and great auk to

192 Dolly Jørgensen

Figure 14.5 Monument to Extinction. Above: full work; below: two panels close-up, artist Bob Lockhart, Louisville Zoo, Louisville, Kentucky, June 2017.

Source: Photograph by author.

the orangutan and Przwalski horse. Most are close-up portraits of animal heads, making the monument a wall of faces. Our gaze is attracted to these animals because they are large and charismatic, a quality which is often mobilised within environmental conservation to get people to care about species.[29] Their form as portraits anthropomorphises these non-humans to an extent, another technique which can be useful for species conservation purposes.[30] There is also an issue of scale at work in this monument. The many faces stretch out over the wall. There is a sense of smallness of the viewer as one faces the many extinct and near-extinct species.

The smallness of a person in the face of the sixth mass extinction event is even more poignant in the 2012 design for the Mass Extinction Monitoring Observatory (MEMO), a spiralling limestone monument to be set on the edge of a dramatic cliff on the Isle of Portland, part of the Jurassic Coast World Heritage site in the United Kingdom.[31] The design featured visitors passing by massive limestone panels, each carved with an extinct species, as they worked their way up the inside of the monument's spiral, which was inspired by a characteristic local fossil, the Portland screw.[32] The original concept was to have 'images of all the species of plants and animals known to have gone extinct in modern times'.[33] The top would be built to 120 metres but remain open so that more panels could be added over time to mark the continuing extinction crisis.[34] The project had received significant financial backing and endorsements, including that of the well-known biologist E. O. Wilson.

MEMO was the brainchild of Sebastian Brooke, a stonemason, who became personally interested in extinction after doing some research on extinct Brazilian fauna for a commission and coming across the story of Spix's macaw.[35] He was struck by the story and wanted to create a stone project that would bring extinction to the fore, pushing people to ask themselves, 'What are we going to do with this knowledge? Where have we come from? What have we become? Where are we going?' He decided that the Isle of Portland, which has been the source of much of London's limestone building material, would be perfect because it is a World Heritage site and 'records a continuous 180 million years of life'. The monument would be 'cumulative', with its ever-higher spiral to stress the profound nature of the problem.

Indeed, the MEMO design is dramatic and cumulative. The first large-scale carving was under construction when I visited Brooke at a Dorchester stonemason's workshop (see Figure 14.6). It was a Wood's cycad (*Encephalartos woodii*), which is extinct in the wild; all existent specimens are clones from cuttings sent to botanical gardens at the turn of the 1900s. The carving was being made life-size – and since this palm-like cycad can grow to about six metres, it was truly monumental. Brooke labelled it 'Egyptian scale', thinking about the massive stone carvings of ancient Egypt. There is a permanence of the remembering in the choice of stone as the material.

But the monumental cycad is not destined for the MEMO spiral that Brooke had envisioned. Instead, in early 2017, he decided to join forces with The Eden Project (an educational charity in Cornwall that has created massive ecological biomes in an old pit mine) to re-scope the project after having difficulties raising the necessary £30 million for the original MEMO design. Together with Eden, the project was changed to take advantage of a soon-to-be-closed underground mine near the original site. Here the walls could be sculpted in directly, reducing the cost considerably. But more fundamentally, the monument would become an experience on 'the values and marvellousness of biodiversity' in addition to

Figure 14.6 Carver at work on a sculpture of a cycad for the Mass Extinction Memorial Observatory (MEMO) project, Dorset Centre for Creative Arts, Dorchester, May 2017.

Source: Photograph by author.

extinct species using a 'theatrical mentality'.[36] Why the shift from extinction to biodiversity? According to Brooke, it was because Eden thought the original idea was 'too gloomy; no one will come'. Although Brooke seemed happy to be moving the project forward when I spoke to him, I could see sadness in his eyes at the loss of his extinction memorial.

A few hours' drive away from Dorset in the hills of Sussex, a different type of mass extinction monument of stones sits near the top of Mount Caburn. But here there are no pictures; in fact, there are no names. Extinct species are instead marked with a pile of unmarked stones, a 'Life Cairn' (see Figure 14.7). Cairns (derived from the Gaelic *càrn*) have been constructed by humans in Europe since the Neolithic era. They are frequently located on hills and contain burials. Even if they do not contain human remains, cairns may still have been constructed to honour the dead. The Life Cairn on Mount Caburn was constructed in this tradition. According to Andreas Kornevall, an environmental activist originally from Sweden but living in England, he and a local church pastor, Peter Jones, dedicated the cairn to extinct species on May 22, 2011, as 'a holy place' that would invoke a 'pilgrim feeling' and 'an emotional reaction'.[37] In his interview with me,

Kornevall stressed that people have the knowledge ('logos') about extinction, but they need the 'poetic feelings and reactions, the mythos' because 'if they only have logos, they only have half the story'.[38] The pilgrimage to the Life Cairn is participatory in a way that seeing a pre-constructed monument is not: individuals are invited to lay a stone on the memorial and to say a lost species' name. For example, when the last Pinta Island tortoise, George, died in the Galapagos in 2012, Andreas led a group of schoolkids to the cairn, and they each placed a letter they had written about George in the pile with a stone.

The Life Cairn has, however, been a place of controversy. It is constructed within the Lewes Downs National Nature Reserve and Natural England, which administer the site, has said that it is 'absolutely not allowed to have a life cairn' because it conflicts with the heritage values of the existing Middle Iron Age fort ramparts.[39] Thus, the stone pile is repeatedly broken down after construction: 'People go there and take away the stone. Others go and put the stones on' in a 'tug of war'.[40] When I arrived at the Life Cairn, almost nothing was left in the stone pile (see Figure 14.7). The stones that had been on it were nearby, however, so Kornevall and I spent a few minutes gathering some of them to reconstruct a small cairn. He contrasted this ebb and flow with the officially sanctioned Life

Figure 14.7 The Life Cairn on the top of Mount Caburn near Lewes, England, was in a rather dilapidated state, so founder Andreas Kornevall is setting a stake to reclaim the location, May 2017.

Source: Photograph by author.

196 Dolly Jørgensen

Cairn in Stockholm that he built after this original one in 2012. That one is still standing.

The Life Cairn as a monument to extinction is a participatory marker of the nothingness of extinction. Standing in front of the pile of stones can only be meaningful if there is an oral component of reading names or outside knowledge to know what species have been lost. The remembering of the names only happens through ritual. This is intentional: Kornevall believes ceremonies are key because they can 'swing our moral pendulum'.[41]

Remembering after none

These monuments are part of the growing wider awareness of ongoing contemporary extinction and attempts to circumvent dystopian futures in which more and more animal species continue to be reduced to zero. Although 'absence is the predominant phenomenological feature of extinction', as observed by Audra Mitchell, 'absence does not only erase subjects but also proliferates them'.[42] There is indeed a proliferation of extinct species in other forms through monumentalisation. The feathered passenger pigeons are replaced by ones in bronze and iron and stone; the thylacine becomes a skeleton in a mausoleum.

Therein lies a potential problem with this response to animal populations reduced to zero. The monuments become testaments to the human power to change environments rather than a mode of respecting the lost. As Rick De Vos notes, extinction narratives 'are shaped by [the species'] absence and their extirpation, by stories of human agency, exploitation and violence rather than those of avian survival and endurance'.[43] All the monuments discussed here mark the end of the species, but none gives much space to the vibrant and long-lived nature of the species before the end event. Yet if a critique of regular extinction stories is that they establish 'spatial and temporal distance – a gap that shields the narratee [us] from the extinct animal and the act of killing', as levelled by De Vos,[44] then these monuments close the gap. They stress the 'avarice and thoughtlessness of man' (Wyalusing monument), 'the current rate of extinction' (Endling), and the 'mythos' of laying a stone (Life Cairn). The monuments do not shy away from laying blame on the viewer.

Because memorials may say more about the people who set them up than about the events they commemorate, what does it say about modern society that memorials to extinction are appearing in more and more places? I think there are two answers to this question. One is that modern society is struggling with the entanglement of remembering and forgetting. Those who set up monuments are afraid that the honouree or event will be forgotten in the future or is already being forgotten by most in the present. The memorial makers want people to remember the acts that brought about a species' end as well as the value and beauty of the species itself. But these remembrances are too late for the species in question – it is gone. The monument's only value is from either prompting new conservation actions in the world today (to avoid future similar ends) or from a purely spiritual or aesthetic appreciation for nature now gone. The second of these values

After none 197

is easier to achieve than the first because it requires only remembering what was in the past while allowing us to forget why it is no longer in the present and not insist on changes to present activities to prevent future extinctions.

The other answer is that memorials to extinction reveal a weakening of human exceptionalism and move towards a post-human perspective over the last 70 years.[45] The oldest passenger pigeon memorials were set up in the same era as monuments to the soldiers of World War II.[46] These birds were also casualties of war, although it was a war on nature, and were understood at the time as worthy as objects of grief. The species was lost, gone from the landscape, and that was worth an expression of sorrow. The Endling display also reveals an attentiveness to the individual within the extinction event, something which affirms the relationality of multi-species communities.[47] The individual bodies laid out in the exhibit, even if they are not the actual endling, make the thylacine personal and specific. The original MEMO design and Life Cairn ask the viewer to recognise the multitude of non-humans in the world as having inherent value. Extinction monuments reveal an awareness of human/non-human entanglement and the wish to engage with it.

Standing in front of the shiny box in the National Museum of Australia, I saw what was perhaps a fitting end for the thylacine. An end with meaning. There is nothing to be done about the thylacine now, but the thylacine deaths need not have been in vain.[48] This is an end that encourages the viewer not to let the same thing happen again. The names on the walls cry out, asking for us to stop adding their living relatives. The monument evokes mourning but at the same time is a celebration of life. As Ursula Heise points out, there are limitations to the elegy as a genre for trying to avoid extinction,[49] so thinking beyond the dead to the still living matters. After there are none, there is not nothing left – there is still a chance to remember, to honour, to grieve, to commemorate, to act.

Notes

1 The fieldwork necessary for this article was generously supported by the Birgit och Gad Rausings Stiftelse för Humanistisk Forskning which funded the author's project 'Monuments to extinction'.

2 Mike Smith, interview with author, Canberra, 16 February 2016. See a full discussion of this exhibit's history and social repercussions in Dolly Jørgensen, 'Endling, The Power of the Last in an Extinction-Prone World', *Environmental Philosophy*, 14.1 (2016): 119–38.

3 James E. Young, 'Memory and Counter-Memory', *Harvard Design Magazine*, no. 9, www.harvarddesignmagazine.org/issues/9/memory-and-counter-memory.

4 American Historical Association, 'Historians on the Confederate Monument Debate', www.historians.org/news-and-advocacy/everything-has-a-history/historians-on-the-confederate-monument-debate.

5 Robert Musil, 'Monuments', in *Selected Writings*, ed. and trans. Burton Pike (New York: Continuum, 1985), 320–3.

6 For the commemoration of animals that fought in armed conflicts, see Hilda Kean, 'Animals and War Memorials: Different Approaches to Commemorating the Human-Animal Relationship', in Ryan Hediger (ed.), *Animals and War: Studies of Europe and North America* (Netherlands: Brill, 2013); Steven Johnston, 'Animals in War:

198 *Dolly Jørgensen*

Commemoration, Patriotism, Death', *Political Research Quarterly*, 65.2 (2012): 359–71; Sandra Swart, 'Horses in the South African War, c. 1899–1902', *Society & Animals*, 18.4 (2010): 348–66.

7 Deborah Bird Rose and Thom van Dooren, 'Encountering a More-Than-human World: Ethos and the Arts of Witness', in Urusla Heise, Jon Christensen and Michelle Niemann (eds.), *Routledge Companion to the Environmental Humanities* (London: Routledge, 2017).

8 Thom van Dooren, 'Care', *Environmental Humanities*, 5 (2014): 291–4; Thom van Dooren, 'Mourning Crows: Grief and Extinction in a Shared World', in G. Marcin and S. McHugh (eds.), *Routledge Handbook of Human-Animal Studies* (London: Routledge, 2014).

9 See Alon Confino, 'Collective Memory and Cultural History: Problems of Method', *American Historical Review*, (1997): 1386–412 and Kerwin Lee Klein, 'On the Emergence of Memory in Historical Discourse', *Representations*, 69 (2000): 127–50 for overviews of this scholarship.

10 Mark Barrow, *Nature's Ghosts: Confronting Extinction from the Age of Jefferson to the Age of Ecology* (Chicago: University of Chicago Press, 2009); Ryan Tucker Jones, *Empire of Extinction: Russians and the North Pacific's Beasts of the Sea, 1741–1867* (Oxford: Oxford University Press, 2014).

11 G. Ceballos, P. R. Ehrlich and R. Dirzo, 'Biological Annihilation via the Ongoing Sixth Mass Extinction Signalled by Vertebrate Population Losses and Declines', *PNAS*, 114 (2017): E6089–96.

12 There are several recent books on the passenger pigeon extinction history, including Mark Avery, *A Message from Martha: The Extinction of the Passenger Pigeon and Its Relevance Today* (New York: Bloomsbury, 2014); Errol Fuller, *The Passenger Pigeon* (Princeton: Princeton University Press, 2014); and Joel Greenberg, *A Feathered River Across the Sky: The Passenger Pigeon's Flight to Extinction* (New York: Bloomsbury, 2014).

13 Aldo Leopold, 'On a Monument to the Pigeon', in Walter E. Scott (ed.), *Silent Wings: A Memorial to the Passenger Pigeon* (Madison: Wisconsin Society for Ornithology, 1947), 4.

14 Leopold, 'On a Monument to the Pigeon', 3.

15 Leopold, 'On a Monument to the Pigeon', 3.

16 Leopold, 'On a Monument to the Pigeon', 4.

17 Hartley H. T. Jackson, 'Attitude in Conservation', in Walter E. Scott (ed.), *Silent Wings: A Memorial to the Passenger Pigeon* (Madison: Wisconsin Society for Ornithology, 1947), 24.

18 Leopold, 'On a Monument to the Pigeon', 4.

19 'Passenger Pigeon Memorial Site', *Gettysburg Times*, 8 October 1947.

20 I have seen photographs of the current monument and have read the text on the plaque from those photographs, http://allenbrowne.blogspot.no/2012/02/pigeon-monument.html.

21 See the Historical Marker Database for examples, www.hmdb.org.

22 R. W. Shufeldt, 'Anatomical and Other Notes on the Passenger Pigeon (*Estopistes migratorum*) Lately Living in the Cincinnati Zoological Gardens', *The Auk*, 32.1 (1915): 29–41.

23 Associated Press, 'Once the Most Abundant Bird in the World, the Passenger Pigeon is Gone', *Lewiston Evening Journal*, 14 January 1975; Joy W. Kraft, *The Cincinnati Zoo and Botanical Garden* (Charleston: Arcadia Publishing, 2010), 24.

24 I have seen only a couple of photographs prior to the 2014 renovation of the exhibit: Joel Greenberg, 'A Trip to the Holy Land, Part II, Piketon and Cincinnati', https://web.archive.org/web/20100506012422/www.birdzilla.com/blog/2010/04/17/a-trip-to-the-holy-land-part-ii-piketon-and-cincinnati/ and Roadside America, 'Martha – Passenger Pigeon Memorial Hut', www.roadsideamerica.com/story/10663.

25 The plaque incorrectly named the Carolina parakeet as 'Inca'.

After none   199

26 Todd McGrain, 'Memorials', www.toddmcgrain.com/memorials/.
27 National Museum of Australia, '*Tangled Destinies*: Land and People in Australia', https://web.archive.org/web/20010620050636/www.nma.gov.au/exhibitions/tangled.htm.
28 I visited the site in May 2017. Descriptions come from that visit.
29 Jamie Lorimer, 'Nonhuman Charisma', *Environment and Planning D: Society and Space*, 25 (2007): 911–32.
30 M. Root-Bernstein, L. Douglas, A. Smith and D. Veríssimo, 'Anthropomorphized Species as Tools for Conservation: Utility beyond Prosocial, Intelligent and Suffering Species', *Biodiversity and Conservation*, 8 (2013): 1577–89.
31 MEMO project brochure, 2012, https://web.archive.org/web/20121228204516/www.memoproject.org/docs/MEMO_brochure.pdf. The architecture firm Adjaye Associates had created the memorial's design.
32 MEMO project website, 2012, https://web.archive.org/web/20121228204516/www.memoproject.org/.
33 MEMO project website, 2009, https://web.archive.org/web/20090704081752/http://memoproject.org:80/.
34 The design is shown in the MEMO project brochure from 2012.
35 Sebastian Brooke, interview with author, 10 May 2017, Dorchester and Isle of Portland. Quotes in this paragraph are from that interview.
36 Brooke, interview with author.
37 Andreas Kornevall, interview with author, 12 May 2017, Glynde, United Kingdom.
38 Kornevall, interview with author.
39 Kornevall, interview with author.
40 Kornevall, interview with author.
41 Keith Parkins, 'The Life Cairn: A Memorial for Extinct Species', Life on a Dark Mountain, https://medium.com/dark-mountain/the-life-cairn-1483610d05ab.
42 Audra Mitchell, 'Beyond Biodiversity and Species: Problematizing Extinction', *Theory, Culture & Society*, 33.5 (2016): 23–42.
43 Rick De Vos, 'Provocations from the Field – Extinction, Encountering and the Exigencies of Forgetting', *Animal Studies Journal*, 6.1 (2017): 1–11, 4.
44 De Vos, 'Provocations from the Field', 8.
45 See Mike Smith, 'Ecological Community, the Sense of the World, and Senseless Extinction', *Environmental Humanities*, 2 (2013): 21–41 for a discussion of these problems for the question of extinction.
46 The effort to construct the first statue to honour World War II soldiers from the United States was started in 1947 to honour the veterans of Iwo Jima. This statue was dedicated in 1954 as the Marine Corps War Memorial. See National Park Service, 'World War II Memorials in the National Park Service', www.nps.gov/subjects/worldwarii/memory.htm and 'History of the Marine Corps War Memorial', www.nps.gov/gwmp/learn/historyculture/usmcwarmemorial.htm.
47 Thom van Dooren, 'Pain of Extinction: The Death of a Vulture', *Cultural Studies Review*, 16.2 (2010): 271–89.
48 There have been and still are ongoing attempts to reconstruct thylacine DNA in the hopes that it can be genetically reengineered through de-extinction techniques and exist again. See Stephanie S. Turner, 'Open-Ended Stories. Extinction Narratives in Genome Time', *Literature and Medicine*, 26.1 (2007): 55–82; Amy Lynn Fletcher, 'Bring 'em Back Alive: Taking the Tasmanian Tiger Cloning Project', *Technology in Society*, 30 (2008): 184–201.
49 Ursula K. Heise, *Imagining Extinction: The Cultural Meanings of Endangered Species* (Chicago: University of Chicago Press, 2016), Chapter 2.

Index

Note: figures are denoted with italicized page numbers.

Abbott, Ian 65
Aboriginal people *see* First Nations, Aboriginal and Torres Strait Islander people
Aborigines Act (1905) 65
abundant animal populations: live sheep exports 6, 99–107; overview of 9; pearl-shell, bêche-de-mer and trochus fisheries 6, 73–82; in swamplands 4, 85–96
acclimatisation, fish 156–7, 158, 160, 161–4, 170–2
aerial insecticides and pesticides: Argentine ants eradication using 45; locust warfare with 30, 32–4, 35, 36, 37; mosquito eradication via 32, 95
aerial surveys 7
Agent Orange 35, 139
Agricultural Gazette of New South Wales 131
Allport, Morton and Joseph 170–1
animal-human relations: Aboriginal or indigenous 2–3, 4, 6, 29, 57–8, 64–6; colonisation influencing (*see* colonisation); conservation efforts in (*see* conservation management); with domestic animals 4; with invasive or introduced animals 2–3, 4, 42–4, 46, 51; media portrayals shaping (*see* media); militarised or warlike approach to 26–8, *27*, 30–7, 46; monumentalisation of extinct species showing 6, 183–97; pigs and 114–15; social ecological systems of 57–8, 64–6, 67; sportlike approach to 17–18, 19, 21, 157–61, *159*, 164–5, 172–3, 175, 176–7; swampland urban development

and 4, 85–96; vineyards and vine feeders in 126–36
Animal Liberation 103–4
Animal Liberation (Singer) 103
animal movement/activism: Animal Liberation as 103–4; Animals Australia as 107; live sheep export opposition by 99–100, 103–4, 107; politicisation of animals with 99–100, 103–4
animal populations: abundant (*see* abundant animal populations); counting 1–10; demonisation of 7–8, 114, 121; domestic (*see* domestic animal populations); equilibrium in (*see* equilibrium in animal populations); excess (*see* excess animal populations); extinct 4, 6, 9–10, 183–97, 199n48; free-living 3, 6–7, 115, 119–21, 122–3n17; human relations with (*see* animal-human relations); invasive or introduced (*see* invasive or introduced animals); native (*see* native animal populations); politicisation of (*see* politicisation of population numbers); scarce (*see* scarce animal populations)
Animals Australia 107
"the Antbeater" figure 49
Ant Hunter Club 49
Ant Menace 49
Argentine Ant Act (1954) 45
Argentine Ant Eradication Act (1962) 47
Argentine Ant Eradication Committee (AAEC) 41, 47–9, 50, 51
Argentine ants: AAEC role in combating 41, 47–9, 50, 51; animal-human relations with 42–4, 46, 51; description and characteristics of 42, 46; domestic

202 *Index*

animals affected by eradication efforts 47–8; economic entomology and 45; history, ontology and phenomenology of 41–4; infestation and eradication of 45–9; insecticides and pesticides against 41, 44, 45–51; as invasive or introduced animals 3, 41–51; media coverage and publicity of 42–3, 44–5, 46–7, 48–9; pest characterisation of 41, 42–5, 49; politicisation of issues with 46, 48–9; popular environmentalism and end of eradication campaign for 49–51

Australasian Meat Industry Employees' Union (AMIEU) 100–3, 104, 105, 107

Australia: Aboriginal people in (*see* First Nations, Aboriginal and Torres Strait Islander people); animal populations in (*see* animal populations); colonisation of (*see* colonisation); Defence of Australia policy 35; Esperance bioregion of 6, 56–67; Great Barrier Reef 73–82; militarised landscapes in 7, 139–49; Murray-Darling Basin in 3, 168–77; swamplands in 4, 50, 85–96, 115, 120; unique characteristics of 1–2

Australian Agricultural Council 45

Australian Council of Trade Unions (ACTU) 101–2, 105, 107

Australian Federation of Animal Societies 104

Australian greyback beetles 19

Australian National Airways 33

Australian Plague Locust Commission (APLC) 36, 37

Australian plague locusts *see* locusts

Australian Workers' Union 102

Banfield, Edmund 78–9

Barr, Neil 67

Bartley, Nehmiah 88

Beard, John 56

bêche-de-mer fisheries *see* pearl-shell, bêche-de-mer and trochus fisheries

Bennett, George 76, 77

benzene hexachloride (BHC) 32, 33

Berger, John 1, 2

Berkes, Fikret 57

bettongs 65

biological controls 16–17, 19, 23n7

birds: counting of 6; demonisation of cats killing 7–8; domesticated 6; fire for land management affecting 57; hunting

of 120; in militarised landscapes 146; monumentalisation of extinct 186–91, *187*, *189*, *190*, 197; urban development affecting 8; vine feeders 4, 126, 127, 130, 131–2, *132*, 133–4, 135; *see also specific bird species*

Birtles, Francis 31

Bishop, Julie 16

black swans 120

Bolton, Geoffrey 160

bounties for pest killing 6, 11nn20–1, 49, 65, 164

Bowen, Alister 161

Boy Scouts 188

Braudel, Fernand 61

Brooke, Sebastian 193–4

Brooks, J. P. 66

brush/bush turkeys 8, 57

bubonic plague 91

Burbidge, Andrew 59

Burgoyne, Iris 66

Burnett, James Charles 87

Busby, James 128–9

bush stone-curlew 146

Bye, Tracey 170, 177

Caire, Nicholas 158

Calvino, Italo, "La formica argentina" 43

'Cane Toad in Oz' website 24n29

'Cane Toad Muster' (Lyons) 18

cane toads: as biological controls for beetles 16–17, 19; conservation management of 18, 20–3; definition and description of 15–17, *16*; demonisation of 7, 8; as invasive or introduced animals 3, 15–23; overview of 15; as pests 3; poisonous threats from 15–16, 19–21; politicisation of population numbers 15, 18; sport of toadbusting to eradicate 17–18, 19, 21; 'unnatural' label for 17–18, 19

Cane Toads: An Unnatural History (Lewis) 17

Card, Mary, Grape Vine and Silvereye Tea Cloth and Table Mat 131–2, *132*

Carmichael, Henry 130

Carmody, Emma: *The Ento(M)-usician* 111–12; *Homecoming (Alpine Strata)* 153–4

Carolina parakeets 188, *189*, 191

Carson, Rachel, *Silent Spring* 41, 51, 134

Carstairs, William 163

Cary, John 67

Index 203

Case, A. L. 50
caterpillars 6, 126, 127, 128–9, 130–1
cats 7–8, 129, 146
cattle: colonisation with 56, 61; counting
of 6; pig population relative to 113–14,
115; swamplands grazing by 88, 89
Caughly, Graeme 58
Cessnock Vintage Festival 133
chickens 6
China: bêche-de-mer popularity in 74;
Chinese market gardens 90–1, 95;
fishers from 78–9, 160–1; pigs in/from
115, 117
Chipp, Don 105
chlordane 44, 45, 46–8, 49, 50, 51
cholera 89
Christmas beetle 8
citizen science 49
Clark, Anna 156–7, 173
Clark, James 75, 76, 78
climate change 22, 23
Closmann, Charles E. 139
cod 160, 163, 169, 174–5
Colding, Johan 57
colonial fishery exploitation: class and
157, 160–1, 175; debate over 156–7;
fish acclimatisation and 156–7, 158,
160, 161–4, 170–2; fishery management
vs. 164; hatcheries in 156, 158,
159, 160; international perspectives
influencing 156, 157; nets used by
commercial fishers in 157–8, 160, 162,
164, 165; pearl-shell, bêche-de-mer and
trochus fisheries 6, 73–82; politicisation
of population numbers for 157, 160–1,
163–4, 165; redfin in 3, 168–77;
regulations and 73, 74, 75, 77–8, 81–2,
156, 158, 160, 162, 164, 165; scarcity
fears *vs.* bounty expectations for 161–4,
165; as slow catastrophe 155–6, 165n2;
for sport *vs.* commerce 157–61, *159*,
164–5, 172–3, 175, 176–7; statistics
on commercial fishers 160–1; tourism
and 73, 79–81, *80*, 157, 163–4, 172–3,
176–7
colonisation: colonial fishery exploitation
3, 6, 73–82, 155–65, 168–77; counting
animals marking prosperity of 5, 5–6;
ecological imperialism with 56; excess
animal populations reduced by 9;
extinct animal populations after 9, 191;
invasive or introduced animals via 2–3,
4, 56–67, 88, 95, 113–21, 163, 168–72,

174–7; locust warfare tied to 3–4, 26–8,
29, 37; native animals affected by 3–4,
8; pastoralism with (*see* pastoralism);
pearl-shell, bêche-de-mer and trochus
fisheries development with 6, 73–82;
pigs as co-colonisers 113–21; sheep and
invasion via 3, 6, 56–67; swamplands
changes with 4, 85–96; urban
development with 4, 8, 85–96, *87*
Columbian Exchange 120
common dunnart 146
Commonwealth Endangered Species
Advisory Committee 145
Commonwealth Heritage Sites 142
Commonwealth Scientific Industrial
Research Organisation (CSIRO):
Argentine ants response of 45–6;
biological controls work of 23n7;
locust warfare role of 32, 34; militarised
landscape research by 141–2, 145
The Compleat Angler (Walton) 157
Conference of Entomologists 46
Connor, Michael 114
Connors, Libby 134, 156, 161
conservation management: Argentine
ants eradication campaign opposition
49–51; biodiversity term in 21;
cane toad population management
as 18, 20–3; colonial fishery
exploitation and efforts for 161–2,
164, 165; ethical considerations
in 18, 22, 23; hyperobjects in 22;
Indigenous Protected Areas in 17;
militarised landscapes for 139–49;
monumentalisation of extinct species
and calls for 191, 196–7; National
Reserves in 17, 141; politicisation of
population numbers and 21–2; redfin
decline applauded by 168–9, 174–5;
scale of efforts in 22
Convention on Biological Diversity 145
Cooke, Brian 66
Cooling, L. E. 91–3
Coombs, H. C. 81–2
Cooper, Wally 176
Council for Scientific and Industrial
Research 33
counting animal populations 1–10; of
abundant populations 9; aerial surveys
for 7; animal-human relations and 1–3,
4, 6; demonisation of animals based on
7–8; digital camera traps for 7; domestic
4, 5–6; of equilibrium state populations

9; of excess populations 8–9; of extinct populations 9–10; free-living 3, 6–7; invasive or introduced 2–3, 4; methods of 4–7; in militarised landscapes 7; native 3–4, 6, 8; politicisation of numbers 4, 7–8, 9; sampling and extrapolation for 7; satellite imagery for 7; of scarce populations 9; *see also specific animals*
Crawford, E. H. K. 171
Crosby, Alfred 56, 58, 120, 135
CSIRO *see* Commonwealth Scientific Industrial Research Organisation
Cullity, Tom 134, 135
Curran, Wally 103

Dabb, Annie 65
Dabungoo (Sambo) 65
Davidson, Jim 172
Davidson-Hunt, Ian 57
DDT 32, 33, 95
Defence of Australia policy 35
demonisation of animals 7–8, 114, 121
Dempster family 59, 60–2, 64–5, 66
dengue fever 91, 93, 94, 95
D'Entrecasteaux, Bruny 57
Derrida, Jacques 2
Deveson, Ted 27, 28, 31
Devitt, Tony 134, 135
De Vos, Rick 196
dieldrin 46–8, 50, 51, 133
digital camera traps 7
Dimer family 62, 63
dingoes 6, 65
diphtheria 89
diseases: Aboriginal people affected by 65; germ theory of 85, 89, 95; marsupials impacted by 65; miasmatic theory of 85, 88–9, 95; mosquitoes transmitting 32, 85, 91–6; redfin population decreased by 168, 169; swamplands as source of 85, 88–96
D'Ombrain, Athel 133
domestic animal populations: animal-human relations with 4; Argentine ants eradication efforts consideration of 47–8; colonisation introducing 4, 56–67, 88, 95, 113–21; counting of 4, 5–6; live exports of 6, 99–107; swamplands grazing by 88, 89, 90, 95; *see also* cattle; horses; pigs; sheep
Dominy, Michele 59
Dowd, John 50
downy mildew 131
droughts 8, 60, 66–7

Drummond, John 60
ducks 120, 127, 139, 189
Dunstan, David 126
dysentery 89

ecological imperialism 56
economic entomology 45
The Eden Project 193–4
"El Argentino" figure 49
Embury, Monty 81
emus 57, 120
endangered animal populations 4; *see also* scarce animal populations
Endangered Species Act (1974, US) 145
Endangered Species Program 145
Endangered Species Protection Act (1992) 145–6, 147
Endangered Species Unit 145
'Endling/The last of a species' exhibit 183–4, *184*, 191, 197
The Ento(M)-usician (Carmody) 111–12
Environment Protection and Biodiversity Conservation Act 4
equilibrium in animal populations: in militarised landscapes 139–49; overview of 9; pigs 113–21; vine feeders 126–36
Erickson, Rica 59, 63
Esperance bioregion: Aboriginal social ecological systems in 57–8, 64–6, 67; description of 56–7; sheep in 6, 56–67
Essig, Mark 113, 120
ethical considerations, in conservation management 18, 22, 23
excess animal populations: Argentine ants 41–51; cane toads 15–23; locusts 26–37; overview of 8–9; sheep 56–67
Export of Live Sheep from Australia report 106, 107
exports, sheep *see* live sheep exports
extinct animal populations: collective memory of 185; colonisation leading to 9, 191; de-extinction efforts for 199n48; grief and guilt over 186–8, 197; mass extinctions of 185–6, 191–6, *192, 194, 195*; monuments memorialising 6, 183–97; overview of 9–10; passenger pigeons as 186–91, *187, 189, 190*, 197; statistics on 4; thylacine as 4, 6, 11n21, 183–4, *184*, 191, 197, 199n48
Eyre, John 58

fairy shrimp 148
Falconer, Peter 104–5
filaria 94

Index 205

fire: Aboriginal land management with 29, 57, 62–4, 86; locust warfare with 29, 30; swamplands shaped by 86

First Nations, Aboriginal and Torres Strait Islander people: animal-human relations with 2–3, 4, 6, 29, 57–8, 64–6; colonisation and relations with 2, 4, 6, 56; counting animals by 5; eco-shepherding of 56, 62–4, 67; fire for land management by 29, 57, 62–4, 86; fishing and fisheries use by 74, 155, 161, 169, 176; Indigenous Protected Areas managed by 17; locust history with 29; oral animal stories of 4; pigs disrupting ecologies important to 113, 115, 120–1; sheep invasion into lands of 6, 56, 58–67; social ecological systems of 57–8, 64–6, 67; swamplands inhabitance by 86–7; traditional pathways of, as TSRs 62; vine feeder hunting by 129, 130

First World War: militarised locust warfare influenced by 30, 31, 37; Puckapunyal Military Training Area development during 144

Fishes of the Murray Darling Basin: An Introductory Guide (Lintermans) 168

fish/fisheries: colonial exploitation of 3, 6, 73–82, 155–65, 168–77; militarised landscapes affecting 139; pearl-shell, bêche-de-mer and trochus 6, 73–82; politicisation of population numbers for 7, 157, 160–1, 163–4, 165; redfin 3, 168–77; sport or recreational fishing 157–61, 159, 164–5, 172–3, 175, 176–7

flamethrowers, locust warfare with 30

Flinders, Matthew 57

Flynn, John 31

Folke, Carl 57

Ford, Lisa 114

"La formica argentina" (Calvino) 43

foxes 19, 146

Franklin, Adrian 99, 113, 119, 156–7, 175

Fraser, Malcolm 101

free-living animal populations: counting of 3, 6–7; invasive or introduced animals as 3; pigs in 115, 119–21, 122–3n17

French cane beetles 19

friar birds 133

Froggatt, Walter 31

Gammexane 32, 33

Georges, George 105–6, 107

germ theory 85, 89, 95

Gibb, Kay 174

Gifford, Peter 66

Gilmore, Ken 174

grayling 160, 163

great auks 189

The Great Barrier Reed: Its Products and Potentialities (Saville-Kent) 76–7

Great Barrier Reef: development of 78–81; pearl-shell, bêche-de-mer and trochus fisheries on 73–82; tourism to 73, 79–81, 80

Great Barrier Reef Committee (GBRC) 79

Greaves, Tom 45, 46

Green, Neville 64

Grewar, Geoff 66

grubs 6, 128–9

Hacking, Ian 42

Haebich, Anna 65

Halbwach, Maurice 185

Hamilton, J. T. 47–8

Hamlyn-Harris, Ronald 94–5

Hanley, Jim 175

Hannickel, Erica 126–7, 128

Hanson, Thor 139

Haraway, Donna 21, 23

hatcheries, fish 156, 158, 159, 160

Hawke, Bob 101–2, 105

Health Act (1911) 45

heath hens 189

Heise, Ursula 197

Hely, Frederick 129

Hendrick, Howard and family 176, 177

Homecoming (Alpine Strata) (Carmody) 153–4

horses: colonisation with 61; pig population relative to 114; swamplands grazing by 88, 89

Hughes, Hugh 116

human relations with animals *see* animal-human relations

Hunter Valley: pigs in 115–21; vineyards and vine feeders in 130–1, 133–4

Hunter Vintage Festival 133

Hutton, Drew 134, 156, 161

hyperobjects 22

Indigenous Protected Areas (IPAs) 17

insecticides: anti-malarial efforts with 32; Argentine ants eradication with 41, 44, 45–51; locust warfare with 30, 32–4, 35, 36, 37; mosquito eradication with 32, 95

International Fisheries Exhibitions 157

International Union for Conservation of Nature (IUCN) 21

206 *Index*

invasive or introduced animals: animal-human relations with 2–3, 4, 42–4, 46, 51; Argentine ants as 3, 41–51; cane toads as 3, 15–23; fish as 3, 163, 168–72, 174–7; naturalisation of 4; pigs as 113–21; sheep as 6, 56–67; in swamplands 88, 95; vine feeders 131

Jackson, Hartley H. T. 187–8
Japan: Argentine ants in 51; fishers from 78–9; pigs in 120; Second World War aircraft of 32
Jones, Peter 194
Jurassic Coast World Heritage site 193

kangaroos: Aboriginal sale of skins 65; bounties for killing 7, 11n20; eastern grey, in militarised landscapes 147; fire for land management affecting 57; pastoralism affecting 120; red, counting of 7
Key, K. H. L. (Ken) 34, 36
Kimberley Toad Busters 18
Kolbert, Elizabeth, *The Sixth Extinction* 185
Kornevall, Andreas 194–6, *195*
Kull, Kalevi 21

labor issues: meat workers' union campaign on 99–103, 104, 105, 107; in pearl-shell, bêche-de-mer and trochus fisheries 73, 75, 77, 78–9, 81; social movements addressing 99–100
Labrador ducks 189
Land for Wildlife properties 142
Larson, Brendan 18
Lean, Dennis and family 175
Leichhardt, Ludwig 130
Leopold, Aldo 186–7, 188
Letters on the Culture of the Vine, Fermentation, and the Management of Wine in the Cellar (Macarthur) 129
Lewes Down National Nature Reserve 195
Lewis, Mark, *Cane Toads: An Unnatural History* 17
'Life Cairn' 194–6, *195*, 197
Life hath its charms (Australasian Chronicle) 71
Lintermans, Mark 168, 169
live sheep exports: animal movement opposing 99–100, 103–4, 107; campaign against 99–107; counting animals for 6; *Export of Live Sheep from Australia* report on 106, 107; farmers

countering opposition to 101; meat workers' union opposing 99–103, 104, 105, 107; parliamentary debates on 104–6, 107; politicisation of campaign against 99–100, 103–7; ratio system with 101
Lockhart, Bob 191
locusts: aerial deployment against 30, 32–4, 35, 36, 37; APLC role in combating 36, 37; colonisation ties to war on 3–4, 26–8, 29, 37; description and characteristics of 28, 31; histories of 28–30; insecticides and pesticides against 30, 32–4, 35, 36, 37; media coverage and publicity of 26, 31, 34, 36; militarised warfare against 26–8, 27, 30–7; plagues of, in religious history 29–30, 37; surveillance and suppression strategies for 33–5, 36
Loomis, Ladd and Betty Ann 48
Lost Birds project 188–9, *190*
Lyons, Dana, 'Cane Toad Muster' 18

Macarthur, William 129–30, 134, 135
Machlis, Gary 139
magpies 130, 133
malaria 32, 91, 93, 94
Malayan Emergency 34–5, 37
Malthouse, Thomas 117
Mandeville, Charles 162–3
The man from Menindie (Souter) 13
Manning, Adrian 21–2
A Manual of Plain Directions for Planting and Cultivating a Vineyard and for Making Wine in New South Wales (Busby) 129
Mark, Patty 104
marsupials: disease impacting 65; fire for land management affecting 57; *see also* kangaroos; possums; wallabies
Mass Extinction Monitoring Observatory (MEMO) 193–4, *194*, 197
Mayr, Gustav 44
McDonald, Jack 33
McGlade, Corporal 65
McGrain, Todd 188–9
McNeur, Catherine 118
meat workers' union, live sheep export opposition by 99–103, 104, 105, 107
media: Argentine ants coverage in 42–3, 44–5, 46–7, 48–9; cane toad coverage in 15; demonisation of animals in 8; live sheep exports opposition coverage by 102, 103, 106; locust warfare

coverage and promotion in 26, 31, 34, 36; pearl-shell, bêche-de-mer and trochus fisheries promotion in 76, 77; pigs' portrayal in 114, 117, 118; swamplands control and development portrayal in 85–6, 93, 95; vine feeder characterisation in 129, 131
Melville, Elinor, *A Plague of Sheep* 56
Menzies, Robert 33
miasmatic theory 85, 88–9, 95
militarised landscapes: animals in 7, 145–9; biological diversity in 140–1, 142, 148; chemicals and poisons in 35, 139; conservation values and management in 139–49; counting animals in 7; culling programs at, controversy over 147; defence capabilities in 141, 142, 148; ecological impacts of 139–49; historical land use impacts in *143*, 144; international perspectives and influences 145, 147–9; monitoring and recording programs at 146; pest control in 146; politicisation of animal populations in 140; post-war land use and settlement patterns 139; privatisation of 148–9; Puckapunyal Military Training Area as 140, 141–7, *143*; restoration and revegetation of 141–5; re-wilding of 148
Minard, Peter 156, 157
Mink, Nicolaas 128
Mitchell, Audra 196
Mitchell, P. B. 59
Mitchell, Thomas 58
Mizelle, Brett 113
monumentalisation of extinct species: collective memory formed via 185; conservation encouraged via 191, 196–7; criticisms of 184–5, 196; 'Endling/The last of a species' as 183–4, *184*, 191, 197; grief and guilt expressed via 186–8, 197; landscape as setting for 188, 189; 'Life Cairn' as 194–6, *195*, 197; Lost Birds project as 188–9, *190*; mass extinction-focused 185–6, 191–6, *192*, *194*, *195*; Mass Extinction Monitoring Observatory as 193–4, *194*, 197; 'Monument to Extinction' as 191–3, *192*; passenger pigeon memorials as 186–91, *187*, *189*, *190*, 197; species-specific 186–91; value of 6, 196–7
'Monument to Extinction' 191–3, *192*
Moody, Lesley 164

Moore, G. F. 62
Morkit 133–5
Morton, Timothy 22, 51
mosquitoes: counting or survey of 91–3, 94; diseases transmitted by 32, 85, 91–6; eradication program for 32, 93–6; swampland development and 4, 85, 91–6
Mullins, Steve 75, 78
Mungomery, Reg 16
The Murray: a river and its people (Sinclair) 174–5
Murray-Darling Basin, redfin in 3, 168–77
Musil, Robert 185
mynahs 7

National Farmers Federation 106
National Museum of Australia 183, 191, 197
National Reserves 17, 141
native animal populations: behavioral retraining of 20–1; colonisation affecting 3–4, 8; counting of 3–4, 6, 8; invasive or introduced species as detriment to 15–16, 19–21, 42, 113, 163, 169, 174; locusts as 28–30; pest characterisation of 6, 127, 128–32, 135, 164; urban development affecting 4, 8
Native Fish Strategy 176
Natural England 195
Nature Conservation Agency 145–6
nets: to deter vine feeders 127, 135; fishing 157–8, 160, 162, 164, 165
Newell, Wilmon 43, 44
Newsome, A. E. 7
newspapers *see* media
Nicholson, A. J. (Nick) 34
Nixon, Peter 104–5
Noxious Insect Acts 37
Nugent, Lord/Nugent inquiry 147–8

O'Gorman, Emily 127
Olivey, George 65
Operation Termite 34
owls 146
oysters 162

pademelons 11n20
Palmer, Arthur 74
parrots 6, 131
Pasfield, Gordon 45, 46, 47, 49
passenger pigeons 186–91, *187*, *189*, *190*, 197

208 Index

pastoralism: biological controls and 17; counting animals and 5; end of 66–7; locust warfare with 28, 37; pig cultivation with 115; sheep spread via 56, 58, 59, 60–1, 62, 64–5, 66–7; swamplands development with 86–7

Patterson, Robert 161

Pauly, Daniel 174

pearl-shell, bêche-de-mer and trochus fisheries: cultivation of 74–6; depletion of 6, 73, 74–5, 76–8, 80–1; development of reef affecting 78–81; early days of 73–4; floating stations in 74, 75, 77, 78; labor issues in 73, 75, 77, 78–9, 81; optimism and romanticisation for 73, 80–1, 82; patroling of 77; regulation of 73, 74, 75, 77–8, 81–2; size limits in 74–6, 77, 81; tourism and publicity references to 73, 79–81, 80

Pearl Shell and Bêche-de-Mer Fishery Act and amendment (1881/1891) 74, 75

Pearson, Chris 140

Peloquin, Claude 26

perch 160, 163, 169, 174–5; see also redfin

pesticides: anti-malarial efforts with 32; Argentine ants eradication with 41, 44, 45–51; fisheries affected by 172; locust warfare with 30, 32–4, 35, 36, 37; mosquito eradication with 32, 95; vineyards using 128, 131, 133–5

Pesticides Act (1978) 49

pests: Argentine ants as 41, 42–5, 49; biological controls for 16–17, 19, 23n7; bounties for killing 6, 11nn20–1, 49, 65, 164; invasive or introduced animals considered 3, 41, 42–5; militarised landscapes and control of 146; native species considered 6, 127, 128–32, 135, 164; vine feeders as 126, 127, 128–32, 133, 135

phylloxera 126, 127, 131, 135

pigeons 120, 127, 186–91, 197

pigs: Aboriginal people affected by 113, 115, 120–1; amusement with 116–17; boundaries tested by 117–19; as co-colonisers 113–21; counting of 6, 114, 116, 121; demonisation of 114, 121; ecological damage by 89, 90, 113, 115, 119–21; free-living or feral 115, 119–21, 122–3n17; free-ranging or pannage of 116, 117, 119; historical writing exclusion of 113–15,

121; human relations with 114–15; in Hunter Valley 115–21; impounding of 118; marking vs. branding of 118; regulations on 113, 117–19; sheep, cattle, and horse population relative to 113–14, 115–16; shooting or killing of 117, 119, 121, 122–3n17; swamplands grazing by 89, 90, 115, 120

pilchards 155

Pinta Island tortoises 195

A Plague of Sheep (Melville) 56

poison: ant eradication efforts with 3; biological controls vs. 19; cane toad poison, threats from 15–16, 19–21; locust warfare using 26, 30, 31; military- or warfare-related 35, 139; poison gas technology 30; vine feeder control using 126; see also insecticides; pesticides

politicisation of population numbers: Argentine ants eradication as 46, 48–9; of cane toads 15, 18; colonial fishery exploitation and 157, 160–1, 163–4, 165; conservation management and 21–2; counting leading to 4, 7–8, 9; live sheep export opposition using 99–100, 103–7; in militarised landscapes 140; scarce animal populations triggering 9

Porter, Barry 176–7

possums 65, 120, 129

powdery mildew 131, 135

Price, Thomas 91, 93, 94

Prober, Susan 57

Puckapunyal Military Training Area 140, 141–7, 143

Punch.'Tis the last fly of summer 181

Putwain, James 162

Qantas Empire Airways 33

Quick, Betty 134

RAAF (Royal Australian Air Force) 26, 32–4

rabbits: Aboriginal benefits of 66; biological controls to combat 23n7; ecosystem impacts of 65–6; as introduced species 19, 131; in militarised landscapes 146; vine feeders 131

race and racial epithets: Argentine ants portrayal 49; demonisation of animals using 7; disease spread and ideologies of 90–1; fisheries labor issues and 73, 78–9

Rat and Mosquito Prevention and Destruction Act (1916) 93
ravens 127, 130, 133
redfin: Aboriginal fishing and 169, 176; acclimatisation of 170–2; conservationists' view of 168–9, 174–5; creeping normalcy of 174; disease decreasing 168, 169; fishers' consumption and memories of 168–70, 173, 174–7; as invasive or introduced animals 3, 168–72, 174–7; origin stories of 170–2; as pests 3; scientific narrative of 169–70, 174–5, 177; shifting baselines for 174; sport or recreational fishing of 172–3, 175, 176–7
red kangaroos 7
Register of the National Estate 142
Richter, Donny 173
Ritvo, Harriet 170
Roe, John Septimus 57, 60
Rolls, Eric 19, 67, 113, 127, 135
Rose, Deborah 21
rosellas 127, 130, 133
Roughley, Theodore 81
Royal Australian Air Force (RAAF) 26, 32–4
Royal Society for the Prevention of Cruelty to Animals (RSPCA) 104, 147
Russell, Edmund 26, 30, 34

salmon 157, 160, 161, 163, 175, 177
sampling 7
satellite imagery 7
Saville-Kent, William 74–5, 76–7
scarce animal populations: colonial fishery exploitation creating 155–65; overview of 9; politicisation of population numbers 9; redfin 168–77; see also endangered animal populations
scarlet fever 89
Scott, James 28, 35
Scott, Robert and Helenus 116
Second World War: militarised locust warfare influenced by 26–7, 32–3, 37; monuments to soldiers of 197, 199n46; pearl-shell, bêche-de-mer and trochus fisheries closed during 81
sewage: fisheries affected by 172; in swamplands 89, 92, 95
sheep: Aboriginal social ecological systems and 57–8, 64–6, 67; colonisation with 3, 6, 56–67; counting of 5, 5–6; eco-shepherding of 56, 62–4, 67; end

of pastoralism for 66–7; in Esperance bioregion 6, 56–67; landscape changes from 59–60; live sheep exports, campaign against 6, 99–107; pastoralism and spread of 56, 58, 59, 60–1, 62, 64–5, 66–7; pig population relative to 113–14, 115–16; politicisation of 99–100, 103–7; stealing and killing of 64; transhumance and movement of 61–2, 63, 66, 67; travelling stock routes for 62; ungulate eruptions with 58–9
Shepherd, Thomas 129
Shine, Rick 3, 19–21
Silent Spring (Carson) 41, 51, 134
silvereyes 4, 126, 127, 130, 131–2, 132, 133, 134, 135
Sinclair, Paul, The Murray: a river and its people 174–5
Singer, Peter, Animal Liberation 103
The Sixth Extinction (Kolbert) 185
Smith, Mike 183–4
Smith, Moia 64
social ecological systems (SES), Aboriginal 57–8, 64–6, 67
Soulé, Michael 21
Souter, D. H., The man from Menindie 13
Sparks, Jack 101, 102–3, 104
Spearritt, Peter 172
Spooner, Peter 62
starlings 127, 133
Stockholm convention on Persistent Organic Pollutants 32
swamplands: animal-human relations in 4, 85–96; Argentine ants eradication campaign affecting 50; diseases tied to 85, 88–96; drainage of 89, 91, 93–5, 120; history of inhabitance in 86–7; media portrayal of 85–6, 93, 95; mosquitoes in 4, 85, 91–6; pastoralism and spread into 86–7; pigs damaging 89, 90, 115, 120; rebranding of 88; sewage management in 89, 92, 95; urban development of 4, 85–96, 87
swamp wallabies 8
Sydney, Australia, Argentine ants in 3, 41–51

Talking Fish oral history project 168–70, 173, 174–5
Tange, Arthur 35
Taylor, Campbell 62, 65
terrorism, locust response echoing campaigns against 36–7

210   Index

Thistle, John 27
Thomas, William 120–1
thylacine (Tasmanian tiger): de-extinction
  efforts for 199n48; exhibit
  memorialising 183–4, *184*, 191, 197;
  extinction of 6, 11n21, 183; mass killing
  of 4, 6, 11n21
'Tis the last fly of summer (Punch) 181
*Toilers of the Reef: A Tale of the Pearling
  Fleet* (Reid/Vennard) 80
Toowoomba: Toowoomba Rat and
  Mosquito Board 93; urban development
  of swampland in 4, 85–96, *87*
Torres Strait Islander people *see* First
  Nations, Aboriginal and Torres Strait
  Islander people
Tosh, James 77
tourism: colonial fishery exploitation
  and 157, 163–4, 172–3, 176–7; Great
  Barrier Reef, fisheries affected by 73,
  79–81, *80*; vineyards and wine regions
  as 133–4
Townend, Christine 104, 105
Towns Police Act 117
Trans Australian Airlines (TAA) 34
transhumance 61–2, *63*, 66, 67
"Trapper Tom" figure 49
travelling stock routes (TSRs) 62
*A Treatise on the Culture of the Vine and the
  Art of Making Wine* (Busby) 128–9
trochus fisheries *see* pearl-shell, bêche-
  de-mer and trochus fisheries
trout 157, 160, 163, 169, 175, 177
tuan 146
typhoid 89–91, 93

ungulate eruptions 58–9
United Kingdom: colonisation of Australia
  (*see* colonisation); Defence Lands
  Committee 147; militarised landscapes
  in 141, 147–8; monumentalisation of
  extinct species in 193–6, *194*, *195*; pigs
  in 115
United States: Argentine ants warfare in
  44; Endangered Species Act (1974)
  145; militarised landscapes in 139, 141,
  148; monuments in 184, 186–93, *187*,
  189, *190*, *192*, 199n46; pigs in 113, 115,
  118, 120; vineyards and vine feeders in
  126–7, 131
urban development: native animal
  populations affected by 4, 8; sewage

management with 89, 92, 95; of
  swamplands 4, 85–96, *87*
Uvarov, Boris 31, 34

Vennard, Alexander 80
Victorian Acclimatisation Society 157,
  160, 164, 171
Victorian Flora and Fauna Guarantee Act
  (1988) 145
Vietnam War: Agent Orange used in
  35, 139; militarised locust warfare
  influenced by 35, 36, 37
Vigger, Ian 19, 21
vine feeders: Aboriginal hunting of 129,
  130; economic *vs.* ecological view of
  126–7, 131–2, 136; gunfire to deter
  126, 130, 134; interspecies relations
  with 126–36; netting to deter 127,
  135; pest characterisation of 126, 127,
  128–32, 133, 135; pesticides for control
  of 128, 131, 133–5; terroir narrative
  free of 127–8, 135; tourism and public
  relations on 133–4
vinegar flies 127
Vissel, Jozef 50, 51, 54n77
von Uexküll, Jacob 21

wallabies 6, 8, 11n20, 57, 120
Walton, Izaak, *The Compleat
  Angler* 157
warfare metaphors: Argentine ants warfare
  as 46; locust warfare as 26–8, *27*, 30–7;
  see also militarised landscapes
Waterside Workers Federation (WWF)
  101
wetlands *see* swamplands
whales 8
Wheeler, William 44–5
White, Lyn 107
White, Richard 173
Wilson, E. O. 193
Wirth, Hugh 104
Woodward, Rachel 140, 141
World War I *see* First World War
World War II *see* Second World War
Wright, Patrick 140
Wyndham, George and Margaret 115–16,
  117

Yates, Colin 59, 64
yellow fever 91, 94
Yonge, Charles 81